Legal Writing for Real Lawyers

A Practical Guide from the Trenches

Russell T. Bowlan, J.D., M.A.

authorHOUSE®

AuthorHouse™
1663 Liberty Drive
Bloomington, IN 47403
www.authorhouse.com
Phone: 1 (800) 839-8640

Published by AuthorHouse 12/13/2018

ISBN: 978-1-4817-5950-2 (sc)
ISBN: 978-1-4817-5949-6 (hc)

Library of Congress Control Number: 2013910138

Print information available on the last page.

Any people depicted in stock imagery provided by Getty Images are models, and such images are being used for illustrative purposes only.
Certain stock imagery © Getty Images.

This book is printed on acid-free paper.

iv

Contents

This book is dedicated to my high school Latin teacher, David Gorham, and my high school English teacher and wrestling coach, Steve Surbeck. Thank you, Gentlemen, for your boundless esprit in the classroom, where you instilled in me bedrock analytical and linguistic skills which have proven invaluable to my career.

In memory of

Allen C. Enegren, Esq.
and
Russell B. Holloway, Esq.,

I submit the following quip
from W.C. Fields:

"A woman drove me to drink
and I didn't even have the decency
to thank her."

Prefatory Note to the Third Edition

As I take competing authors to task in the coming pages, I realize one or more may have revised their books since mine was first published in 2010. I have not bothered to consult these redrafts because, in my experience, Trolls, Curmudgeons and Yapping Chihuahuas are loath to forsake the shelter of even the most fugitive of bandwagons. Thus, I need not waste my time or money reviewing these niggling emendations; more importantly, thanks to *Legal Writing for Real Lawyers*, neither do you.

Prologue

After spending over a decade as a trial attorney for the insurance industry, I'd had my fill of disloyal corporate clients and treacherous colleagues. So I decided to leave the courtroom and refocus my career on writing. Some months later, a product liability firm hired me to write trial and appellate briefs, setting me on a path that would dramatically change my way of thinking about the tools of my trade. A year later, I noticed I had become acutely critical of other people's grammar. When I read books for pleasure, I would mark all over them with pen and highlighter. One afternoon, it occurred to me that I had not consulted any of my grammar books since college. As I warily retrieved my 1979 vintage *Strunk and White*, I dared pose a terrifying question: *Could I be wrong about some of these issues?*

I was relieved to find that I was correct about the core elements of grammar. But as I delved more deeply, the education and experience of the intervening years led me to uncover three intriguing realities. First of all, the leading authorities do not agree on every grammatical element. Second, some of the rules make absolutely no sense. And last, over time I had made up my own rules to fill the gaps.

Ever since my third-grade homeroom teacher had sparked in me a keen fascination with the written word, I had taken comfort in the presumption that the avuncular grammarians of my youth would always provide an answer for any writing dilemma I might face.

Little over three decades later, the facts in front of my face proved otherwise. Desperate to find a better set of rules, I naturally turned to my colleagues. After all, who better than a lawyer to devise a comprehensive rubric to anticipate the remotest contingency? After reading a few of the more popular contemporary books on legal writing, I was disappointed that these "authorities" did not offer the bulletproof grammatical code I sought. But what really unnerved me were some of the legal writing "rules" they seek to shove down the throats of today's law students.

Since then, I've read a number of similarly acclaimed "authorities." On the whole, I find among them general agreement on certain basic elements of the writing process. But a disturbing conclave of these authors peddle advice so irresponsible that only two conclusions can fairly be drawn: (1) these authors haven't the faintest grasp of what persuasive communication is all about and (2) they wrote their books, not because they had anything particularly enlightening to say, but because they needed to publish books. As a result, what is perhaps the most absurd notion in the history of the English language has become, not merely a trend but a movement.

This is not your run-of-the-mill how-to book. If you want one of those, you can go to any bookstore and find the usual suspects, who will tantalize you with cute little gimmicks they dreamed up at faculty mixers. Mind you, the gimmicks themselves won't help you become a better legal writer, because there is no magical method. Good writing takes sweat, practice, heartache and failure upon failure. In fact, you will never become an "expert" legal writer. Such a label indicates a pinnacle one has reached, from which he can never fall. But all writers have good days and bad. The best you can strive for is to become a better writer than you were yesterday. For example, amid the new material I have added to Chapter Three, you will find samples of briefs from the original publication. Many of those reproductions will flow even more smoothly than in prior editions because the interstitial years have seen me further hone my editing skills; therefore, no matter how many times I have blue-penciled a brief, I find room for improvement each time I revisit it. The purpose of this book, then, is to elevate your level of thinking about, not just legal writing but the English language.

Since childhood, I have been far more fascinated with fact than fantasy. Accordingly, as I mature as a lawyer, my briefs return often to the themes of common sense and logic. In this book I will use common sense and logic to expose the myths perpetuated by the self-proclaimed "authorities" on legal writing. This is not a simple task. To obtain a proper understanding of legal writing, we must journey back to the origins of both linguistics and law. In the process, I will reintroduce you to grammar. Not the regimented version teachers have crammed down your throat all your life, but the system that began when the very first caveman gestured and grunted. The system that worked perfectly, naturally, for millennia until a succession of pedants in the most recent hiccup of time defiled it.

Before we proceed, try this simple exercise to gain perspective. Sit in a comfortable chair and breathe deeply for a few moments. Now close your eyes and imagine yourself as a newborn child. You are able to make noise, but you are unable to control or articulate it. Nor can you decipher the meanings behind the variety of noises others make at you. You experience raw emotions, but you can't begin to understand them because you have no vocabulary to differentiate between fear, hunger and contentment. Linguistically, you are cut off from the world around you. Our preverbal ancestors were every bit as isolated.

Now open your eyes, pick up the nearest dictionary and read a single page. Then fan through it from A to Z. As you do so consider, not merely the symbols but the countless generations of human beings who forged this lexicon. Perhaps now you can begin to appreciate what a colossal accomplishment modern language represents. It is such reverence for linguistics that compelled me to write this book.

Chapter One

The Mythmakers

I find that the best time to shop for groceries is on Sunday morning, when the streets are deserted because all the conventionalists are holed up in churches listening to philosophical prudes tell them how to live. One such morning, the checkout clerk asked to see my I.D. before she rang up my beer. I shared a laugh with the lady behind me. The clerk could tell I wasn't a minor (a) with one eye closed (b) from five miles away. Still, someone in risk management had rescinded this clerk's right to rely on her own judgment; hence, this farcical situation in which a man has to prove he is half his age before he is permitted to spend his hard-earned money on one of human history's most enduring potations.

This anecdote illustrates a malady which is pervasive in modern society: the quest to either find or fabricate a panacea for every conceivable ill so that we might live on automatic pilot. Inherent in this thought process is the ambition to configure a world in which everyone can enjoy the fruits of this life without having to earn them.[1] This idea is reflected in the attempts by authors of legal writing books to create a *Rule for All Seasons*. To illuminate the folly in this notion, one need only observe nature. All around us, every day, we see the following truth demonstrated again and again: If you stop moving, growing and adapting, other creatures who have not stopped moving, growing and adapting will kill you and devour your carcass. Like it or not, you must accept this reality before you can hope to become an effective legal writer.

Another prerequisite to becoming a persuasive legal writer is to disabuse oneself of the various myths about law and writing. History teaches that the best way to dispel a myth is to unmask the

---

[1] This mindset lies at the heart of the various derivations of socialism, whose purveyors ignorantly seek to replace equality of opportunity with equality of outcome.

mythmaker and expose his underlying motives. Our prime suspects are Trolls, Curmudgeons and Yapping Chihuahuas.

The Troll[2]

In Nordic literature, trolls were commonly described as humanlike forest dwellers with exaggerated features such as big heads, overly broad shoulders or awkwardly long arms. Often ascribed otherworldly qualities, trolls were portrayed both as harmless pranksters who would sneak into the kitchen before a feast and gorge half the food, and as coldblooded misanthropes who would steal infants and new mothers.

As with many tales of lore, the origin of the troll may have a factual basis. It has been suggested that our Cro-Magnon ancestors may have actually encountered the last surviving tribes of their evolutionary predecessors, the Neanderthals.[3] For a less ambitious explanation one need only look to the recent historical record – explorers are notorious for flaunting their ethnocentrism when they describe the indigenous races they discover in their travels. Whatever its origin, the legend was popularized in modern literature by a fairytale I remember fondly – *Three Billy Goats Gruff*.[4] In that tale, three goats wish to cross a bridge to greener pastures. The troll who lives beneath confronts each in turn. The first two convince the troll to let them pass, each promising that the next goat will yield a bigger feast. The last goat proves too big for the troll to capture. It butts the troll off the bridge into the fast-flowing water, where he drowns.

Like the fabled he-goats, the innocent law student dreams of that glorious day when she attains the brass ring: the coveted *Juris*

---

[2] The following narrative is directed solely at the post secondary education industry. Career academicians and administrators at the primary and secondary levels of education are vital to any thriving society. I certainly hold those of my youth in highest regard.

[3] *El Collar del Neandertal* ("The Neanderthal's Necklace"), Juan Luis Arsuaga 1999

[4] *Norske Folkeeventyr* ("Norse Folktales"), Peter Christen Asbjørnsen and Jørgen Moe 1845-8

Doctor degree that will render the world an oyster in the palm of her hand. No sooner has she passed the LSAT than she finds herself at the shallow end of a long and treacherous bridge, peering up at the bristly brow of the modernday Troll: The Legal Research and Writing Professor. When he speaks, she turns aside and covers her face, not out of fear but to escape his fetid breath.

"Bow down before me, silly little human, for I am the Keeper of the Code of Written Form. Do not let reason cloud your mind; the colon always goes here. Despite everything you were ever taught about syntax, the case citation is always inserted like this. These things are so because I say they are so. I am always right, because I have TENURE."

Today's Troll is to real-world legal practitioners what the Toy Poodle is to the canine species: a useless, annoying breed that we revere merely because our intuition suggests it was once good for something. Lest we judge an individual Troll too harshly, we must understand that he was not born this obtuse. His present way was paved by the horde of magisterial grammarians who preceded him. In the distant past, grammarians did make certain contributions to the overall development of communication. And they will always be indispensable at the primary and secondary levels of education. But, as we shall see, the very nature of linguistics relegates the role of the grammarian and his progeny, the Legal Research and Writing Professor, to that of a historical commentator.

Today's Troll is anyone who presumes to own the last word on any issue. Today's Troll is the college or graduate school professor who would have you believe there is only one way to write and he is the authority on that system. The stronger one's emphasis on rules, the surer you can be that he is a Troll. By and large, you will find Trolls to be career academicians, a thousand miles long on theory but bankrupt on practical experience. Here's the distinction I'm getting at. In the late 1980s I taught introductory courses on creative writing as a graduate assistant. On receiving my M.A., I was called into the dean's office. Dr. Warren tried to convince me to get an Ed.D. and let him groom me to become a college educator/administrator like him. Enamored as I was with the classroom, I had to decline.

"The way I see it, Clif', I have to leave this nursery and accomplish something *out there* before I can come back *in here* and teach people how to accomplish something *out there*."

He dismissed me as though I were duller than the idiot who invented the slotted screw.

Let us now turn back the clock a few millennia to witness the evolution of interpersonal communication.

Essential History of the World Part A – The Birth of "Higher" Education

It is the dawn of mankind … I mean womankind … I mean … let's start over.

It is the dawn of humankind. One sultry afternoon between 4.5 million and 100,000 B.C.E., a caveman points at an animal and grunts. His hunting companion repeats him. They jump up and down, pointing at the animal and grunting in delight, while the cavewomen wag their heads disapprovingly. On this momentous occasion (1) men have agreed on the meaning of the very first word, thus inventing verbal communication, and (2) women have agreed to treat men like morons despite their accomplishments, thus establishing a ubiquitous and abiding pastime. A generation later, Cavewoman thwacks Caveman on the noggin, grunts twice and makes a stabbing gesture in the air. In the years since they first set up cave, *thwack-grunt-grunt-stab* has always meant Cavewoman is hungry and Caveman needs to kill something edible. Dutifully, Caveman picks up his pointed stick and turns to leave. But Cavewoman thwacks him again and knocks the stick out of his hands. Puzzled, Caveman focuses every last ounce of his brainpower upon the task of understanding Cavewoman. Such intense concentration robs his extremities of blood circulation, causing his jaw to hang askew, his face to wash pallid and his eyes to glaze over, thus originating the timeless *Baby, what the hell are you trying to tell me?* stare.

4

As Cavewoman repeats the *thwack-grunt-grunt-stab* sentence, Caveman realizes she has subtly changed her inflection on the second grunt. What she really means is: *I don't love you anymore, so take your pointed stick and your clubs, and get out.* An alternative meaning is: *I need me-time, so buzz off for a week.* Unfortunately for Caveman, he can not decipher which meaning is correct, so he packs his belongings and saunters into the wilderness, uncertain if she'll ever want him back, but secure in the knowledge that, if she allows him to return, she'll blame him for every nanosecond he was gone. As he plods a lonely path, he happens upon another distraught caveman. The comrades eventually stumble across a fermented apple. Curious, they squeeze it and drink its nectar, thus inaugurating the kegger – a phenomenon that survives today as one of the most effective recovery mechanisms for jilted men.

What can we learn from this brief glimpse into the naissance of human dialogue? For one thing, we see that as life changes so must the language that depicts it. We also observe the bedrock principle of efficient expression: communication does not take place unless and until the people trying to communicate reach a consensus on the meaning of the words they use.

Centuries pass. World population increases exponentially. As society grows ever more complex, so does its vocabulary. When one culture is exposed to another, they inevitably borrow from each other's language, each adding yet more depth to its glossary. As individual cultures develop, each invents a system of modular symbols to replace drawings. Pictographic art and writing diverge. With the written word comes the realization that today's generation is no longer isolated in history. When scholars contemplate the breadth of information they can pass on to their descendants with this emerging alphabet, it becomes more important than ever before to preserve commonality of meaning.

Linguists take the first step, scouring hamlets and villages to compile collections of words that will come to be known as "dictionaries." Knowledge, jealously hoarded for so many centuries by kings and priests, spreads among the commoners faster than graft through a government assembly. With each generation, the written record builds upon itself. Meanwhile, technology improves, causing travel to increase, leading to the intermixture of ever more educated cultures. To keep pace with this knowledge explosion, the linguists find it necessary to warehouse records of all the accomplishments it engenders. Repositories of knowledge spring up all over the globe. Before long, the thinkers, creators and doers of the world are amassing such vast amounts of knowledge that the linguists fear they themselves will have to forsake thinking, creating and doing to devote their full attention to maintaining the Repositories. Unwilling to squander their talents on such a perfunctory task, they comb the streets and alleyways for layabouts and ne'er-do-wells, on whom they dub various titles roughly translated into modern English as Myopic Busybodies. It is no mere coincidence that these same streets and alleyways produce the Moralistic and Megalomaniacal Busybodies who will become what we know today as religious and political leaders. But I digress.

Within just a few generations, many of the Repositories have grown so large as to become cities unto themselves. While a smattering of Repositories are bankrolled by churches or local governments, Myopic Busybodies in a growing number of Repositories have to resort to begging, borrowing and stealing to feed their families. Thus, variations of the words "alumnus," "endowment" and "pledge" creep into our vocabulary.

As people flock to the Repositories to partake of their teeming stores of knowledge, the Myopic Busybodies are faced with two enormous problems. First, they simply can not find enough time in a day to both solicit funds and maintain the Repositories, so they decide to charge patrons a fee ("tuition"). The establishment of fee-based education turns knowledge into a commodity and gives the Myopic Busybodies a property interest in the accomplishments of others. This leads to the second dilemma. In order to maintain the appearance of exclusive ownership, the Myopic Busybodies must "administer" this knowledge to the hungry masses (hence, "professors" and "students"). But there are not nearly enough Myopic

6

Busybodies to meet the demand. They must increase their ranks, but they fear that if they hire outsiders their racket will be exposed. So they choose the only available option: they groom and recruit the students who show the most promise of becoming parasites like themselves. Naturally, these will be the students who are most adept at memorizing and then regurgitating the fruits of other people's intellectual labor ("A-students"). The Quack ("career academician") is born.

With the Quacks now acting as their strawmen in the higher education charade, the Myopic Busybodies have unwittingly carved out for themselves the hollowest existence in history: that of the parasite which feeds off of other parasites. The "higher education administrator" has entered the world stage.

In perhaps the most colossal irony of all time, the students begin to confuse the Quacks, who do nothing but ingest and vomit the accomplishments of thinkers, creators and doers, with the very thinkers, creators and doers they emulate. The Quacks do nothing to dispel this misconception because, in their own minds, they are in fact thinkers (about the accomplishments of others), creators (of ways to imitate those who create) and doers (in the sense that they recycle knowledge attained by others). Thus, a parallel universe (hence, the term "university") emerges in which living off the sweat and heartache and genius of others becomes a vocation, even an art, in its own right.

Before long, the Quacks who specialize in upchucking the written word grow weary of the dizzying pace at which language is developing. They begin to grumble in the taverns.

"We chose the wrong field. I asked one of the Quacks in Numbers to calculate the total variations possible with a 26-letter alphabet. He laughed so hard he choked on his mutton."

"Those smug mathematicians. All they do is sit around drinking grog. They haven't seen anything new since the Greeks were conquered. Why, just yesterday, a German philosopher coined ten new words! The pace is killing me."

7

"We must devise a way to keep the thinkers from ideating, the creators from inventing and the doers from achieving."

"You're not helping matters any."

"What did I do?"

"You just used three synonyms in one sentence."

"Sorry. What we need is a diversionary tactic."

"Stop it with the big words already!"

"I mean we need to distract them with dumb stuff so they'll have less time to think up cool stuff."

"I like it. What do we do?"

"You know those round things they sometimes put at the end of a self-sustaining statement?"

"Yeah?"

"Let's invent more symbols like that."

"I can't stand the round things and you want to invent more? Are you drunk?"

"Of course I am. How else would I have come up with this? Fetch us more grog. Here's what we do. We make a little crescent … then a round thing on top of a round thing …"

"How about a round thing on top of a crescent thing?"

"You're catching on. Then we cook up silly rules for when to use them."

"I see. Get them sidetracked on form at the expense of substance. Brilliant!"

Thus grammar is born. In this trifling instant of time, the grammarian serves her historical purpose by recognizing the role of punctuation. Alas, in the generations to come, a whimsical frolic will burgeon into an entire industry devoted to, not the lifeblood of communication – the word – but its peripheral ornamentation.

Meanwhile, as the individual thinkers, creators and doers strive to both understand and improve the human condition, parasitic industries develop better methods of feeding off of them. The ranks of the three biggest such industries (Religion, Politics and "Higher" Education) swell to the point that they become institutions. By the time the individual thinker, creator and doer realizes these institutions are in cahoots, it is too late to stop their momentum. He wakes up one morning to find that a world which once made sense has been turned on its head. He can no longer ply his trade the way his ancestors have for countless generations. Before he can go to work to earn money, he must first pay money to go to school and re-learn everything his predecessors have already taught him from Quacks who, by and large, have never themselves plied his trade (or succeeded at it). If he does not do this, the Megalomaniacal Busybodies will throw him into a dungeon. Thus, the term "licensure" enters our lexicon and, with it, the do-nothings of society become the gatekeepers through which the do-everythings must pass.

At long last, the Megalomaniacal Busybodies have bestowed legitimacy upon the Quack. With this new power, he takes his post at the small end of your bridge to greener pastures. Ladies and Gentlemen, I give you *The Troll*.

The Moral of the Story

That "laws" of physics remain constant within the confines of Earth's atmosphere is not a testament to the ingenuity of the human species. It is merely an observation of how matter reacts time and again under a given set of variables. In other words, human beings did not invent these precepts and then fashion matter to fit their mold. We merely assigned names and values so that we could describe to each other behaviors that existed millennia before we were here to witness them.

By contrast, "rules" of grammar are neither universal nor constant. This is because language is not a piece of matter. The semicolon does not exist in nature. Frontiersmen did not round up wild quotation marks and tame them for domestic service. Thus, the sounds and symbols we take for granted as "language" do not exist independently from us. Before I utter the word "chair," there is silence. At the very moment I say "chair," the image it invokes exists only for speaker and audience. As my voice fades away, so does the word "chair,"

9

along with whatever mental image speaker and audience assigned to it. Thus, language is abstract and it is dynamic.

So is structure. Anyone who has studied a foreign language understands that the order of subject, verb and modifier changes from culture to culture. When an unpracticed Spaniard or Croatian speaks our native tongue, we refer to it as "broken English." If we merely pay attention, though, it isn't hard to understand what she is saying. Thus, when my neighbor asks "For what that you do?" I understand her to mean "Why did you do that?" My neighbor has communicated with me because she and I are both active participants in our conversation. It matters not that she failed to raise her voice at the end of the sentence to indicate an aural question mark. She formulated the question in her mind, chose symbols we both understood to reflect that question and verbalized. I heard and understood. This is communication, which brings us to another crucial point.

The only function of language – be it oral, written or punctuated with a knuckle to the jaw – is to exchange information. It follows that the mechanisms of language delivery (e.g., grammatical principles) should not impede that process. I said earlier that the proper role of the grammarian is that of a historian. As we have seen, language is an abstraction that is always moving and expanding. It is neither an animal that can be caged nor a piece of rock whose boundaries can be defined. Therefore, it is foolish for someone to tell you that the way a thought is conveyed today is the way it should be put forth ten years from now. As we proceed, you will see the futility of trying to establish, let alone enforce, such standards.

The Curmudgeon

Like scientists, lawyers live and work in a world of proof, where mere assertions are not enough. Therefore, the legal system is most properly understood from the empiricist point of view. Empiricism holds that the mind of the newborn individual is a *tabula rasa* – a clean slate. This applies equally to society and its various constructs. Thus, knowledge is neither innate nor inevitable: we acquire it exclusively through experience. To fully appreciate today's Curmudgeon, then, we must first consider the origin of the system in which he operates.

Essential History of the World Part B –
The Seeds of Our Legal System

It is the dawn of caveperson domesticity. Cavewoman thwacks Caveman on the noggin, grunts twice and makes a stabbing gesture. Caveman dutifully begins to pack his belongings. But when he goes to retrieve his sporty new wheels, Cavewoman kicks him in the groin and drapes her arms over his precious discs of stone. Caveman is confused. Cavewoman whistles. Sophisticated Caveman with Silk Loincloth swoops in from his ritzy grotto across the water. He explains to Caveman that he can no longer just walk away when Cavewoman turns fickle. In the argument that ensues, the epithets "chauvinist" and "gold digger" are coined. Just before Caveman is swindled out of everything but his nose-ring, Sophisticated Caveman with Off-the-Rack Loincloth appears to argue that Cavewoman is being too greedy. Legal terms such as *retainer fee* and *quantum meruit* edge their way into our vocabulary.

As the drama unfolds at Cave 90210, the argument between the Sophisticated Cavemen escalates to a point at which they have run out of threats. There is nothing left to do but club each other on the head. But neither is so fond of his client that he is prepared to shed his own blood. They must figure out how to resolve the dispute in such a way that (a) neither has to get his hands dirty and (b) each walks away with his reputation as a fierce advocate intact. *Eureka!* Sophisticated Caveman with Silk Loincloth gets an idea. While Caveman and Cavewoman stare in bewilderment from a dim corner of the cave, their advocates huddle together, conferring in hushed tones:

"I can't back down. How would that look?"

"Well neither can I."

"We need a patsy."

"I'd rather find a wise and objective arbitrator."

"Either way, we need someone else with apparent authority to make the decision."

"I concur. We need someone with a keen enough intellect to salvage truth and equity from our indiscriminately partisan contest of semantics."

"I don't know about all that. I just want someone else to blame if my case goes south."

The advocates exit the cave and return moments later with Wise Old Caveman. As each explains to his client:

"We left the cave to do battle. I was prepared to champion your cause to my early demise. Just as we were about to commence our deadly duel, Wise Old Caveman stepped between us. He reasoned with us. He showed us an alternative to our *all or nothing* trial strategy. He taught us about *compromise*. He must be the wisest member of our clan, because he has outlived his peers. So we must trust him to *judge* our dispute."

In reality, this *judge* was merely the first distinguished looking human they stumbled upon who had nothing better to do.

More disputes inevitably arise and, as the ranks of the Sophisticated Cavemen swell, so does their need for judges. The arrangement works swimmingly for a generation or two. Alas, chronic grumblers and agitators by nature, Sophisticated Cavemen who lose their cases soon begin itching for ways to get a do-over. So they scour the *caveterias* and assisted-living dens for yet older judges, and give them appellate power. With each new appointment come all the perks of higher social status, a wink from a political boss and a reminder:

"Don't forget who put you here, Pops."

As the losers set about populating ever higher panels of review, the winners devise a way to increase their odds of remaining winners: they convene at the local watering hole and invent "laws." To sell both the concept and the process to their doubters, they devote this inaugural lawmaking session to the most universally acceptable notions:

"It will be a crime to steal another man's club. Agreed?"

"Hear, hear!"

"Splendid idea."

"It will be a crime to kill another caveman?"

"Except for those valley dwellers with the funny eyes."

"It will be a crime to kill another clan member?"

"Good form, good form!"

Having garnered legitimacy for themselves, the *legislators* meet for a second session … but this time with a perfidious motive. To the law against stealing another man's club, they attach an exception: "Unless he is in debt to you." And to every popular law they attach ten secret laws (disguised as "riders" or "amendments") aimed at making life easier for their cronies at the expense of their cronies' enemies and business competitors. If a trial or appellate judge decides a case contrary to their grand scheme, they simply (a) pass a new law to override that decision and/or (b) force the decisionmaker out of office at arrow point and install a *friendlier* judge.

Over time, a younger and smarter breed of jurist begins to populate the bench. No longer satisfied to operate as mere pawns in the tug-o-war between opposing political machines, they strike back by recording their decisions and publishing them. A new source of law ("judicial precedent") takes hold and, with it, the judicial branch carves for itself a position of relative (though by no means absolute) autonomy. These trailblazers establish a legacy of, not mere legitimacy, but prestige for their successors.

Unfortunately, as happens with any institution, the occasional recipient of that power suffers the delusion that he was entitled to this high office by merely being born. Ladies and Gentlemen, I give you *The Curmudgeon*. The Curmudgeon is the judge who patronizes lawyers and postures for her constituency. The typical Curmudgeon walks half a beat slower than most people to accentuate her air of superiority. The Curmudgeon refers to herself by the royal pronoun *We*. The Curmudgeon elects to dine on the open-air patio, then complains to the wait staff about flies. Like the Troll with his precious tenure, the Curmudgeon presumes that the robe she wears gives her carte blanche to say and do anything she likes with total impunity.

The Big Picture

The human condition is a contradictory one. We toss around catchphrases like *equal opportunity* and *self-determination*. We develop systems of government ostensibly based upon *freedom*. But where two or more people gather, a leader inevitably emerges. Why? Our world is random and chaotic. Human beings are so afraid of this natural state of disorder that even in our dreams we invent gods and gurus to follow. Because we ourselves can't solve the riddle of existence, we imagine something greater than us has done so. Thus, society thrives on untold forms of hero worship. The truth is that ultimately no human being has control over anything. We have no say in the circumstances of our birth. We may be lucky enough to forestall death or even choose its manner, but we can't stop it. Between birth and death, we are at the mercy of the elements, disease and genetics. But the typical human being can not accept this reality, so we distract ourselves with idols of sport, stage and screen, as well as rules and statistics. In our headlong quest for order and predictability, we walk a tightrope holding a pole from whose ends dangle Safety and Autonomy.

Here and in later parts of this book, I will quote from *Man and People* by Jose Ortega y Gasset.[5] As I prepared to write the inaugural draft of this book, I intended to base it upon Sr. Ortega's masterpiece. I soon realized that, if I borrowed everything I found salient, I would end up reproducing the entire work altogether. Instead, I will now try to distill that 272-page opus into a paragraph or two in which I will apply Sr. Ortega's observations to the evolution of our present legal system. Regardless of your interests or educational background, I strongly recommend that you read *Man and People* yourself – I guarantee that you will be a better human being for having done so.

---

[5] W. W. Norton & Company, Inc. 1957, translated by William R. Trask

Only I know Me.[6] Though You may physically resemble Me, and though You may share my language, I do not know You as well as I know Me. Naturally, when I encounter You (a) I hope You will be kind to Me but (b) I can imagine 100 ways in which You could just as well harm Me. As a result of each successive meeting during which You treat Me fairly, I grow to trust You … but never as implicitly as I trust Me. When He comes along, then She, We are confronted with the innumerable potential vagaries of Them. Weary of sleeping with clubs at our sides (assuming We are able to sleep at all), We and They strike a bargain whereby (a) We and They agree to restrict our actions toward each other for the general safety of Us (b) labor is divided among Us according to our skills and mutual needs, and (c) We and They elect a certain number of individuals among Us to act as the enforcers of our compact. When We and They agree to give up a certain amount of autonomy for the good of Us, Society is born. And Society is inevitable. As Sr. Ortega puts it:

> So now we can set it down that man, aside from the man that I am, appears to us as the other, and this means … the "other" means, he whom I can and must – even against my will – frequent, since even if I should prefer that the other did not exist … it turns out that I irremediably exist for him, and this obliges me, willy-nilly, to reckon with him and with his intentions toward me, which perhaps are malevolent. This mutual "reckoning with," *reciprocity*, is the first fact that we can classify as *social*. (*Man and People*, p. 103)

This is not a human construct; it is a fact of nature. For two or more human beings to survive each other, we must agree to impose upon ourselves what Sr. Ortega calls "the power of the collectivity"

---

[6] For you insufferable pedants out there, I am quite aware this subject-object sequence ordinarily requires a reflexive pronoun. If you fail to appreciate why I suspend its use in this particular context, then you are a bozo.

or "public power." (*Man and People*, p. 269) When I say to you, "I want you to treat me kindly," I know intuitively that I can not expect you to oblige unless I, in turn, give up my natural tendency to do that which pleases me at your expense. Thus, tomorrow morning I hop in my faithful pickup truck and motor to the office. Traveling westward, I confine myself to the westbound lanes of traffic, not because I fear some deity named West will otherwise strike me down, but because I know this behavior will keep my motorized beast from colliding head-on with another motorized beast. As I go about my daily life, I obey these various rules and customs simply because doing so maintains order and predictability; thus, I reduce the odds that I will clash with my societal cohorts. But keep in mind that I am not physically constrained by these rules and customs. I am ultimately free to ignore them. When I do, I tell my fellow human beings one of two things: (1) "I withdraw my assent to this contract because I no longer care about you" or (2) "Because I care about us, I urge that we rewrite this clause to better serve us."

The social contract is at once fragile and resilient. By and large, most human beings prefer order and predictability; therefore, we gladly participate in the contract. But a contract has no inherent clout; its only power consists in the parties who mutually agree to maintain it. If they withdraw their consent, the contract vanishes and society as all citizens have known it ceases to exist. Hence, the inevitable consequences of revolution – for the "winners" and "losers" alike. With each new generation we decide how much conformity or dissent we can bear. Thus, despite its impregnable appearance, the fabric of every establishment ebbs and flows with the times.

Likewise, the office of Judge is a masquerade in which clerks, bailiffs, litigants and lawyers voluntarily participate. The oath of that office serves to remind the judge that the power of the bench is a temporary privilege – that his is but one of many roles that constitute our system of justice. Neither does the vaunted black robe magically imbue a fallible human being with boundless knowledge. It is most instructive to bear in mind that judges are either appointed or elected,

16

which endeavors most often have less to do with merit than with massaging porcine egos and devising catchy campaign slogans.

So what am I telling you? The mere fact that an impatient, robe-clad man wields a gavel does not mean he is necessarily an authority on procedure, precedent or statutory interpretation. Neither does it remotely qualify him to lecture you, the legal writer, about the tools of your trade. In every encounter with either a trial or appellate judge, therefore, you will be best served to remember the distinction between the person and the office he serves. While the latter deserves reverence as a matter of principle, the opinions and conclusions of the former should be promptly and thoroughly doublechecked.

The Yapping Chihuahua: An Absurdity Wrapped in Farce and Garnished with Mockery

You can set your watch by the following truism: Those who have no talent for creative expression (or are so afraid of failure and embarrassment that they never found the guts to attempt it) will seek refuge in the pedestrian world of form and convention. *Merriam-Webster* defines *pedant* as: "**2 a:** one who makes a show of knowledge **b:** one who is unimaginative or who unduly emphasizes minutiae in the presentation or use of knowledge **c:** a formalist or precisionist in teaching." You may think this definition applies well enough to the Troll. In a sensible world, you might be correct. Alas, I must introduce you to a character this definition fits even more snugly.

Essential History of the World Part C – The *Nothing* Expert

As education warehousing grows into an established vocation, certain students find themselves in a dire predicament. On the one hand, they are only mediocre at recycling information by rote. On the other, they both fear having to make it in the real world and covet the existence of their mentors in academia. So they contrive a universe even more arcane than that fabricated by the Myopic Busybodies.

17

Soon, a more insidious incarnation of the Troll is seen lurking about the aureate halls of universities. They tout themselves as experts on how to cite the authority one uses to support his propositions. Thus springs yet another barrier (in addition to the grammar barrier already in place) for the writer and his reader to overcome in their mutual effort to communicate.

Though the Toy Poodle is of no use to the canine world, it retains a modicum of value to humans because it can be trained and groomed and paraded in dog shows. The Chihuahua, on the other hand, has no redeeming qualities whatsoever. Its hair is too short to style, its head is too large for its body, it's too scrawny to pull a sled and it's too stupid to learn how to do anything worthwhile. All it does is eat, crap and yap incessantly. Next to the mosquito and the fly, it is perhaps the most annoying waste of organic matter to ever infect our fair planet.

Come to think of it, I'm not so sure Chihuahuas are organic.

Anyway, if the Troll is to the legal practitioner what the Toy Poodle is to the canine species ... Ladies and Gentlemen, I give you the citation expert, also known as *The Yapping Chihuahua*. To underscore the Yapping Chihuahua's immateriality to the realm of letters (which can not be overemphasized), I will now reconstruct for you an account that hails from the turn of the last century.

Posted – Keep Out

I was setting outside watching the sun fall when I heard a rustling north of the barn. Been having a coyote problem, so I got the 12-gauge and throwed some shot that way. Didn't hear nothing else, so I went to bed.

Come find out it was Nate's boy had skinnied through my fence to pester my cattle and took some of my shot in his left hand. A time later he summoned me to the courthouse. Seems he wanted me to pay him a lot of money for shooting him. I brung the big sign the boy walked right past, what says KEEP OUT,

18

and I showed it to Jedediah Paugh, the newly elected justice of the peace in my county.

Jed says, "You assaulted and battered an invitee on your property. You gotta pay him for his injuries."

I says, "Jed, he weren't no invitee."

Jed throws up his finger and says, "Boy, this here is a court of the law. You address me proper."

So I says, "Judge, look at the sign says KEEP OUT. It was nailed to the very fence that boy climbed through."

Jed says, "How do I know it was posted?"

So I says, "'Cause I'm telling you so. 'Cause you seen it a hundred times when you come by to drink my whiskey."

Jed says, "Less'n the sign says POSTED I don't have no probative evidence it was posted."

"I'm telling you it was posted."

"Don't make no neither."

"Why not, Judge?"

"Nate's boy cain't read nohow. I hereby rule that you owe Nate's boy half your stock."

"How so?"

"'Cause there's a law says so."

"I ain't never read no such law. Heck, Jed, I cain't even read."

"Don't make no neither, 'cause I can. And your sign may as well not be, 'cause it don't say POSTED."

The Stinking Elephant in the Room

The preceding story illustrates the age-old battle between form and substance. The earliest example of this debate in American jurisprudence can be found in the landmark case of *Marbury v. Madison* (1 Cranch 137 – U.S. D.C. 1803):

> If congress remains at liberty to give this court appellate jurisdiction, where the constitution has declared their jurisdiction shall be original; and original jurisdiction where the constitution has declared it shall be appellate; the distribution of jurisdiction, made in the constitution, is form without substance.

Pick any State on your favorite legal research engine and plug in the query "form /3 substance." I dare you to find a published, undisturbed opinion that does not favor substance over form.

Nothing interrupts the flow of a paragraph more than a citation. But this does not mean they should always be banished to the 10-point gutter at the bottom of the page, because it is equally annoying to stop in the middle of a poignant argument, find a magnifying glass and decipher the footnote. When I was in law school, the prevailing wisdom was that footnotes had no place in a legal brief: if it wasn't important enough to put in the main body, it did not belong in the brief. Today, some Yapping Chihuahuas proclaim that all citations, without exception, belong in the gutter. One such busybody (who is so taken with himself that he cites his own previous books as supportive authority) has even bragged that he has enough idle time on his hands to debate the issue with an equally recalcitrant busybody on the opposing side.[7]

Out here in the trenches of real-world law, judges and lawyers have no time for such nugatory squabbling. For example, I practiced law for over 12 years before I ever consulted a book on citation, and that was purely by happenstance. In the midst of a fracas over editorial control of a posttrial brief, my colleague responded to one of my suggested improvements: "You obviously follow *The Bluebook*[8] in

---

[7] Bryan A. Garner's *The Winning Brief* (Oxford University Press 2003), p. 141
[8] Gannett House, 18th Edition, 2005

all instances. Well, in Florida, our local rules trump *The Bluebook*." I didn't know a *bluebook* from a *tangerinebook*. Like any good lawyer, though, I promptly bought one so I would be armed for my next scuffle with the Florida attorney. After trudging through 40 pages, I closed it in disgust, vowing that the only reason I would ever open it again would be to poke fun at its inanities ... the silliest of which I will address in the next chapter.

The bottom line on the Yapping Chihuahua is that she is an anachronism, utterly irrelevant to any serious discussion about legal writing. The tripe she hawks – form above substance – should therefore be ignored until logic and common sense swallow her whole, forever silencing her infernal prattle.

Chapter Two

The Myths They Propagate

Let us now investigate the most prevalent myths in reverse order, from 5 (somewhat silly) to 1 (so silly its proponents should be spanked at midfield during the halftime show at the next Super Bowl).

Myth 5 – Language Is Static

To set the tone for this section, I invite you to contemplate a most penetrating observation from Sr. Ortega:

> Linguistics had to begin by isolating this skeletonic and abstract side of real language. This procedure enabled it to elaborate grammar and vocabulary – which it has done thoroughly and admirably. But scarcely was this achieved before linguists saw that they had only made a beginning, because actual speaking and writing is an almost constant contradiction of what grammar teaches and dictionaries define – and to such a degree that it could nearly be said that speech consists in offending against grammar and outraging the dictionary. At least, and in all formality, what is called being a good writer, that is, a writer with style, is to subject grammar and vocabulary to frequent erosions. Hence such a great linguistic scientist as Vendryes could define a dead language as one in which it was not permissible to commit errors; and this, turned around, is equivalent to saying that a living language lives by committing them. (*Man and People*, p. 240)

Every generation leaves its distinctive mark on language. Again, this is because language does not exist apart from the sentient beings who use it. Thus, the ebb and flow of the human enigma apply to our lexicon, proving the futility of the Trolls' attempt to confine it in neat little boxes. Let us ponder a few examples of how the English language is evolving before our eyes.

"People Say I Am Redundant, That I Repeat Myself, That I Say Things Over and Over Again ..."[9]

When I was only a year and a half out of law school, I engaged an elder attorney in a debate over "reiterate" vs. "iterate." My position was that "reiterate" was an unnecessary, redundant word and, therefore, should be stricken from the English dictionary. He replied, "*Iterate* means to repeat oneself. *Reiterate* means to repeat someone else." Mere minutes of cursory research proved that we were both wrong, but for different reasons.

My twenty-pound *Webster's*[10] and *Merriam-Webster* Online[11] agree that "iterate" means to say again repeatedly and "reiterate" means to iterate *ad nauseam*. Though our modern English dictionaries cite a Latin root *reiteratus*, no such word is listed in my middle/high school Latin texts or *Cassell's Latin and English Dictionary*.[12] Aside from the stray reference I uncovered during a more recent search online (which source I find inherently dubious), *reiteratus* appears to be an anomaly in the Latin language – a seldom used conjunction of *re-* ("again") and *iteratus* ("repeat").

My colleague was wrong because the common sources do not make the distinction he advanced. I was wrong in arguing that a word should be excised from our lexicon, which makes even less sense than trying to un-ring a bell. Still, there was no denying the visceral effect the word "reiterate" had on me. The word is, in fact, gratingly

---

[9] I believe a stand-up comic coined this quip in the late 1980s, but I have since forgotten his name and have failed to find a source in my subsequent research.

[10] *Webster's New Universal Unabridged Dictionary* (Barnes & Noble Books 1992)

[11] www.merriam-webster.com

[12] MacMillan Publishing Co. 1987

redundant. But it is that redundancy which reinforces its meaning. I find the word irritating to this day. But that is precisely its function.

By its very definition, one would expect to see "reiterate" rarely. Ironically, we use it more often than we use "iterate" because we associate repetition with the prefix "re-." How long, then, will it be before "reiterate" subsumes the meaning of its root "iterate" (meaning to repeat again and again) and we forget altogether the original meaning of the anomaly (to repeat to absurdity)? I submit that, as I write this sentence, the transition is virtually complete.

Hopefully One Hopes that a Hopeful Day Will Come

In 1989, I was sitting in the cubbyhole office I shared with two artists-in-residence when the illustrious Chairman of the Creative Studies Department, Christopher F. "Kit" Givan, Ph.D., blustered in and treated me to a diatribe on the irresponsible use of the word "hopefully." Contrary to my habit with most of the professors in that department, I listened keenly when Kit assumed his soapbox because I found him both entertaining and enlightening. The thrust of Kit's argument was that the only correct usage of the word "hopefully" is adverbial: "The optimist does his daily chores hopefully," meaning that he performs the daily grind with a buoyant attitude. It chapped his hide whenever he saw the word used in place of the subject and verb: "Hopefully, [in lieu of "I hope"] that lunatic Givan won't flunk me just because I can't stand Shakespeare."

As he raved, I at once marveled at his passion for the language and feared that my mentor was on the losing side of the battle. Like any good educator, Kit encouraged his students to debate him as a matter of course. So I complied:

"But, Kit, what about the argument that language is dynamic?"

This launched Kit into another animated tirade. Alas, as Kit waxed indignant a generation ago, an arm's length away sat a seven year-old dictionary that offered the following alternative definition for the word "hopefully": "2. it is hoped; if all goes well: *Hopefully, we'll win.*"[13]

A few years later, I found that my Legal Research and Writing professor shared Kit's outrage:

> **hopefully** This poor, battered word means "with hope," as in: "he hopefully entered the interview." It does not mean "we hope." "Hopefully, nothing will happen tomorrow," is nonsense: what is intended is "we hope nothing will happen tomorrow." What is actually said is, "with hope in its heart, nothing will happen tomorrow."[14]

Who is right? I agree with my elders that the alternative use does not jive with the way we have employed that term for a number of generations. But who are we to assail millions of fellow English speakers (some of whom carry more "credentials" than we) for embracing the new usage? While it is certainly not inappropriate to explain why the original usage makes more sense, to insist that the alternative use is *wrong* is to ignore the reality of how language develops.

Minuscule vs. Miniscule

This is another example of how authoritarians shrink from factuality. Both *Random House* in 1982 and *Websters* a decade later list only "minuscule." It is derived from the Latin word *minusculus* (meaning "rather small"). Thus, Trolls proclaim: "**minuscule.** Not miniscule."[15] But when we consider the fact that the English word "minimum" is derived from the Latin superlative *minimus* (meaning

---

[13] *The Random House College Dictionary, Revised Edition* (Random House, Inc. 1982)

[14] *The Literate Lawyer* by Robert B. Smith – Butterworth Legal Publishers 1986 – p. 51

[15] Id., p. 56

"smallest," "least" or "very little"), we understand that the form "miniscule" was inevitable in English usage, because the human mind thrives on comparison and association. Thus, the word "minuscule" has been "misspelled" so consistently that "miniscule" is now referred to as an alternate spelling.[16] In fact, the variant "miniscule" first appeared in English usage over a century ago.[17] Thus, to peer down from one's ivory tower and demean the form "miniscule" is asinine. I share Mark Twain's outlook on the issue: "I don't give a damn for a man that can only spell a word one way."

Cannot vs. Can Not

The *Webster's* on my credenza *defines* "cannot" as "a form of can not." The latter form is logical in a world in which we routinely build negative verbs such as "would not" or "did not." No self-respecting wordsmith would dare write: "This precedent mustnot stand." Nevertheless, the authorities of my childhood insisted the proper form was "cannot." And the Trolls, notorious for their aversion to even token due diligence, perpetuate this piece of illogic today:

> *Cannot* is the correct form in almost all cases.
> **I cannot represent you in this case.**
> *Can not* appears only when *not* is part of another phrase.
> **He can *not only* request a new hearing but also require a change of venue.**[18]

But when you ask the Troll why, she snaps, "Because that is the way it is done!" then marches away grumbling, "Pesky students with

---

[16] *The American Heritage Dictionary of the English Language, Fourth Edition* (Houghton Mifflin Company, 2004)
[17] www.merriam-webster.com/dictionary/miniscule
[18] *Legal Writing: Getting it Right and Getting it Written* by Mary Barnard Ray and Jill J. Ramsfield – Thomson/West 2005, 4th ed. – p. 51

their annoying questions … I don't have time to make sense, I have a deadline to meet on my fifth edition."

As usual, the student is left to her own devices in getting to the bottom of this mystery. It takes her only a matter of seconds in any reputable library to discover that an obsolete definition of "can" is "to know," which is derived from the Old English word "cunnan," which is related to the Icelandic word "kenna" (hence, the English word "ken" meaning "range of knowledge") and the German word "kennen." As with many words in the English language, the spelling "cannot" derives from a natural merging of languages. But the fact remains that it is an illogical form in modern English usage. This is why (a) those to whom English is a second language typically use the form "can not" and (b) I adopted the form "can not" some years back.

If you take the time to look, you'll find that *can not* is just as common a usage as *cannot*: "… a court can not elevate its interpretation of those policies over the plain wording of the statute and established precedent." (*Shay v. Shay* – 863 N.E.2d 591 at 598 – Ohio 2006) Further, this usage is by no means a novelty: "… because he can not be charged as Heir unless he is in by Descent …." (*Rose v. Cooke* – 2 Va. Colonial Dec. B192 (1736 WL 10) – Va. Gen. 1735) Hence, the Troll's position is silly and untenable. Because the meaning is the same, neither form is more "correct" than the other. Remember, language works because the once arbitrary definition of "onomatopoeia" does not change. As for how we will be spelling "onomatopoeia" in two hundred years, one can not predict.

Irregardless

Every time I hear this word, I want to pull my hair out, gnash my teeth and abuse small, defenseless creatures. I despise it. If I hear it more than once in any given 24-hour period, I fall into a catatonic stupor from which I must be nursed back to consciousness with a very stiff belt of bourbon. Much to my chagrin, the term has persisted in usage for so long that even *Merriam Webster* has been swayed (albeit begrudgingly) to grant it "word" status:[19]

> One entry found for **irregardless**.
> Main Entry: **ir·re·gard·less**
> Pronunciation: "ir-i-'gärd-l&s
> Function: *adverb*
> Etymology: probably blend of *irrespective* and *regardless*
> *nonstandard*: **REGARDLESS**
>
> **usage** *Irregardless* originated in dialectal American speech in the early 20th century. Its fairly widespread use in speech called it to the attention of usage commentators as early as 1927. The most frequently repeated remark about it is that "there is no such word." There is such a word, however. It is still used primarily in speech, although it can be found from time to time in edited prose. Its reputation has not risen over the years, and it is still a long way from general acceptance. Use *regardless* instead.

The 1992 hardback edition of *Merriam Webster* is not so forgiving:

> *Nonstandard.* regardless [IR(RESPECTIVE) + REGARDLESS]
>
> **-Usage.** Irregardless is considered nonstandard because it is redundant: once the negative idea is expressed by the *–less* ending, it is poor style to add the negative *ir-* prefix to express the same idea. Nonetheless, it does creep into the speech of good English speakers, perhaps as a result of attempting greater emphasis.

---

[19] www.merriam-webster.com, July 9, 2006

This is significant in light of the fact that just a few generations ago the same dictionary did not even acknowledge *irregardless* as a variation.[20]

Other Curiosities

As your writing skills develop, two things will inevitably happen: (1) you will forget old, rarely used words and (2) you will both learn and create new words. One of my favorite examples of the latter process is the cute little word *guesstimate*. In 1959, Webster's did not recognize the term. Then, late one night a crafty communicator – seconds shy of a deadline, out of coffee and desperate for a concise way to inject more doubt into the already tenuous term "estimate" – was visited by a stroke of genius as a Charlton Hestonesque voice rang out from on high: "Brave little human, thou canst combine the word *guess* and the word *estimate*." The new term spread among persons of letters like wildfire until, two decades later, it had edged its way into our dictionaries as slang.[21] Today, this lovable little term has been granted the status of a full-fledged word,[22] and rightly so.

A law student/intern once asked me to proofread one of his briefs. I was appalled at how this bright young man's ability to communicate on paper had been emasculated at the hands of Trolls. So obsessed were his professors with championing their favorite version of *The Rules* that this student had spent very little time actually reading, writing and contemplating *words*. For instance, the word *dissimilar* has been around a long time. The oldest dictionary I have shows it was an accepted word form two decades before this student was born (*Webster's* 1959). Yet this student spells it *dis-similar*. Furthermore, the style manuals I grew up with agreed (and still do) that the accepted abbreviation for *pages* is *pp*. But this student spells it, rather sensibly, *pgs*.

What was my role as his linguistic elder? My first task was to

---

[20] *Webster's New Collegiate Dictionary* (G. & C. Merriam Co. 1959)
[21] Random House 1982
[22] www.merriam-webster.com

remind him of the cardinal rule of writing: Consolidate – If you can convey your meaning with two letters (words, sentences, pages, etc.), don't use three. From this perspective, the widely accepted forms *dissimilar* and *pp* win the day. But what if this student had used a slightly different form of "dissimilar," such as *unsimilar*? Every dictionary I know of agrees that *unsimilar* is *not* an English word. Does this mean that when I say *unsimilar* the grammar goblins cast a spell upon all within earshot, rendering them incapable of understanding what I said? Will my utterance of it cause you physical or emotional injury? I submit to you that the word *unsimilar* deserves a place equal to its more popular form *dissimilar*. A number of appellate courts agree. On October 16, 2018, a random search on *Westlaw* returned 27 cases in which the word *unsimilar* was used. The most recent was *U.S. v. Campbell* (2009 WL 595980 – E.D. Tennessee – Not Reported); the earliest, *In re McLaughlin's Estate* (77 N.Y.S.2d 623 – N.Y. Sur. 1947).

Thus, in this scenario, my response to the student would be twofold. First, I would make him aware of the more common form. Second, I would encourage him to use whichever form worked for him. The Trolls would call the use of *unsimilar* a demonstration of illiteracy (thereby unwittingly exposing their own). I call it a logical and inventive way of obeying the cardinal rule of consolidation. Who cares if you offend the Trolls? Last I checked, there was no law imbuing tenured grammar junkies with police powers. What matters is that, when I say "The apple is unsimilar to the orange," the listener understands what I mean. This, my friend, is communication. *Hopefully*, the Trolls will someday understand this.

Here is another interesting example of how English usage borrows from Latin and morphs it over time. In *Gibson v. Texas Pacific Coal Co.* (266 S.W. 137, 138 – Tex. Comm'n App. 1924), one finds the following passage:

> Stubblefield shall receive ... 40 per cent. of such sums as may be realized on account of said claim, even if the said case is compromised, after such appeal.

Searching for an efficient way to compare a portion to the whole, our predecessors adopted two Latin words: *per* meaning "through" or "in the presence of" and *centum* meaning "one hundred." *Per centum* was abbreviated to *per cent.* and, over a few more generations, it was refined into the word we now know as *percent.*

As a final example, let us explore the modern English words "agenda," "memorandum" and "criterion." *Agenda* is the neuter plural of the Latin *agendum* (gerund[23] of *agere* meaning "to do"). The English adoption of *agenda* as a singular form took place so early in modern usage that the original singular *agendum* has practically faded into linguistic oblivion. Because no one I've met in my entire life uses the form *agendum,* I use the modern English singular form *agenda* – to do otherwise would impede communication. The plural form of "memorandum" is not so cut-and-dried.

Cassell's defines *memorandus, -a, -um* as the gerundive form of *memoro,* which means "to mention, call to mind or relate." The plural of the neuter form *memorandum* is *memoranda.* Neither our mainstream English dictionaries nor *Cassell's* explain this last detail. I knew it instinctively, but to confirm it I had to retrieve my fifth grade Latin primer and revisit the second declension.[24] Thus, the distinction is lost upon a growing number of attorneys and legal authors who, having never received a single lesson in Latin, employ the plural version "memorandums."

Those of us who first encountered "memorandum" during our Latin studies will go to our graves using only the plural spelling "memoranda." Nevertheless, I suspect that in English usage the plural form "memoranda" will eventually pass into obscurity.[25] That's neither good nor bad. It is simply the way language evolves. But the

---

[23] The term "gerund" is a fancy way of referring to a verb that has been turned into an adjective or a noun.

[24] *Latin, Our Living Heritage, Book I* by Breslove, Hooper & Barrett (Bell & Howell Co. 1968)

[25] On April 25, 2013 I performed separate Westlaw searches for "memorandums" and "memoranda." Each returned the maximum limit of 10,000 cases. A search for "memorandas" yielded 38.

fact remains that the Latin plural form *memoranda* is far from falling into the same state of obsolescence as the Latin singular *agendum* – a reality of which every conscientious legal writer should be aware.

Once upon a time, English speakers were looking for a more concise way to say "a standard on which a judgment or decision may be based." They adopted the Greek word *kriterion*, whose plural form is *kriteria*. As happened with the Latin form *memorandum*, English usage imposed its own grammatical logic upon the Greek word, creating the plural *criterions* and adopting *criteria* as an alternate singular form. *Merriam-Webster* observes:

> The plural *criteria* has been used as a singular for over half a century <let me now return to the third *criteria*— R. M. Nixon> <that really is the *criteria*— Bert Lance>. Many of our examples, like the two foregoing, are taken from speech. But singular *criteria* is not uncommon in edited prose, and its use both in speech and writing seems to be increasing. Only time will tell whether it will reach the unquestioned acceptability of *agenda*.

There is no rule of thumb for when our Latin and Greek word forms wither into extinction. But of one thing we can be sure: the conscientious legal writer goes the extra mile to investigate these trends.

Myth 4 – Rules of Grammar Are Absolute

The main premise of this book is that today's legal writer should spend more time honing his skills for persuasive communication and less time splitting hairs over arcane formalistic minutiae. Because there are plenty books out there which address the rudiments of grammar, this section should by no means be treated as a comprehensive primer. Rather, it is my hope that from the examples I provide, you will derive a commonsense standard to apply to all of the sticky little messes that inevitably arise when time is shortest and stakes are highest.

The sentence is the lifeblood of written language. Just what is a sentence? When I was in high school, I read a William Faulkner novel in which a single sentence ran longer than a page. Over a decade later, I sent a four-page settlement demand to a colleague. His written reply consisted of one word: "No." So we may presume the sentence is not defined by length. Let us consult a prominent lexicographer. According to the dictionary I too often ignored in college (*Random House* 1975), a sentence is: "a grammatical unit of one or more words, bearing minimal syntactic relation to the words that precede or follow it, often preceded and followed in speech by pauses, having one of a small number of characteristic intonation patterns, and typically expressing an independent statement, question, request, command, etc., as *Fire!* or *Summer is here.*"

Fear not, faithful reader – I don't know what the hell that means either. *Merriam-Webster Online* captures it better as: "a word, clause, or phrase, or a group of clauses or phrases, forming a syntactic unit which expresses an assertion, a question, a command, a wish, an exclamation or the performance of an action that in writing usually begins with a capital letter and concludes with appropriate end punctuation, and that in speaking is distinguished by characteristic patterns of stress, pitch and pauses."

In our formative years we were taught that a sentence should, at a bare minimum, have a subject and a verb. This is not a bad rule of thumb, especially if you have not attained a certain comfort level with written expression. But I prefer to define the sentence as a complete thought, or self-sustaining assertion, which either (a) stands alone or (b) fits cogently between the assertions which immediately precede and follow it. For example:

> Mr. Cain then struck the victim. Because he made
> fun of his pants.

The second statement was known as a *dependent clause* when

33

I was in grade school. One might also recognize it as a *sentence fragment*. Whatever arbitrary label we assign to it, there's something about that second sentence that just ain't right. The troublemaker is the word *because*. Eliminate it and you have the grammatically correct sentence, "He made fun of his pants." But who made fun, whose pants looked funny, and what do those pants have to do with Mr. Cain's insensitive act? We don't need to memorize twenty-five artificial constructs to know intuitively that this is a bad combination of statements. As we apply logic and common sense, we may pick from a variety of ways to clean up this mess:

> Mr. Cain then struck the victim because he made fun of his pants.

> Because the victim made fun of his pants, Mr. Cain struck him.

> Mr. Cain then struck the victim. Why? Because he made fun of his pants.

The first two examples would please the most crotchety of Trolls. Though the final construction at least places your fragment in an understandable context, it might earn your syntactic knuckles a good rapping. Why? For one thing, it violates our sacred Rule of Consolidation: If you can say it in one sentence, don't use three. I happen to agree with this principle *most of the time*. But blind allegiance to it will rob you of the extra punch you need in certain situations.

> Mr. Cain then struck the victim. Why? Because he made fun of his pants.

Inserting the question *Why* adds an extra beat to the passage, emphasizing the outrage of Mr. Cain's act by making the reader pause for a microsecond longer than he otherwise would. Thus, upon

34

the real-world writer devolves the privilege and the responsibility to reach beyond the mechanics of writing, to arrange the nuts and bolts of his trade according to, not the vapid droning of the Troll but the cadence of music and poetry. As Mark Twain instructs:

> The right word may be effective, but no word was ever
> as effective as a rightly timed pause.

The fundamental punctuation marks are the period, the comma, the question mark and the exclamation point. Your typical grammar book will propose any number of "proper" uses for the comma. For instance, Michael Strumpf and Auriel Douglas have compiled rules for the comma under no less than 31 subject headings.[26] The U.S. Constitution recognizes that you have the inalienable perquisite to sit down and memorize each and every rule. But it won't do you any good because writing is not a robotic process. If you are paying adequate attention to your work, it is highly probable that tomorrow you will not place a comma where you placed it in the same sentence yesterday.

The self-proclaimed experts out there agree that the exclamation point does not belong in legal writing. Bully for them. But they can not agree on something as simple as the placement of the comma. A good example of this is the ongoing *last comma in a series* debate. When I learned grammar in the 1970s, I was taught that I should always omit the last comma, thus: "I will have eggs, toast and Novocaine for brunch." Though the gods and goddess of style and usage during that era[27] disagreed, the goddess deftly recognized that this rule was subject to stylistic preference: "... some writers, however, prefer to omit the comma before *and.*"[28] Among today's legal writing commentators, the saner ones agree that the last comma

---

[26] *The Grammar Bible* (Owl Books 2004)

[27] William Strunk, Jr., and E.B. White, authors of *The Elements of Style* (Longman Publishers 2000); and Margaret Shertzer, author of *The Elements of Grammar* (Macmillan Pub. Co. 1986)

[28] *The Elements of Grammar*, p. 79

is optional. I particularly like the way Martha Faulk and Irving Mehler addressed the issue:

> Most legal writers prefer to keep the serial comma before *and* because they feel it's safer to do so, and because their readers expect to see the comma there. However, many writers (and some editors) routinely omit the comma before *and* in a series of words *unless the omission would cause a misreading.*[29]

Unfortunately, when commentators spout such heresy (known in the real world as common sense), Trolls rush to the defense of inanity. So pervasive is their banter that not even a seasoned jurist is immune from their noxious influence. In his book *The Legal Writer*,[30] Judge Mark Painter directs, "Always Use the Serial Comma." To support his argument, he cites three cases in which he contends that the lack of a serial comma created confusion for the reviewing courts. But a fair reading of each proves otherwise.[31]

In the first (*Sunshine Enterprises of Missouri, Inc. v. Board of Adjustment of the City of St. Ann* – 64 S.W.3d 310, 313 – Mo. 2002), at issue was whether an under-$500 lender could be classified as a "pawn shop" or an establishment "whose primary business is check cashing and related services" under a zoning ordinance. Though the court indulges itself in a brief discussion of the comma, this is nothing more than a random frolic: because the business at issue did not fall under either classification, the placement of the serial comma between "check cashing and related services" was completely irrelative to the case.

---

[29] *The Elements of Legal Writing* – Longman Publishers 1994 – p. 69 (emphasis added)

[30] Cincinnati Book Publishing 2005, p. 97

[31] Ever mindful of my ethical obligations as an officer of the court, it is not my intent to denigrate Judge Painter's office or his performance on the bench. I restrict my opinions to the views he has expressed outside the courtroom, not about the law or a particular controversy, but about forensic discourse in general.

In the remaining cases the only confusion was caused, not by the inclusion or omission of a comma, but by turgid advocates who, in an attempt to pervert the rules of statutory construction, enlisted the serial comma argument merely because it facilitated their ruse. Don't take my word for it. Read them for yourself. Here is an excerpt from *New York State Dairy Foods, Inc. v. Northeast Dairy Compact Commission* (198 F.3d 1, 9-10 – C.A.1 Mass. 1999):

> Appellants seize on this last provision, arguing that the lack of a serial comma after "partially regulated plants" and before "and all other handlers" suggests that the latter modifies the former. *** The district court found this construction to be contrary to the logic of the Compact, and we agree. Failure to construe the statute in this way would leave a gaping hole in the regulatory regime.

And here are the salient portions of *Peterson v. Midwest Security Ins. Co.* (636 N.W.2d 727 – Wis. 2001):

> Peterson reads the definition of "property" differently. He argues that the phrase "buildings, structures and improvements" merely modifies "real property," so that a person who owns a building, structure or improvement but does not also own the underlying real property does not own "property" within the meaning of the statute. He interprets the statute to create two categories of "property": 1) real property, *along with* any buildings, structures, or improvements thereon; and 2) the waters of the state. He bases this interpretation on the lack of punctuation between the phrases "real property" and "buildings, structures and improvements" in the definition.
>
> We decline to give the absence of a comma such interpretive significance. Peterson's punctuation-based

interpretation operates to impose a requirement that does not appear on the face of the statute: that the owner of a building, structure or improvement implicated in a recreational injury must also own the underlying real property in order to own "property" as that term is defined in the statute. But the statute does not say "'[p]roperty' means real property and buildings, structures and improvements thereon *that are owned by the real property owner*," and we cannot rewrite it in the exercise of interpreting it. (Id. at 575)

The dissent argues that our reading of the statute violates the rules of grammar and punctuation. We do not disagree that courts sometimes look to grammatical rules when interpreting legal texts. But interpreting a legal text is not like diagramming a sentence or correcting an English paper. The rules of grammar and punctuation should not be applied at the expense of a natural, reasonable reading of the statutory language (taking into account the context in which it appears and the purpose of the statute), or when the result is an expansion or contraction of the statute contrary to its terms. Here, strict adherence to the "rule of the serial comma" as advocated by the dissent operates to add a substantive requirement to the statute that it otherwise does not contain. (Id. at 732, fn. 7; internal citation omitted)

This is one example of how litigants and partisan judges will grasp at any straw, however brittle, to lend credence to a groundless argument. With one incisive stroke, the majority has (a) upbraided the dissent for attempting to use a grammatical rule to pervert the clear meaning of a statute and (b) clarified its own position in the ongoing *form vs. substance* battle.

I often find that inserting a comma where my grade school

grammarian once told me to merely obscures an otherwise fluid statement. In other situations I insert a comma where she would not, because I am using the wonderfully versatile tool for emphasis. These ideas are by no means new; they have merely been suppressed by the Trolls. In 1975, a mild-mannered English professor named John R. Trimble, Ph.D., published a little book titled *Writing with Style – Conversations on the Art of Writing.*[32] The good professor was well acquainted with Trolls, to whom he referred as *literary prudes.* Anyone who is serious about becoming an effective writer should read his book.[33] Here is Professor Trimble's introduction to his section on the comma (Id. at 107):

> Most students have trouble with commas. Where do you put them in? When can you leave them out? If you demand a definitive answer, lock yourself in a padded cell with one of the thick handbooks on grammar. If you'll settle for something incomplete but practical, read on.
>
> One simple rule, comprehensive enough to cover most contingencies, is this: Insert a comma wherever there is a light natural pause. Test it this way: Read your sentence aloud, in a measured voice, as if to a large audience. If you find that you naturally pause in a given place, or *must* pause to make the sense of your sentence instantly intelligible to the listener, insert a comma. Let your ear and good sense be your guides. If still in doubt, have a friend read the sentence aloud, slowly and emphatically. The pauses, if there are any, will begin announcing themselves.

Though I was only in the ninth grade when I first read this passage, I had suffered the "comma always goes here" tyranny

---

[32] Prentice-Hall, Inc., 2nd edition 2000

[33] Caveat – I merely said to read it, not to adopt it wholesale as gospel.

long enough to recognize its soft-spoken genius. Alas, I rapidly forgot this commonsense approach under the tutelage of the Trolls I encountered in college, graduate and law schools. So thoroughly did they reindoctrinate me that I would not consult the above passage again until a quarter-century later, when I realized that (a) I myself was thinking like a Troll and (b) I needed to be deprogrammed in quick order.

In the same breath that I salute Dr. Trimble, I must sadly acknowledge that, on the very next page he succumbs to the urge to endorse a Rule for All Seasons when he advocates the use of the serial comma in every situation. While this is perhaps good advice for new initiates to the polemic process, it presents a stumbling block to their development because it spawns the mindless overuse of the comma in a vast array of situations in which it is simply unnecessary. Fortunately for me, English teachers such as Coach Surbeck and his colleague Perry Oldham preserved my rationality on this issue by training me to cull the helpful advice from the unconstructive; therefore, I may wholeheartedly (a) embrace my predecessor's adroit perception of the natural pause while (b) dismissing his espousal of the Rule for All Seasons, because part of my duty as a writer is to rectify the missteps of my progenitors. (I am less forgiving of my contemporaries, because they should know better.)

What's that? You've never heard of Dr. Trimble? That's no surprise. As I've established, rational viewpoints are heretical in trolldom. So it is little wonder that among the current "authorities" on legal writing only one even mentions Dr. Trimble.[34] Sadly, rather than using the opportunity to improve on his mentor's reasoning, this Troll vacuously perpetuates the serial comma myth.[35]

When we consider the comma as nothing more than a way to mark a natural pause, our sentences become smoother. So it follows with other punctuation marks. When we focus on function rather than form, applying nothing more than common sense and logic, a

---

[34] *The Winning Brief,* p. xi
[35] Id., pp. 293-5

natural hierarchy emerges whereby a few core rules become vital, the majority fall into the *advisory* category and the remaining rules are negligible if not altogether obsolete. The preceding sentence illustrates what I mean. The two commas surrounding "applying nothing more than common sense and logic" are necessary, not so much because it is a dependant clause but because one naturally pauses at these junctures. Here are two other ways one might express this thought, contingent upon the degree of emphasis one wishes to place upon it:

> When we focus on function rather than form (applying nothing more than common sense and logic) a natural hierarchy emerges ....

> When we focus on function rather than form – applying nothing more than common sense and logic – a natural hierarchy emerges ....

One might also wish to express the entire thought as a list. When I was in middle school, I was taught the following method for essay writing:

> When we focus on function rather than form, applying nothing more than common sense and logic, a natural hierarchy emerges whereby: (a) a few core rules become vital; (b) the majority fall into the *advisory* category; and, (c) the remaining rules are negligible if not altogether obsolete.

I remained faithful to this rigid structure until 2005 when my career move freed me to focus more on writing. As I analyzed my craft day in and out, I first dropped the final comma: "... and (c) the remaining rules are negligible ...." I then asked myself if all the other stilted punctuation was necessary. Thus, depending on a variety of factors (e.g., the underlying tone of a particular case or my gut sense for

41

how this particular brief should flow), I might drop the colons and semicolons altogether because the list indicator is all I need to mark the transition:

> When we focus on function rather than form, applying nothing more than common sense and logic, a natural hierarchy emerges whereby (a) a few core rules become vital (b) the majority fall into the *advisory* category and (c) the remaining rules are negligible if not altogether obsolete.

And, if I want to place greater emphasis on the final phrase, I might do it in any of the following ways:

> (c) the remaining rules are negligible, if not altogether obsolete.
> (c) the remaining rules are negligible – if not altogether obsolete.
> (c) the remaining rules are negligible *if not altogether obsolete.*
> (c) the remaining rules are negligible, *if not altogether obsolete.*
> (c) the remaining rules are negligible – *if not altogether obsolete.*

Finally, we've all known since our tender years that the verb must agree in number with its subject. But collective nouns present a challenge to the implementation of this rule. Try as they do to come up with the best explanation for why a verb following a collective noun should be singular or plural, the proponents of either postulate fight a useless battle. In the sentence we've been playing with appears the phrase "the majority fall." Depending on whose book you read in which climate, you may be convinced that "the majority" requires a singular verb. On the other hand, you know intuitively that 1 can not be a majority of only 1 or 2. Thus, the term *majority* (a) connotes a quantity of at least 3 and (b) requires a plural verb. Which do you choose? Let the Trolls waste their time bickering about it amongst themselves – chalk it up to a matter of personal style and use singular or plural according to your own instincts.

Here's the bottom line on punctuation and rules of grammar. In whatever situation you find yourself, ask this question: Will my obedience to this rule (e.g., putting a comma here or a semicolon there) add to or detract from the meaning I wish to convey? Whatever obstructs your attempt to communicate should be discarded. You don't need to memorize a thousand arbitrary rules aimed at homogenizing and mechanizing English usage. All you need do is take an extra millisecond to THINK about each and every word you utter.

Myth 3 – There Are Rules for All Seasons

For all of the scoundrels I've encountered in the practice of law, I've been fortunate enough to work with a good number of honorable attorneys. One of the latter is a gentleman named Mark. Though Mark's native tongue is Spanish, he is quite fluent in English. He once told me that he never had spelling tests growing up in Mexico, because Spanish is largely phonetic. It was frustrating for Mark to learn English, because it seemed to him there were more exceptions than rules. And he is right. The best example of this is the little jingle I recited every morning in first grade: *i before e, except after c*. It was a hopeful theory, but in practice it turned out to be just plain silly: *believe* vs. *seize, friend* vs. *their*. Thus, I was not surprised to find the following article posted at BBC News on June 20, 2009:[36]

Schools to rethink 'i before e'

The spelling mantra "i before e except after c" is no longer worth teaching, according to the government.

---

[36] http://news.bbc.co.uk/2/hi/uk_news/education/8110573.stm

Advice sent to teachers says there are too few words which follow the rule and recommends using more modern methods to teach spelling to schoolchildren.

The document, entitled Support for Spelling, is being distributed to more than 13,000 primary schools.

But some people believe the phrase should be retained because it is easy to remember and is broadly accurate.

Bethan Marshall, a senior English lecturer at King's College London, said: "It's a very easy rule to remember and one of the very few spelling rules that I can remember and that's why I would stick to it.

"If you change it and say we won't have this rule, we won't have any rules at all, then spelling, which is already terribly confusing, becomes more so."

Judy Parkinson, author of the best-selling book I Before E (Except After C), told the Daily Telegraph it was a phrase that struck a chord.

"There are words that it doesn't fit, but I think teachers could always get a discussion going about the 'i before e' rule and the peculiarities of the English language, and have fun with it. That's the best way to learn."

The guidance is being issued as part of the National Primary Strategy for under-11s.

It says: "The i before e rule is not worth teaching. It applies only to words in which the ie or ei stands for a clear ee sound. Unless this is known, words such as sufficient and veil look like exceptions.

"There are so few words where the ei spelling for the ee sounds follows the letter c that it is easier to learn the specific words." These include receive, ceiling, perceive and deceit.

The document recommends other ways to teach pupils spelling, like studying television listings for compound words, changing the tense of a poem to practise irregular verbs and learning about homophones through jokes such as "How many socks in a pair? None — because you eat a pear."

Some education experts have supported the government and questioned the effectiveness of the rule.

Jack Bovill, chairman of the Spelling Society, said words such as vein and neighbour made it a meaningless phrase.

"There are so many exceptions that it's not really a rule," he said.

He added that it would be helpful if spelling were allowed to evolve.

You would do well to ponder that final line for a few moments. By voicing the aspiration that spelling be allowed to evolve, Mr. Bovill has captured the essence of a living language.

The *i before e* maxim is an example of a misguided attempt to create what I call a Rule for All Seasons: a magical theorem that applies so universally that it *frees* the writer of the *burden* of *thinking*. Though I address such rules in other parts of this book, I wish to focus here on three in particular.

A Question of Fundamental Respect

One of the most juvenile tactics I have seen attorneys employ is to refer to an expert who holds a doctorate degree, not as "Dr. Smith" but as "Mr. Smith" or even "Smith." That is why I must take issue with Bryan A. Garner. At page 266 of *The Winning Brief,* he endorses this puerile litigation ploy. *Quoting style manuals for journalists as his support,* Mr. Garner[37] explains that omitting these titles creates "a brisker, more matter-of-fact style. Journalists aren't being rude when they do this, and neither are you."

To the contrary, I think it *is* rude, especially when journalists do it. I also think the last source a thoughtful writer should consult for advice is a style manual which caters to one of the most elitist (undeservedly) professions in society. One may argue that, when the appellate rules limit you to only so many words, dropping the honorifics can save crucial space for substantive argument. But I have never found such terms of respect to be the culprits. In an Indiana case I'll address in greater detail in the next chapter, we had only 4,200 words in which to convince the next higher court that the lower court had defied long entrenched standards of review. Our local counsel urged that we could save about 70 words by dropping the titles. Days later, I produced a final brief that hammered home every salient point, kept the honorifics and was one word shy of the limit.

As I've said, I am a strong advocate for verbal economy. But one can take concision to an absurd extreme. As our lives move ever faster, and as our habits of communication are assaulted by a burgeoning number of rap and hip-hop artists, one appreciates more than ever simple acts of courtesy and respect. Yes, it takes longer to write "Mr. Smith" than it does "Smith." Yes, it is galling to stop in

---

[37] Every graduate of an accredited law school is awarded a doctorate in the field of law. Practicing lawyers customarily deemphasize this eponym, preferring to be called "Ms." or "Mr." Thus, in referring to the professor as "Mr." Garner I mean him no disrespect. Rather, I grant him the urbane benefit of the doubt. Though he has spent the majority (if not all) of his professional life in classrooms as opposed to courtrooms, I credit him with the same magnanimity shared by my colleagues.

the midst of constructing an argument to scan a *curriculum vitae* or deposition to ascertain whether he has the credential that entitles him to be called "Dr. Smith." But here is what Mr. Garner and his sycophants at the Plain Language Institute (see Myth 1) fail to understand: *When a judge experiences me as an attorney who takes the time to pay my adversaries this type of respect, I'll never have to shout to get that judge's attention.*

We must remember who we are and what our responsibility is. Precision is the lawyer's stock-in-trade. Leave the truncated headline-speak to the drudges scavenging for a scoop – write your briefs like a dignified, grown-up professional.

The Unisex He/She vs. They Conundrum

In my 20s and 30s, it seemed that every time I turned around someone was debating how to handle the unisex pronoun. For many years I resisted the so-called *Equal Timers* and used the pronoun *he* in all instances: "One often does not know as much as he thinks." For trivial personal reasons, I now sympathize with the *Equal Timers*. Most if not all authors agree that the usages "he or she" and "he/she" are cumbersome. As you've seen in this book, I simply alternate them at random. I approached this section with the intention of championing *they* as a practical, time-saving unisex pronoun. My argument was that, so long as we strove for equal grammatical representation between the sexes, universal acceptance of *they* as an alternative was inevitable.

But when I heeded the advice I often give to others about doing one's homework before opening one's mouth, I discovered that uptight people such as I have been wrestling with what appears to be a dead issue. Though the 1959 edition of *Webster's* does not recognize this usage, the 1982 edition of *Random House* does:

> 3. *Nonstandard.* (used with an indefinite singular antecedent in place of the definite masculine "he" or the definite feminine "she"): *Whoever is of voting*

47

age, whether they are interested in politics or not, should vote.

I recently consulted www.dictionary.com. The third definition tracked that above word-for-word with one exception – the word *nonstandard* had been eliminated. I also found the following note on usage:

Long before the use of generic he was condemned as sexist, the pronouns they, their, and them were used in educated speech and in all but the most formal writing to refer to indefinite pronouns and to singular nouns of general personal reference, probably because such nouns are often not felt to be exclusively singular: If anyone calls, tell them I'll be back at six. Everyone began looking for their books at once. Such use is not a recent development, nor is it a mark of ignorance. Shakespeare, Swift, Shelley, Scott, and Dickens, as well as many other English and American writers, have used they and its forms to refer to singular antecedents. Already widespread in the language (though still rejected as ungrammatical by some), this use of they, their, and them is increasing in all but the most conservatively edited American English. This increased use is at least partly impelled by the desire to avoid generic *he* or the awkward *he/she* and *he or she* when the antecedent's gender is not known or when the referent is of mixed gender: *The victim had money and jewelry taken from them. It's hard to move an aging mother or father from their long-term home.*

Despite the above fact, you will not have to go far to find someone who will try to convince you he has devised the perfect "non-they" argument. Don't waste your time trying to make heads or tails of it, because common sense instructs that there is no such magic bullet. I doubt I will ever bring myself to use the unisex *they* in a legal brief, despite the fact that I employ it quite freely in both conversational speech and non-legal writing. By the same token, I would not presume to ridicule another legal writer for embracing a usage my fellow nit-pickers and I have stubbornly resisted for two decades.

Block Quotes vs. Quotation Marks

In *Legal Writing: Getting it Right and Getting it Written* (p. 187) Mmes. Ray & Ramsfield proclaim:

> When a direct quote is longer than forty-nine words, indent it, single-space it, and omit quotation marks.

However they conjured it up, this rule is just plain silly. The fact is that the gods of written expression did not hand down a magic number. For the lawyer who applies common sense, there are many factors that go into deciding whether to use block quotes or quotation marks. For instance, you may choose the block quote to call special attention to a particular thought. You may insert a less poignant statement in quotation marks so that you do not interrupt the flow of your presentation. On the other hand, you may block-quote a nonessential statement simply because you notice your paragraph is running a bit long. If you're trying to pare down an appellate brief to conform to a particular court's page limitation, the block quote will almost always be preferred because every court I'm aware of allows you to single-space such quotes.

Finally, the block quote should not be overlooked as an aesthetic tool. Curves and undulations on interstate highways are not wholly coincidental. Many were either created or preserved because highway planners understood that, when you are careening down the tarmac in a motorized beast at 75 mph, monotony kills. Likewise, when the human eye is trudging through a legal brief, the occasional widening of the margins is as refreshing as a scenic turnoff to the weary driver.

With this and the innumerable other decisions you will make as a legal writer, you must disabuse yourself of the notion that an easy answer can be found in the pages of a rulebook. Like it or not, you have chosen a profession that demands independent, creative and meticulous thought. If that sounds like too much work my friend, you should strongly consider another career.

Myth 2 – Today's Lawyer Must Be a
Master of Mindless Trivia

Citation Structure

Let us pretend you are a judge. Not a Curmudgeon, mind you, but a sensible and intelligent jurist. I, the forthright and fastidious lawyer, would like to discuss with you a case named *Hawk v. Seaboard System Railroad, Inc.* Now you, the sensible and intelligent judge, have no reason to disbelieve anything I tell you. You know you can trust me because ... well ... I am a lawyer. Nevertheless, because I have nothing to hide from you, my opponent or the next higher court, I want you to be able to read the case and satisfy yourself that what I say about it is accurate. Thus, it is imperative that I draw a map that leads you directly to it. This requires only 3-count-em-3 pieces of information: (1) Volume (2) Reporter (3) Page.

But what if you find my brief so riveting that you don't want to stop in its midst to look up the case? *This brief is so poignant, so compelling ... Why isn't this lawyer writing Presidential speeches or grant proposals? I'm of a mind to give his client everything she wants ... Hawk v. Seaboard ... it fits the argument perfectly. I can't recall who wrote the opinion or when. That quote looks accurate ... the argument is so eloquent that I'd rather not stop now to check it, but I've got to know who wrote it and when, because I will not cite it in my ruling if it was penned by that nitwit who vied for my seat when I was a district judge.* Anticipating such a dilemma, I provide you with two additional pieces of data: (4) Court (5) Date. Putting it all together, we have the following citation for *Hawk*:

547 So.2d 669 (Fla. App. 2 Dist. 1989)

To point you directly to a quoted portion, I can further refine my citation in any of the following manners:

547 So.2d 669, 674 at fn. 2 (Fla. App. 2 Dist. 1989)

547 So.2d 669 at fn. 2 (Fla. App. 2 Dist. 1989)

With the above examples I have told you (a) where to find the case (b) where to find the text I have quoted (c) what appellate division decided the case and (d) when the decision was rendered. Citation is that simple. Now let's take a look at a few examples of how the Yapping Chihuahuas have needlessly complicated it. In my brief I make two arguments, the first of which is:

Argument 1

This Court does not sit as Juror No. 7. Because the jury enjoys great latitude in fashioning a pain-and-suffering award, this Court may not overturn its verdict simply because the Court disagrees with it:

> While this wide latitude is subject to review, the trial court **does not sit as a seventh juror with veto power** and may not substitute its judgment on damages. [*Hawk v. Seaboard Sys. RR., Inc.*, 547 So.2d 669 at 671 – Fla. App. 2 Dist. 1989 (citation omitted; emphasis added); review dismissed, 549 So.2d 1014 – Fla. 1989]

The purveyors of *Bluebook* would advance the following criticisms of my form:

1) "Juror No. 7" should read "Juror No. Seven."[38]

---

[38] Id., Rule 6.2(a)

2) Because my direct quote from the *Hawk* case is less than 49 words long, it should not be set off as a block quotation.[39]
3) There should be a space between "So." and "2d."[40]
4) The ordinal "2nd" implied in "2 Dist." should *always* read "2d."[41]
5) My citation of *Hawk* should not be included with the block quote, but should be set off in the main text.[42]

The pushers of *ALWD Citation Manual*[43] march in lockstep with the *Bluebook* fanatics ... with one minor exception: after innumerable, marathon summits, they have come to the epochal conclusion that the block-quote threshold should be raised by one word.[44]

But the inanity does not end with *ALWD*. As often happens with a segment of society that has nothing important to do, the Yapping Chihuahuas have proliferated exponentially to the point that they have begun to infect legislative and administrative bodies. Florida provides a good example of this. F.R.A.P. 9.210 sets out the requirement for the content of appellate briefs. The rule addresses basic parameters such as paper and margin size, font, length and structure. At the very end, as though it were an afterthought, subsection (h) provides: "Counsel are requested to use the uniform citation system prescribed by rule 9.800." F.R.A.P. 9.800(b)(1) requires that "Fla. App. 2d Dist." be written "Fla. 2d DCA."

Thus, Argument 1 would appear in one of two forms:

(A)

This Court does not sit as Juror No. Seven. Because the jury enjoys great latitude in fashioning a pain-and-suffering award, this Court may not overturn its

---

[39] Id., Rule 5.1(b)

[40] Id., Rule 6.1

[41] Id., Rule 6.2(b)

[42] Id., Rules 5.1 & 5.2

[43] Darby Dickerson (Aspen Publishers 3rd Edition 2006)

[44] Id: Rules 4.2(a), 4.3(a) 47.4(a) & 47.5(c); Chart 12.1

verdict simply because the Court disagrees with it: "While this wide latitude is subject to review, the trial court **does not sit as a seventh juror with veto power** and may not substitute its judgment on damages." [*Hawk v. Seaboard Sys. RR., Inc.*, 547 So.2d 669 at 671 – Fla. 2d DCA 1989 (citation omitted; emphasis added); review dismissed, 549 So.2d 1014 – Fla. 1989]

(B)

This Court does not sit as Juror No. Seven. Because the jury enjoys great latitude in fashioning a pain-and-suffering award, this Court may not overturn its verdict simply because the Court disagrees with it:

> While this wide latitude is subject to review, the trial court **does not sit as a seventh juror with veto power** and may not substitute its judgment on damages. [Though irrelevant, a successive sentence or two would be inserted here to meet the arbitrary 49/50-word requirement.]

> [*Hawk v. Seaboard Sys. RR., Inc.*, 547 So.2d 669 at 671 – Fla. 2d DCA 1989 (citation omitted; emphasis added); review dismissed, 549 So.2d 1014 – Fla. 1989]

Let us revisit the purpose of language. Is it to obfuscate? Is it to speak in secret code? No, it is simply to communicate. Citation is no different. If I refer you to "So.2d" rather than "So. 2d," will you not find your way to *Southern Reporter Second*? If I describe a court as the 3rd Circuit rather than the 3d Circuit, will I inflict physical or mental damage upon a member of the judiciary? Though our venerated Rule of Consolidation would favor "2d DCA" over "App.

2 Dist.," I submit that "2d DCA" presents a stumbling block to the attorney who practices nationwide. Here is what I mean.

The majority of jurisdictions follow the convention that, if you're referring to an intermediate State appellate court, you cite it as [St.]+[App.]+[# Dist.]+[Date]. As I sat in Oklahoma writing trial briefs for a Florida case, I noticed stray references to "DCA" in my research. I dismissed these instances as internet laziness until I ran across the above rule in my appellate research. Here's the interesting thing. I did not discover F.R.A.P. 9.800(b)(1) until after I had submitted hundreds of pages of briefing to the trial court. Yet neither the trial judge *nor our local counsel (who had, by that time, practiced law in Florida for over a quarter century)* took issue. Why? Because we were concerned with legal issues that far outweighed such piddling distinctions in citation format.

It is simply not human nature to follow such trifling rules. Some years back, I plugged 771 So.2d 44 into *Westlaw*. Though this case was described as "4 DCA" in another opinion, the *Westlaw* heading referred to it as "Fla. App. 4th Dist." When I entered the same citation two years later, only the ordinal suffix had been dropped: "Fla. App. 4 Dist." After reading in the committee notes that R. 9.800 was conceived in part to conform to *Bluebook* format, I had to chuckle when I saw that the author of that opinion (and/or the *Westlaw* transcriber) had violated *Bluebook* Rule 6 (Id. at 46):

> This case is distinguishable from *United Services Automobile Ass'n v. Behar,* 752 So.2d 663 (Fla. 2nd DCA 2000).

I will be the first to applaud if "2d DCA" supersedes "App. 2 Dist." on a national scale, just as "C.A.10" seems to have replaced "10th Cir." But such a change will owe its impetus, not to a court rule but to the natural, evolutionary process of usage.

Here is the second argument from my brief:

Argument 2

The trial court should ignore the appellate court
in this case because *"stare decisis* does not command
blind allegiance to precedent." [*State v. Gray* – 654
So.2d 552, 554 – Fla. 1995; *Puryear v. State* – 810
So.2d 901, 904-5 – Fla. 2002; *Rotemi Realty, Inc., v.
Act Realty Company* – 911 So.2d 1181, 1188 – Fla.
2005]

With a dangerously profuse amount of idle time on their hands,
the Yapping Chihuahuas have conjured up peculiar little things they
call "signals."[45] For them it is not enough that I cite authority for
my propositions; I must introduce each with a codeword to tell my
reader whether that authority's content is redundant, supplemental or
inferential. Let us revisit Argument 2 and apply the rules regarding
signals. Because I have directly quoted *Gray*, I need no such signal
to introduce its citation. The remaining cites clearly support the
proposition for which I quoted *Gray*, but the same quote does not
appear in either of those opinions. So I must insert a magic word
to *signal* this general agreement to my reader: "Accord: *Puryear
v. State*, 810 So.2d 901, 904-5 (Fla. 2002); *Rotemi Realty* ...." The
Yappers have developed a whole array of magic signals: *E.g., See,
See Also, Compare, Contra, But See*. They even offer mix-and-match
sets: *See e.g., Compare e.g.* But have they enhanced the process of
communication or degraded it? Let us consider a passage from *Payne
v. Tennessee*:

Evidence about the victim and survivors, and any
jury argument predicated on it, can of course be so
inflammatory as to risk a verdict impermissibly based
on passion, not deliberation. Cf. *Penry v. Lynaugh*,

[45] *Bluebook* at Rule 1.2 & ALWD at Rule 44.3

492 U.S. 302, 319-328, 109 S.Ct. 2934, 2947-2952, 106 L.Ed.2d 256 (1989) (capital sentence should be imposed as a "'reasoned *moral* response'") (quoting *California v. Brown,* 479 U.S. 538, 545, 107 S.Ct. 837, 841, 93 L.Ed.2d 934 (1987) (O'CONNOR, J., concurring)); *Gholson v. Estelle,* 675 F.2d 734, 738 (C.A.5 1982) ("If a person is to be executed, it should be as a result of a decision based on reason and reliable evidence"). [501 U.S. 808, 836 (1991)]

According to the Yapping Chihuahuas, "Cf." denotes authority that "supports a proposition different from the main proposition but sufficiently analogous to lend support."[46] So the highly educated writer of that opinion (a) dutifully follows the rule, but then (b) adds a parenthetical to his *Penry* citation specifying the proposition it sets forth, thus (c) obviating any need for the introductory code, thereby (d) wasting the reader's valuable time.

I submit to you that the very idea of imposing a system of signals on legal writing is just plain silly. Practicing lawyers and sitting judges so seldom encounter signals that it takes more time to decipher the abstruse definition for one than it does to just read the page or paragraph to which the author refers. The conscientious writer must consider how many variations of the bleeding obvious his reader is prepared to stomach. Forget signals. Remember that you're arguing your case to a judge, not a kindergartener. You, the judge and your opponent find yourselves in this particular arena because you share a distinctive analytical dexterity. Therefore, you may presume the judge is savvy enough to take into account the entire spectrum of a citation's potential applicability without your trying to spoonfeed him. In fact, I submit to you that any attempt to narrow that spectrum is an insult to that judge's intelligence. In the real world, 90% of your citations need no further commentary – provided, of course, that

---

[46] *Bluebook*, R. 1.2

they are precisely placed.[47] For 9% of the remainder, you'll be better served to work the commentary into the main discussion – if it's not important enough to be there, you don't need to say it anyway. Only in the rarest of instances will the practicing lawyer see the need to employ a *signal*. In that event, common sense suggests that you craft your own introductory word or phrase, and here is why. What makes sense to you at this particular stage of your argument will make far better sense to your audience than will some watchword whose context is often more tenebrous than the Hearsay Rule.

Before moving to the next topic, I will leave you with an example of how dangerous a *signal* is in the hands of a lawyer who (a) is inexperienced (b) is inattentive to detail (c) is overworked (d) dictates his briefs to an inept assistant or (e) all of the above. I once reviewed an application filed with the Supreme Court of Tennessee in which the composer used the signal "accord" to introduce two cases in the body of the discussion: *Masson v. New Yorker Magazine, Inc.* (85 F.3d 1394 – C.A.9 1996) and *Securities Industries Ass'n v. Board of Governors of Federal Reserve* (900 F.2d 360 – D.C. Cir. 1990). Whoever (and/or whatever software) later pieced together the Table of Authorities thought "accord" was part of the case style. Thus, the writer and his client looked like fools when the high court of Tennessee read the following entries in the Table of Authorities: *Accord Masson v. New Yorker Magazine, Inc.*, 85 F.3d 1394 (C.A.9 1996) and *Accord SEC v. Board of Governors of Federal Reserve*, 900 F.2d 360 (D.C. Cir. 1990). (I don't know how this person drew "SEC" from "Securities Industries Association," but that certainly did not shore up the defendant's credibility.)

Citation Placement

What distinguishes our profession from most is that we are taught to analyze an issue from every possible angle. Our vast body of codified and decisional law has grown and diversified, and

---

[47] See my discussion of the Wayward Associate in the Epilogue section titled "Every Lie We Whitewash Erodes the Truth."

continues to do so, because lawyers do not take things at face value. We are at once celebrated and reviled for our ability to forge new interpretations for precedents and statutes. To us, nothing is sacred. We question everyone. We dissect everything. Lawyers are what a poet I know once called "two-fisted thinkers." Sadly, very few of us test the conventions of legal writing with the same bulldog attitude. All too often we simply adopt forms and structures used by people we consider "authorities" (judges or professors) without taking a second thought. Most illustrative of this haphazard approach is how we present our citations. It is such an elemental question that every "authority" I have consulted has overlooked it.

Let us revisit the concept of citation. Standing alone, "*State v. Gray*, 654 So.2d 552, 554 (Fla. 1995)" communicates nothing. While the quote from that case ("Yet *stare decisis* does not command blind allegiance to precedent.") certainly qualifies as a statement, it again is meaningless unless the writer explains to the judge how it advances her argument that she is entitled to an attorney fee award. So we see that the citation is subordinate to the body of the brief; hence, we refer to it as "supportive" authority. Consequently, when judges and lawyers read briefs, we focus first on the argument being made and second on the citation. As I submitted earlier, the citation interrupts the flow of your argument like a speed bump in a parking lot or a commercial in the middle of a climactic movie scene. This is why those Trolls who are either lazy or need a new gimmick to sell a book intone, *Always in a footnote, always in a footnote.* As with any Rule for All Seasons, this one fails to account for the fact that it is annoying to stop in the midst of a sentence, travel to the bottom of the page, squint to decipher the footnote, then try to pick up the flow of the sentence again.

You as the writer must choose which placement adds the greatest impact to your overall presentation. The first step in making this determination is to know your audience. Your county judge around the corner may have different predilections than the federal judge downtown. In one situation, you may wish to emphasize the date of the decision. Another court may be keenly interested in the jurisdiction. If the 3rd District Court of Appeals issued a particularly favorable ruling, you may wish to remind that tribunal that the 2nd and 5th Districts followed its reasoning. With subsequent history, "reversed on other grounds" may justify inclusion in the body of the brief, while "rehearing denied" may not. If your opponent has already cited the case in the body of his brief, you may decide to stick the entire citation in the gutter. The bottom line is this: If you have the slightest inkling that some or all of the citation will matter to the judge, you will best serve your client to keep it in the main body of your brief where she can refer to it with ease.

The seasoned practitioner knows intuitively that if your argument makes sense, it is more likely than not supported by statute or precedent. Sometimes you will find yourself discussing an issue that is obvious to both your opponent and the judge – painfully so if you are citing a case that has been quoted 10,000 times to define a standard of review. In any event, your reader's natural tendency will be to either (a) scan the cited matter to note a significant case name or date, or (b) skip over it for now. To assist the reader, you will want to clearly distinguish the citation from the argument. As you have already seen, my solution is to set (a) all of it off in brackets (or, depending upon length, parentheses) if it concludes my quotation or thought and (b) all but the case name off in parentheses if it is introductory. This way, the reader sees the road bump in time to either slow down and study it or swerve and avoid it. Consider the following example from *Payne v. Tennessee*:[48]

> But this is just as true when the defendant knew of the specific facts as when he was ignorant of their details, and in each case there is a traditional guard against the inflammatory risk, in the trial judge's authority and responsibility to control the proceedings consistently with due process, on which ground defendants may object and, if necessary, appeal. See

---

[48] 501 U.S. 808, 836-7 (1991)

Darden v. Wainwright, 477 U.S. 168, 178-83, 106 S.Ct. 2464, 2470-2, 91 L.Ed.2d 144 (1986) (due process standard of fundamental fairness governs argument of prosecutor at sentencing); *United States v. Serhant,* 740 F.2d 548, 551-2 (C.A.7 1984) (applying due process to purportedly "inflammatory" victim impact statements); see also *Lesko v. Lehman,* 925 F.2d 1527, 1545-7 (C.A.3 1991); *Coleman v. Saffle,* 869 F.2d 1377, 1394-6 (C.A.10 1989), cert. denied, 494 U.S. 1090, 110 S.Ct. 1835, 108 L.Ed.2d 964 (1990); *Rushing v. Butler,* 868 F.2d 800, 806-7 (C.A.5 1989). With the command of due process before us, this Court and the other courts of the state and federal systems will perform the "duty to search for constitutional error with painstaking care," an obligation "never more exacting than it is in a capital case." *Burger v. Kemp,* 483 U.S. 776, 785, 107 S.Ct. 3114, 3121, 97 L.Ed.2d 638 (1987).

The string cites and parenthetical summaries make the process of scanning or skipping quite tedious. Enclosing them in brackets makes it easier for the reader to differentiate the argument from its supportive jumble:

> But this is just as true when the defendant knew of the specific facts as when he was ignorant of their details, and in each case there is a traditional guard against the inflammatory risk, in the trial judge's authority and responsibility to control the proceedings consistently with due process, on which ground defendants may object and, if necessary, appeal. [See *Darden v. Wainwright,* 477 U.S. 168, 178-83, 106 S.Ct. 2464, 2470-2, 91 L.Ed.2d 144 (1986) (due process standard of fundamental fairness governs argument of prosecutor at sentencing); *United States v. Serhant,*

740 F.2d 548, 551-2 (C.A.7 1984) (applying due process to purportedly "inflammatory" victim impact statements); see also *Lesko v. Lehman,* 925 F.2d 1527, 1545-7 (C.A.3 1991); *Coleman v. Saffle,* 869 F.2d 1377, 1394-6 (C.A.10 1989), cert. denied, 494 U.S. 1090, 110 S.Ct. 1835, 108 L.Ed.2d 964 (1990); *Rushing v. Butler,* 868 F.2d 800, 806-7 (C.A.5 1989).] With the command of due process before us, this Court and the other courts of the state and federal systems will perform the "duty to search for constitutional error with painstaking care," an obligation "never more exacting than it is in a capital case." [*Burger v. Kemp,* 483 U.S. 776, 785, 107 S.Ct. 3114, 3121, 97 L.Ed.2d 638 (1987).]

To make it even cleaner we can (a) eliminate the signals because they are foolish (b) forego the punctuation at the end of each because a citation is not a grammatical sentence and (c) eliminate the parallel cites because they are just plain silly in the 21st century:

But this is just as true when the defendant knew of the specific facts as when he was ignorant of their details, and in each case there is a traditional guard against the inflammatory risk, in the trial judge's authority and responsibility to control the proceedings consistently with due process, on which ground defendants may object and, if necessary, appeal. [*Darden v. Wainwright,* 477 U.S. 168, 178-83 (1986) (due process standard of fundamental fairness governs argument of prosecutor at sentencing); *United States v. Serhant,* 740 F.2d 548, 551-552 (C.A.7 1984) (applying due process to purportedly "inflammatory" victim impact statements); *Lesko v. Lehman,* 925 F.2d 1527, 1545-7 (C.A.3 1991); *Coleman v. Saffle,* 869 F.2d 1377, 1394-6 (C.A.10 1989), cert. denied,

494 U.S. 1090 (1990); *Rushing v. Butler,* 868 F.2d 800, 806-7 (C.A.5 1989)] With the command of due process before us, this Court and the other courts of the state and federal systems will perform the "duty to search for constitutional error with painstaking care," an obligation "never more exacting than it is in a capital case." [*Burger v. Kemp,* 483 U.S. 776, 785 (1987)]

Of course, if you suggest using brackets and dropping parallel citations to your resident Yapping Chihuahua he will call you dirty names because, when we illuminate the boundary between argument and citation, we discern that the former requires ingenuity and the latter only a gag reflex:

Argument

But this is just as true when the defendant knew of the specific facts as when he was ignorant of their details, and in each case there is a traditional guard against the inflammatory risk, in the trial judge's authority and responsibility to control the proceedings consistently with due process, on which ground defendants may object and, if necessary, appeal.

Authority

[*Darden v. Wainwright,* 477 U.S. 168, 178-183 (1986) (due process standard of fundamental fairness governs argument of prosecutor at sentencing); *United States v. Serhant,* 740 F.2d 548, 551-552 (C.A.7 1984) (applying due process to purportedly "inflammatory" victim impact statements); *Lesko v. Lehman,* 925 F.2d 1527, 1545-1547 (C.A.3 1991); *Coleman v. Saffle,* 869 F.2d 1377, 1394-1396 (C.A.10 1989), cert. denied, 494 U.S.

1090 (1990); *Rushing v. Butler,* 868 F.2d 800, 806-807
(C.A.5 1989)]

Sacrilege! Heresy! This yahoo has gone too far. My Legal Research and Writing professor swears by the Citation Manual and, more important, he gives me good grades and kudos when I memorize arbitrary rules and regurgitate them on paper at semester's end. "Sit, stay, roll over! That's a good little law student, good little toady!" The Citation Manual has been with us in one form or another for the better part of a century. Some law schools employ entire committees devoted to it. Every law student I know has one. In fact, I was required to buy one and I have the plasma donation receipts to prove it. Now this schmo comes along and tells me it's useless and I should throw it away. Isn't that what he's saying?

Yes. I am telling you to throw it away for a number of reasons, the foremost of which inheres in the old adage about not jumping off a cliff just because everyone else is doing it. The plain fact is that the original citation manual, *Bluebook,* was conceived as an internal reference to standardize footnotes in the Harvard Law Review. Because legal practitioners and students are far more obsessed with rules and regulations than your average person, it is no coincidence that the legal profession welcomed it with open arms. Then, like one-hit-wonder pop-artists, the Harvard Yapping Chihuahuas leapt to the fallacious conclusion that everything they had to say was important.

"These law junkies are crazy about rules, man."

"I hear you, brother. And I'll tell you something else. Pass me that roach."

"Here you go, dude. What's that?"

"When it comes to rulebooks, lawyers like them big."

"Right on, sister."

"Far out."

"Power to the Chihuahuas."

So they expanded their repertoire beyond footnotes. As their collection of rules grew and diversified, the little manual grew into a tome over 400 pages in length. Because popularity breeds jealousy, other Yapping Chihuahuas developed their own competitive versions of it. As a result, today's law student saunters away in bewilderment while rabid gangs of Yapping Chihuahuas scrap over whose mascot is the prettiest. Why? What particular linguistic crisis does each system solve? Are we to believe that, before the advent of *Bluebook*, lawyers, judges and juries were unable to communicate with one another? To the contrary, as I have illustrated, some rules are so petty that they actually hinder communication. In the face of this reality, what motivates these pedants to champion one set of rules over another? Let's ask one.

In 1996, a Legal Research and Writing professor named Darby Dickerson wrote a rather exhaustive critique of the 16th *Bluebook* edition.[49] Including the appendices, this *article* exceeded 200 pages. The footnotes alone numbered 322. Why would Ms. Dickerson, with the responsibility of training woefully ill equipped students to become eloquent legal writers, commit so much of her valuable time and energy to analyzing a book that devotes itself entirely to, not the substance of legal argument and analysis, but the form of the subordinate reference that tags along like a remora on a Sailfish? We find our clue at page 94 where she contrasts *Bluebook* with *Maroonbook*:[50]

> The Maroonbook's failure to convert the masses, however, does not necessarily mean that the Bluebook's future is secure.

It appears that Ms. Dickerson's underlying concern is with bragging rights and market share. Why would this be? After all, her mission is to turn students into effective legal writers, and she has only a handful of semesters in which to do so. Thus, she has no dog in this fight. Or does she?

---

[49] "An Un-Uniform System of Citation: Surviving with the New Bluebook" (26 Stetson L. Rev. 53)

[50] *The University of Chicago Manual of Legal Citation* (Lawyers Cooperative Pub. Co. 1989)

Four years after writing the article, Ms. Dickerson emerged as the author of a 572-page behemoth titled *ALWD Citation Manual.* Touted as a more sensible approach to citation than its competitors, all this manual really does is slap a new brand of perfume on the smelly gorilla in the room. Like her countless predecessors, Ms. Dickerson could not care less whether her book improves legal writing or blasts it back to the Stone Age.[51] Why? Because sharpening the implements of communication was never its purpose.

So what was its purpose, yahoo?

With a major publication on her résumé, Ms. Dickerson's academic star soared. The same year her first edition was published saw her ascend to Associate Dean. A few years later she was enthroned as Vice President and Dean of Stetson University College of Law. And she owes it all to a ragtag brood of academic outcasts in Cambridge who dared dream 10,000 tortuously complicated ways to talk about absolutely nothing.

Human nature abhors uniformity for its own sake. Here is what some of our appellate courts have said on the subject:

> *Payne v. Tennessee* (501 U.S. 808, 827-8 – 1991) (citations omitted):

> [W]hen governing decisions are unworkable or are badly reasoned, "this Court has never felt constrained to follow precedent." *Stare decisis* is not an inexorable command; rather, it "is a principle of policy and not a mechanical formula of adherence to the latest decision."

---

[51] The punch line to this anticipatory pun may be found in my discussion of a muttonhead I refer to as the Indiana Ringer in Chapter Three.

Delgado v. State (776 So.2d 233, 241 – Fla. 2000) (citations omitted):

While we are aware of the importance of *stare decisis*, this principle must give way to common sense and logic. "Perpetuating an error in legal thinking under the guise of stare decisis serves no one well and only undermines the integrity and credibility of the court."

Puryear v. State (810 So.2d 901, 905 – Fla. 2002) (citations omitted):

Our adherence to stare decisis, however, is not unwavering. The doctrine of stare decisis bends where there has been a significant change in circumstances since the adoption of the legal rule, or where there has been an error in legal analysis. "[I]ntellectual honesty continues to demand that precedent be followed unless there has been a clear showing that the earlier decision was factually or legally erroneous or has not proven acceptable in actual practice."

State v. Gray (654 So.2d 552, 554 – Fla. 1995):

Yet *stare decisis* does not command blind allegiance to precedent.

Haag v. State (591 So.2d 614, 618 – Fla. 1992):

Moreover, as we have said before, stare decisis is not an ironclad and unwavering rule that the present always must bend to the voice of the past, however outmoded or meaningless that voice may have become.

Unless and until human beings are replaced by automatons, the citation manual will remain nothing more than a vanity press for Law Review nerds. Show me an appellate court that is prepared to dismiss an appeal because the brief writer omitted a space between "So." and "2d," and I'll show you an appellate court that is begging to be overturned for elevating form over substance.

Myth 1 – The Illusory Dichotomy

Because our job is to persuade, those of us who use language in the real world of thinkers, creators and doers study the tools of our trade with a singular intensity. We never stop learning new words. We never tire of analyzing the various ways our colleagues use words. We experiment with everything. We use the tangible (word) to express the intangible (thought), and the tangible exists only to serve the intangible. We push language to its limits, sometimes succeeding and sometimes failing, with a cardinal passion – to say it better today than we did yesterday. In a speech he delivered at La Sorbonne in Paris on April 23, 1910, President Theodore Roosevelt observed:

> It is not the critic who counts; not the man who points out how the strong man stumbles, or where the doer of deeds could have done them better. The credit belongs to the man who is actually in the arena, whose face is marred by dust and sweat and blood, who strives valiantly; who errs and comes short again and again; because there is not effort without error and shortcomings; but who does actually strive to do the deed; who knows the great enthusiasm, the great devotion, who spends himself in a worthy cause, who at the best knows in the end the triumph of high achievement and who at the worst, if he fails, at least he fails while daring greatly. So that his place shall never be with those cold and timid souls who know neither victory nor defeat.

The Trolls are the "cold and timid souls" – the play-by-play announcers who merely chronicle our blunders and victories in standardized form. Likewise, a "rule" of grammar is nothing more than a snapshot of language: out of context and frozen in time.

You know as well as I that, while Trolls may be delusional, most are not idiots. Why, then, do they inveterately ignore the truth about linguistics? One of the most poignant communicators of all time, Mel Brooks, provides the answer:

> "We've got to protect our phony-baloney jobs, gentlemen!"[52]

Entrenched in the world of academia is the misconception that, if someone's thoughts are mass produced in bound volumes, those thoughts must be worth the pulp they are printed on. Hence, the tacit edict *Publish or perish*. The unfortunate result is that Trolls scurry to get their names embossed on the spines of books, not because they have anything particularly important to say about legal writing, but merely to protect their phony-baloney jobs. As often happens when a Troll has nothing new or helpful to say on a subject, many of these authors simply repeat the same bilge they were spoonfed by their mentors. For the most part they are relatively harmless, and their cute little editions may be displayed on a bookshelf to lend a learned ambiance to one's den or office.

But good intentions often lead to absurd notions when idle minds put pen to paper. Tragically for the student of legal writing, one of the silliest notions in the history of the English language is gaining ground:

> Lawyers use a lot of odd words and phrases that
> no one else uses and few understand. Your writing
> should pass what I call "the McDonald's test." If you
> were to read the document you're drafting aloud in
> McDonald's, would people understand what you're

---

[52] Governor William J. Le Petomane in *Blazing Saddles* (Warner Brothers 1974)

saying? If not, your prose is too removed from ordinary language. (*Writing to Win* by Steven D. Stark – Broadway Books 2000 – p. 24)

Mr. Stark claims to have actually practiced law, so we can assume he has obtained at least one advanced degree. This proves that "higher" education does not necessarily confer wisdom. More discomfiting is the apparent fact that this same gentleman lectured at Harvard, which demonstrates another time-honored truth: Though you may lead a moron to a hallowed trough of reason, you will come away with nothing more than a wet moron. When I first read the above quote, I thought I had missed something, so I read it again. Then I decided he had to be talking about a specific type of legal writing, such as a client letter. Alas, no. To calm my nerves, I laid the book aside and assured myself Mr. Stark was an anomaly.

The very next book I opened proved me wrong. In fact, there appears to be a concerted campaign in trolldom to eliminate from all forms of legal writing polysyllabic words and so-called "legalese." For instance, Judge Painter echoes the above concept by referring to the "plain-language movement."[53] One of his chapter titles typifies the fatuity of the argument: "Latin is a Dead Language – Keep it Buried."[54] Whatever one chooses to call it, the very premise of the "movement" is flawed. And phrases like the one about Latin, devised to buttress the "plain-language" argument, are as vacuous as they are irresponsible.

When I was growing up in the 1970s and 80s, the following directive was drilled into my misshapen skull by every English, French and Latin teacher I encountered: "If you don't understand a word, open a dictionary and LEARN." Back then, everyone understood that the main goal of written discourse is to educate

---

[53] *The Legal Writer*, p. 19
[54] Id., p. 118

rather than placate. But today's Trolls would upend that logic. For example, Judge Painter insists:

> Remember to make the *reader* feel smart.
> When in doubt, use English. No one will have to
> go look it up ....[55]

Where am I? Who turned out the lights? Whither the rug that was once underfoot? Did I just read what I think I read?

Yes, I am sorry to inform you that an influential man with roughly the same cranial capacity as you has actually posed the inane suggestion that you throw away 80% of our wonderfully diverse lexicon and confine the expression of your thoughts to a format as barren as "See spot run." Why? For fear that you might insult the least sophisticated reader among us. I will not stand for such nonsense, and neither should you.

Granted, it is uncomfortable to admit you do not know the meaning of a word. But the fact is that no one could possibly know every word in her particular language.[56] Our intrepid friends at *AskOxford.com* once counted the number of full entries in the Second Edition of the Oxford Dictionary: 171,476. This excludes 47,156 words classified as obsolete, as well as 9,500 derivative words. Hence, there should be no shame associated with cracking open a dictionary. Furthermore, history proves that discomfort is one of the surest stimuli toward innovation and growth. As another great communicator, Terry Gilliam, lamented in an interview: "Offense makes people think. Offense makes people argue, and we're losing that."

Should I lose a cycling race, it would be ludicrous of me to fault the winner for training harder than I. By the same token, the legal writer is not a nursemaid for the illiterate and the blithe. I would surmise that what these "plain-language" exponents are actually railing at

---

[55] Id.

[56] This assertion applies even to those with so-called "photographic" memories, because it is one thing to recall and regurgitate; it is another altogether to comprehend.

(though they don't know it) is the abysmal failure of a distressing majority of today's primary and secondary educators to, not only teach their pupils the basic mechanics of language, but inspire them with the beauty of finely crafted expression. An alarming number of college graduates have never been exposed to the classical languages of Latin or Greek; therefore, they don't have the slightest clue that there would be no English as we know it today without the influence of those languages. Still fewer have been exposed to the classics of literature. I submit to you that the lawyer who has never pondered the cadence of *"Arma virumque cano,"*[57] or brooded over the meaning of "I will show you fear in a handful of dust,"[58] is ill qualified to write so much as a demand letter, let alone a legal brief.

So we have a lot of aspiring lawyers out there who don't know how to use the big, fancy words. The quick, easy fix is to ban the big, fancy words.[59] Lots of luck, Troll. Language is far too resilient, and the human mind far too curious, to tolerate such a defeatist attitude. The only realistic alternative is to roll up one's sleeves and assist the student in the arduous task of trying and failing, again and again and again, until the student attains a certain command of those alluring beasts. Legalese, *schmegalese.* There is no such thing as "pure English." The English language we use today is an amalgam of "foreign" languages, both classical and modern. So don't shrink from the Latinate terms and concepts. Embrace them, adapt them and internalize them. In this way, you will continue the natural, evolutionary legacy that began when our earliest ancestor dared dream a better way to express his thoughts.

To those who declare Latin to be dead, I say, *Re-read your history.* A good place to start would be Baugh and Cable's *A History of the English Language* (Routledge 2002). All you need do is open your dictionary and scan the etymologies at random to discover that

---

[57] "Of arms and the man, I sing." Opening line to *The Aeneid* (Virgil, c. 29-19 B.C.E.)

[58] *The Waste Land* (T.S. Eliot 1922), l. 30

[59] This is the same myopic attitude possessed by modernday politicians, who find it more expedient to pass new laws rather than to rigorously enforce existing ones.

Latin is alive and well. Here is a microscopic sample of modern English words that would not exist if our ancestors had followed the "plain-language" proscription of Latin: agriculture, consent, custody, deliberate, education, fraudulent, *grammar*, hiatus, immunity, judicial, liberator, manifest, negligence, opinion, prudence, querulous, rational, science, testator, ulterior, vicarious.

Nature abhors stasis. If you're not growing, you're dying. The lazy writer will only reinforce the sloth of the reader, and the attorney of a succeeding generation may well find himself uttering the following words to an appellate panel: "It's what is J. feel me?" Within a few more generations, language will have relapsed to grunting and pointing.

In the real world, there are no such distinctions as "ordinary" or "plain" language. Language is simply language. We can either cultivate it or let it wither and die. To paraphrase Sr. Ortega again, language is more than just a system of lines, dashes and dots. It is a primal window through which we experience life. It is an inseparable part of us. The rational man can no more abridge his lexicon than he can voluntarily lop off his own healthy limb. Recall the newborn infant from the Prologue. Without a vocabulary, the infant can neither understand the world around her nor communicate her needs to that world. Thus, as one's linguistic skills are attenuated so is her overall experience of life. Conversely, as one's repertoire grows, not only does she blossom, but her evolution enriches the world around her.

If you ponder linguistics long enough, you'll eventually understand that words are only approximations of what we really want to say. As mercaptan helps us detect leaks of otherwise odorless gases, words are tags that allow us to identify thought. Like the ocean, pure thought is smooth and unbroken, and it is always on the move. If you don't believe me, take up meditation. Try to stop your mind from generating the slightest sound or image. A Zen Buddhist guru will confirm that the best one can do is coax his mind into focusing on a single figment. From this primordial torrent of emotions and mental impressions, language seeks to pluck concepts and share them with others. Common sense instructs that the bigger one's net, the more fish he will catch.

Here's a radical thought. Instead of gutting our vocabulary lest we offend an entry level cashier, why don't we encourage that cashier to improve his own, thus elevating the overall level of *McDonald's-speak*?

I will close this chapter with one final word on grammar. It is axiomatic that one can not improve upon a system he knows nothing about. Therefore, your first task is to thoroughly familiarize yourself with the "rules" of grammar as they exist today. It makes no difference whether you are a Rhodes scholar or you can barely spell your own name. Wherever you find yourself right now, there is always something new for you to learn. So go out and buy two grammar books at random. Study them, but don't surrender your better judgment to them. As Mark Twain advised: "Don't let schooling interfere with your education." Your purpose is not to memorize the various rules and declare yourself "enlightened." Rather, your goal is to ponder what each rule adds to the broader mosaic of communication. This process will never end. With each new brief you write, logic and common sense will demand that you refine your understanding of the building blocks. From this point forward, you have become a lifelong student of the watershed phenomenon that is language.

Now, roll up your sleeves and let's get to work.

Chapter Three

Prefatory Note

In this chapter, I will feature full briefs and excerpts of briefs filed of public record in actual cases. To avert frivolous defamation lawsuits by certain rabidly litigious knuckleheads, I have substituted generic terms for the opposing parties, their expert witnesses and their products. I have also changed the names of our clients and witnesses to protect their privacy. To insure ease of reading (and to preserve your sanity when you peruse the longest excerpt from the Indiana Ringer), I have (a) omitted title pages, tables of contents and authorities, and record references (b) eliminated footnotes in all but one (for exemplary purposes) and (c) corrected all spelling/ grammatical errors that I deemed unnecessary for illustrative use. Finally, I have not attempted to correct grammatical errors in transcript excerpts for the simple reason that they fall into the *vocal speech* category.

Return to Sanity – All You Need to Know about Legal Writing

In his bestselling book *The Tao of Jeet Kune Do*,[60] martial arts legend Bruce Lee wrote: "Simplicity is the shortest distance between two points." Regardless of what you are composing, be it a sentiment on a greeting card or a brief to the U.S. Supreme Court, your task as a writer is to pack the greatest punch into the fewest words possible. How does one develop this skill? The *last* place one should look for instruction is an appellate opinion, because these are typically written by obsequious law clerks who (a) have never represented a client and, typically (b) aspire only to rise among the ranks of their local packs of Yapping Chihuahuas; thus, they can drone all day long about the hundred mindless nuances of a footnote, but their prose is less dynamic than a piece of overcooked pasta. So where do you go?

I once received an email from a colleague. Bright and articulate,

---

[60] Ohara Publications, Inc., 1975, p. 12

Jeff's only deficit as a lawyer was that he couldn't write as eloquently as he could speak. Like that of a distressing majority of today's lawyers, Jeff's undergraduate education emphasized math and science at the expense of linguistics. While a fortunate few of us were diagramming sentences in three different languages as early as the 5th grade, Jeff never wrote a structured essay until he was in high school. Thus, he was denied the opportunity to internalize the mechanics of written expression at a tender age. As a result, Jeff had such little grounding in the fundamentals of the English language (e.g., subject-verb agreement, word placement and core punctuation) that his briefs stumbled and stammered as though his native tongue were anything but English. Laudably, Jeff recognized this shortcoming and decided to do something about it.

The upshot of his email was that he was thinking about blowing an exorbitant wad of cash on a legal writing seminar hosted by a Troll. By coincidence, I had recently read one of this particular Troll's publications. My response was twofold. I first cautioned that, from the perspective of a practicing lawyer, a lot of what this Troll spouts is bunk. I then told Jeff that, despite the previous fact, he would certainly benefit from interacting with other attendees who share the goal of improving themselves as legal writers. Though I thought it a crying shame to see him line the pockets of a Troll, I did not discourage Jeff from attending, because he needed to learn to crawl (the mechanics of writing, such as what generally defines a sentence and where the period goes) before he could hope to fly (the art of poignant expression). Trolls are suitable tools for such remedial instruction. As I stated earlier, my assumption is that you are beyond the crawling stage. Hence, my advice for you is completely different.

Persuasive expression was with us in a variety of forms millennia before the conception of what we recognize as the legal brief. Therefore, you would be best served to immerse yourself in the select creative writers of the past few centuries. Here are some titles to start you off: *The Old Man and the Sea* by Ernest Hemingway,[61]

---

[61] Charles Scribner's Sons 1952

Heart of Darkness by Joseph Conrad,[62] Nathaniel Hawthorne's *The Scarlet Letter*,[63] T.S. Eliot's *The Waste Land*,[64] *Paradise Lost* by John Milton.[65] I once asked a colleague what book he would want if stranded on a desert island. He replied, "A dictionary. All the other books are in it." Were the same question posed to me, I would have to choose the *Norton Anthology of American Literature*[66] which has been in my library ever since my freshman year of high school. Published in two volumes, this collection devotes nearly 5,000 pages to the most notable American authors dating back to the 16th century C.E. I suggest you get the hardback version. This is heirloom quality content; to bind it in paper is downright profane. The set will be relatively pricey, but I guarantee that somewhere between John Winthrop (1588-1649) and Sylvia Plath (1932-63) you will find what you need.

And just what is it you need? What will you find in literature that is lacking in your average legal brief or case opinion? First and foremost, you will find inspiration. From the essays you will glean analytical prowess. In the short stories you will see how smoothly a master wordsmith can interweave plot and character to form a captivating tale. Finally, the poet is the consummate verbal economist. It is not uncommon for a poet to agonize for weeks over a single line or phrase. Eliot's *The Waste Land* was nearly twice as long before he and Ezra Pound whittled it down to 434 lines. Expose yourself to every genre. Lose yourself in Walt Whitman's rhythm. Study how effortlessly Emily Dickinson stabs you in the throat with a lone image. This, my friend, is storytelling at its finest. And what good is a legal brief if it doesn't tell a story?

The next time you hear someone utter the catchphrase "Monkey see, monkey do," don't laugh: most human learning is accomplished by imitation and repetition. And this will be your next task. When

---

[62] 1902
[63] 1850
[64] 1922
[65] 1667
[66] W.W. Norton & Company, Inc. 1979

you run across an author you particularly like, emulate his style. For example, if your favorite novel is *A Farewell to Arms*,[67] pretend you are Papa Hemingway the next time you sit down to write a brief or memorandum. This is in no way false personation. The fact that you are drawn to a particular author means you share that author's interpretation of (and approach to) prose. In the same way one person likes folk music while another prefers jazz, this author's word-choice and cadence parallel your own. This is what people usually mean when they say someone's work *speaks to me*. So what may seem at first blush like mimicry is nothing of the sort: it is the process of enlisting an old pro to help you discover your own *writing voice* – the perfect conduit for the expression of your legal arguments. You can be confident that, as you emulate that author, what ends up on the page will be uniquely you. It is crucial that you develop and hone your writing voice, because tone and timber are essential elements of written discourse.

Dictating vs. Writing

Before we delve further into the composition process, I must address a topic that does not receive enough attention. In fact, I'm aware of only one contemporary writer who even addresses this issue. On page 148 of his book *Writing to Win*, Steven D. Stark advises, "Don't dictate litigation documents." I would take this one step further and admonish you to not dictate anything at all. When you set out to create a brief, memorandum or opinion letter, you bring to the process everything you know, not only about this particular case, but about every case you've handled in your career. I'm not just talking about facts and figures. In deciding what to say and how to say it, you consider many unquantifiable aspects, such as the temper of the judge or the pathos of your client. With every word, punctuation mark and space you add to the page, you imprint your

---

[67] Charles Scribner's Sons 1929

feel for the case. No secretary, paralegal or other type of assistant can duplicate that.

In November 2005, a Florida jury awarded our client an eight-figure wrongful death verdict. The defendants moved for a new trial and, failing that, appealed. The client hired a local attorney to handle the post trial and appellate phases. Despite this development, the client wanted a cooperative effort between trial and appellate counsel. So, about two weeks before our new-trial response brief was due, the Florida Ringer sent it to me for review. The draft needed more than just a touch-up here and there; it required a major overhaul. Many sections needed to be rewritten altogether. Most disturbing was her omission of a crucial case. I fixed everything time would allow, added the pivotal case and sent it back to her. When I received our copy of the filed response days later, I couldn't believe my eyes. Countless punctuation marks I had moved were again misplaced. Though some of my additional arguments remained, many of the phrases I had rewritten were again as rambling and stilted as before. And the one case I had inserted to lend support to our most tenuous element of damages had disappeared.

On reviewing her first draft of our appellate brief,[68] I noticed something odd. In a direct quote from the trial record, the Florida Ringer misquoted one of the plaintiff's attorneys. A phrase from the transcript, "the GM case as well," had been transposed in this draft to read: "the GM cases well." How, I wondered, with electronic transcripts and *copy-paste* technology at her disposal, could anyone botch a direct quote in this fashion? I soon deduced she had dictated the entire brief to her inept legal assistant. This explained why the majority of my revisions of the trial-level brief (which I had presumed were being made directly to the master draft) had been overlooked. On closer analysis, I discovered that she had also (a) misquoted the trial judge twice (b) misquoted her own client (c) botched a statute

---

[68] Third District Court of Appeal, Florida, Case No. 3D06-1656 – *Appellee's Answer Brief* – July 31, 2007

citation and (d) misquoted 5 appellate opinions (e) *one of which had been issued by the very panel to which our appeal had been assigned.*

In her haste to attach her name to a verdict she had not helped to win, one of the Florida Ringer's shortcomings in this instance was that she was so reckless as to rely on an inefficient transcriber to deliver a flawless product. As happens all too often, the panelists in our case had made their decision on the briefs long before oral arguments commenced. While one certainly hopes an appellate court will focus on substantive issues rather than matters of form, you and I both know that such careless mistakes had a visceral effect on these particular judges. They demonstrated inattention to detail and utter disregard for, not only the court but the client.

This brings us to the final point on dictation: If you choose to ignore my advice and dictate your briefs, for crying out loud, *have the good sense to proofread the final product before you sign and file it.* Lest you go thinking I'm a paranoid purist, consider the following order:

UNITED STATES DISTRICT COURT
MIDDLE DISTRICT OF FLORIDA
ORLANDO DIVISION

CAROLYN NAULT,
Plaintiff,

-vs-   **Case No. 6:09-cv-1229-Orl-31GJK**

THE EVANGELICAL LUTHERAN
GOOD SAMARITAN FOUNDATION,
Defendant.

ORDER

This matter came before the Court without oral argument upon consideration of Plaintiff's ... Response to this Court's Order and

---

Motion for Voluntary Dismissal (collectively, the "Motion") (Docs. 21 and 22). Upon review, it is

ORDERED that the Motion is **DENIED** without prejudice for failing to comply with Local Rule 3.01(g), for failing to secure a stipulation of dismissal from Defendant pursuant to FED. R. CIV. 41(a)(ii), and for otherwise being riddled with unprofessional grammatical and typographical errors that nearly render the entire Motion incomprehensible.

It is **FURTHER ORDERED** that Plaintiff's counsel, [redacted], shall re-read the Local Rules and the Federal Rules of Civil Procedure in their entirety. Furthermore, [redacted] shall personally hand deliver a copy of this order, together with the Court's exhibit attached thereto, to his client, Carolyn Nault, by no later than **Monday, September 21, 2009**. By no later than **Wednesday, September 23, 2009**, [redacted] shall file with theCourt a "Notice of Compliance," certifying to the Court that he has fully complied with this Order.

DONE and **ORDERED** in Chambers, Orlando, Florida on September 15, 2009.

Copies furnished to:

	S/Gregory A. Presnell
Counsel of Record	Gregory A. Presnell
Unrepresented Party	United States District Judge

Here are some illuminative snippets of the pleading to which Judge Presnell refers:

7.   That the court directed the Plaintiff to show cause as to why there should not be sanctioned for failing to conduct adequate pre-suit investigation and for opposing Defendants motion to dismiss.

10.   That prior to filing this action, counsel for the Plaintiff had determined that "Good Samaritan Society" was a fictitious name

for "The Evangelical Lutheran Good Samaritan Society" and had attended on filing this action against that entity.

11. That a review counsel's file subsequent to the court order indicates that for some reason full which counsel is unaware, the defendant named in the complaint was changed to the current defendant. Counsel believes that this was changed by counsel's prior assistant it was no longer with counsel's firm.

I've never used a dictation machine, and I never will. Just the other day I saw an advertisement for the latest voice-recognition software program. The ad was directed at business professionals and students alike. If you have the slightest inkling that you might try such a program, *don't do it.* Automation is inimical to accurate, persuasive writing. Here's one of the countless examples I often see. In 2006 I reviewed an appellate brief prepared by our local counsel in Indiana. Their version of Microsoft *Word* did not recognize the legal term "tortious," so the auto-correct application had substituted "tortuous" *in a direct quote from an appellate opinion.*[69]

A computer program will never be an adequate substitute for human eyeballs and fingertips when it comes to the written word. If we heedlessly skip down the road of automation we will ultimately lose even the most rudimentary compositional skills. Leave dictation to the trial attorneys who don't have the time to compose (and who, therefore, have the foresight to avail themselves of impeccable transcribers) and the used-car-lot-lawyers like the Florida Ringer who need to hold gadgets in front of their faces to feel important. If you're going to create a brief, do it with your own hands.

---

[69] No word processing program should be trusted. The legal writer should never presume a software developer is more linguistically adept than he. If you are, indeed, the vigilant drafter your client expects, it will not be uncommon for you to add words to your program's dictionary on a weekly, if not daily, basis.

Overcoming the Blank Page

When you sit down to write, the first thing you must do is decide what you want to say to the court. So talk to the court. Forget about the law for now, and just tell the court from your gut how it should rule and why.

Late in 2005 I began writing briefs in one of a number of cases that involved rollover accidents in Mexico. The defendants, vehicle and tire manufacturers incorporated and headquartered in the United States, had filed a joint motion to dismiss based on the theory of *forum non conveniens* ("FNC" for short). Their position was that, because the plaintiffs were residents of Mexico and the accidents had occurred in Mexico, it would be *more convenient* for these U.S. corporations to defend the lawsuits in Mexico, despite the facts that (a) the vehicles and tires were designed in the U.S. and (b) the vast majority of the evidence we would use at trial was obtained from the defendants' U.S. offices (thus, it would have to be translated into Spanish at no small expense). In the battle that ensued, I watched these defense lawyers: misrepresent both U.S. and Mexican law, attempt to destroy the career of a Coke-bottle-bespectacled-mild-mannered legal professor merely because he disagreed with them, and lie through their teeth to a Texas trial judge in open court. It soon became apparent that these defendants would stop at nothing in their attempt to avoid a fair trial.

The chicanery of the defense attorneys was exacerbated by the complacency of U.S. judges. Every time we exposed one of their nasty tricks, the defense attorneys would succeed in diverting the court's attention onto a collateral issue. Every time we expected a judge to levy sanctions against them for blatant discovery violations, he would simply mumble a bland edict: *Now, now, you boys and girls play nice.* When the battle of experts on Mexican law degenerated into back stabbing and name calling, we submitted a lengthy affidavit from a sitting appellate judge in Jalisco, Mexico, explaining in detail why everything the defendants had told our U.S. court about Mexican law was tommyrot. Still, thousands of pages and 3½ years after the defendants had filed their motion, our judge had yet to issue a ruling. All the deadlines on the briefing schedule had passed. There was nothing left to do but wait.

As I sat in the office early one morning brooding over the case, I said aloud in disgust, "Enough is enough." For kicks, I plugged that statement into a search box. To my surprise, two appellate cases popped up. Inspired, I called my friend Mark and laid out my idea. He not only motivated me; he helped to set the tone for the entire project:

"At this point, Russ, who cares if we piss the judge off and get the case dismissed? At least we'd be out of limbo."

Less than a week later, I filed *Plaintiffs' Motion for Final Ruling on FNC*. The brief opened:

"Enough is enough."

The court in *Potter v. Houston* (847 N.E.2d 241 – Ind. App. 2006) came to the above conclusion after putting up with arguments similar to those contended by Defendants in their recent briefing. Characterizing the complaining party's arguments as "illogical and puerile," that court cited a pattern of ignoring "unfavorable factual determinations and rulings," "numerous attacks on orders and judgments that can be fairly characterized as collateral" and an "overarching theme" of motions and arguments "calculated to cause great expenditure of time and money" by the opposing party (Id. at 250).

I then hit the Court with a rapid-fire list of facts that proved the defendants wrong. Because the ultimate goal was to get the judge to act, I put more edge on the closing discussion than I ordinarily would:

In truth, neither Plaintiffs[71] nor Defendants need discuss the civil code of Nuevo Leon: the Mexican trial and appellate courts have already considered and applied it. But Defendants refuse to accept this reality. As Plaintiffs have pointed out before, Defendants have thus far attacked every ruling from the Mexican State and appellate courts. Yet, despite the vehemence with which they assail both Mexican law and the judges who interpret that law, Defendants would have this Court believe that they consider those very courts more convenient, available and adequate to protect their rights. With all due respect, whom are they trying to kid?

The facts stated on page 2 above have been repeated *ad nauseam.* Experts have spoken at considerable length. Even a judge who has been trying cases in Mexico for over twenty years has shared his thoughts on the matter, and that very judge's reasoning and conclusions have been affirmed by an appellate court. But that isn't enough for Defendants. So determined are they to keep the issue alive that their rhetoric has disintegrated into an exercise in one-upmanship, wherein they will not hesitate to vilify anyone who disagrees with them. In their latest brief, they go so far as to suggest, without a shred of evidence of any improprieties, that this Court should initiate an ethics investigation into a judge in a sovereign foreign country (despite the fact that they carefully avoided hurling such allegations before a Mexican forum). This is further proof that Defendants will stop at nothing to manipulate *reality* to comport with their untenable *theory.* Plaintiffs suspect that if they found and produced a long lost treatise penned by Learned Hand himself, in which Judge Hand stated categorically that a case such as this one should be tried in an American court, Defendants would demand an immediate séance-deposition and accuse the venerable jurist of colluding with Plaintiffs, "thereby violating the code of ethics for retired souls."

---

[70] There is no Rule for All Seasons regarding whether you should refer to your clients anonymously or by name. You will base this decision on any number of factors. Generally, I refer to my clients by name in both trial and appellate briefs. In this particular case I used the generic "Plaintiffs" because there were three of them. To recite their names with each reference would have proven cumbersome.

> Plaintiffs are fellow human beings who happen to speak a different language, and who live a more modest lifestyle, than we. They were severely injured, both emotionally and physically, by defective products designed and sold by Defendants. Each new round of briefing on the *FNC* issue only aggravates their emotional wounds. With the evidence Plaintiffs have against them, the last thing Defendants want is a fair trial. Thus, every day they manage to delay Plaintiffs' day in court is a victory in Defendants' ledger books. Defendants have already managed to prolong this *FNC* debate for over 1,000 days. Plaintiffs submit that the Court has all the facts and law that it will ever need to make a ruling. Plaintiffs implore the Court to do so. After three tortuous years, even an adverse decision may be considered progress.

The defendants were quick to point out that my brief was not permitted by the briefing schedule. The court agreed. In the first footnote to her subsequent order, the judge noted *for the record*:

> Neither have we considered any arguments contained in the Plaintiffs' superfluous motion entitled Motion for Final Ruling on *FNC* ....

While this statement suggests my brief had no effect at all, the timing proves otherwise. It is notable that the judge did not say she hadn't *read* the brief. The issue had been pending for over 3 years. We filed the motion on June 6. The judge issued her ruling on July 16, *denying* the defendants' motion to dismiss.

Research

So you have decided what you want to say. Now you need to find authority to support your proposition. Because the term *research* dredges up traumatic memories from my misspent legal youth, I choose to call this the hunting/gathering phase. Depending on the complexity of your issues, or the scarcity or abundance of law that

85

is directly on point, this could prove to be the most time-consuming stage of your project. Don't be alarmed, however, if the hunt takes you in unanticipated directions. I have often emerged from the hunt/ gather phase with a proposition different from the one I started with. This is the *art* of research: though I may approach it with a clear idea of what I will tell the court and how, I remain attentive to the faintest nuance that could either tweak it a bit or transform it altogether.

When I begin to work on a reply brief, I ignore my opponent's cited authority. My goal is to start with the broadest view of a particular subject and narrow my scope from there. If no particular statute applies to the issue and my own queries come up dry, I go to the digests. *If all else fails*, I plug in a case from my opponent's brief, search the headnotes for a general proposition of law and *keycite* from there. My overriding goal is to not get trapped at this initial phase in (a) my opponent's biased selection of authority or (b) my own knee-jerk reaction to the issue, which may or may not take me down the right path.

Above all, make sure you have all of the facts pertaining to the particular issue you're researching. In 2006, two Michigan attorneys asked us to help them try a catastrophic injury case in southern Texas. The case was mistried, then settled the following summer. Before the defendants wrote the checks, an old partner of the Michigan firm (who had not spent so much as one second working on the case) filed an attorney lien based on a dissolution lawsuit he had filed against the Michigan firm in their home jurisdiction. We knew that a resolution of the old partner's claims in Michigan could take years. My task was to find authority for the Texas judge to determine the merits of the Michigan fee dispute solely as it affected the settlement funds in the Texas case.

My first idea was to attack the problem from a jurisdictional perspective. I cracked my knuckles and entered the query "plenary power." In little time, I found eleven cases supporting the proposition that this attorney fee dispute fell within the trial judge's continuing jurisdiction. I fired off a memo and moved on to other things. One of the Michigan attorneys called the following morning. He liked where

I was going with plenary power, but he couldn't shake the feeling that we were missing the target. I asked him to tell me more about the old partner. In the course of the conversation, he mentioned two client contracts. I stopped him there.

"So, when the client originally hired you, the old partner was with your firm, but he had nothing to do with the case. Then you severed ties with the old partner. Then the client signed a new fee contract which excluded the old partner?"

"Yeah."

I had run across a body of case law dealing with this precise scenario the previous day, but I had ignored it because I didn't have all the pertinent facts. I jotted down the following research note:

> The key to keeping this in front of the Texas judge is whether it could potentially affect the client. The real question goes to the nature of the old partner's claim. It's not a contract dispute among former law partners; it's a contract dispute with the client, who effectively discharged the old partner before the case went to trial.

I found supportive authority and combined it with the plenary power cases. Our Texas judge wasted no time in telling the former partner where to stick his lien.

It is during the hunt/gather stage that my briefs usually begin to take shape. I typically have two documents under simultaneous construction: (1) a research log and (2) my working brief. Here is why. One of the meditation techniques Zen Buddhists employ is the *kōan* – a paradoxical phrase, word or image such as, "What is the sound of one hand clapping?" By focusing his conscious attention on the *kōan*, the Zen practitioner frees his unconscious mind to achieve enlightenment (*satori*) behind his conscious back, as it were. Likewise, as we direct our attention to the gathering and processing of information we free the deeper, creative processes. Thus, it is not unusual for me to come up with my most incisive openers and segues during the research phase. When I do, I simply open that window, plug in my thought, minimize it and continue with the research. And when I find a good case summary, I copy/paste a snippet into the research log. Before and after each snippet, I jot down arguments and follow-up questions in a stream-of-consciousness fashion:

Notes for MPSJ Reply

Filing Deadline June 28

Thoughts on Δ's assertion that our driver was at fault for traveling in the left lane:

1.   It ignores the mechanism of this particular accident. Another driver cut into his lane and hit his brakes. Our driver hit his own brakes and steered left-right-left to avoid a collision. This scenario might just as easily have happened if he were in the right lane. The initiating cause of the accident was the vehicle's inability to stay on all four wheels during a run-of-the-mill evasive maneuver. Thus, the foreseeability of this accident scenario might be the key to our argument that 3P's involvement is irrelevant.

2.   There was no contact between the vehicles.

Excerpts from
Boryszewski ex rel. Boryszewski v. Burke
882 A.2d 410 (N.J. Super. 2005)

Before the initial trial of the matter, plaintiffs' claims against all defendants except Daimler were either settled or dismissed.

Against Daimler, plaintiffs had alleged a product liability cause of action based on a design-defect/"crashworthiness" theory. [413]

***

The accident occurred at about 5:50 p.m. on August 5, 1998. Annette Boryszewski was driving her family's 1998 Plymouth Grand Voyager, a minivan, on Route 280 westbound in East Orange. Her three sons-Matthew, age fourteen; Brian, age eleven; and Timothy, age seven-were riding in the Voyager with her. Brian was in the front passenger seat, Matthew was seated in the second row behind the front passenger's seat, and Timothy was seated in the second row behind the driver.

At the same time, defendant Cody Burke was driving his Jeep Wrangler in the far left lane of Route 280 eastbound. The left front tire came off Burke's vehicle, bounced over the median divider, hit a vehicle on the westbound side of the highway, bounced again several times, and then crashed into the windshield and windshield header of the Boryszewski vehicle. The tire shattered the windshield and crushed the roof downward, fracturing Annette's skull and killing her.

A week before the accident, the tires on Burke's vehicle had been rotated at defendant Gazzani Motors, which leased space at the North End Mobil gas and service station in Bloomfield, operated by Jeffrey Argast, also named as defendants. A State Police investigation into the accident concluded that the mechanic whohad rotated Burke's tires did not securely fasten the lug nuts on the front tires, causing the left front tire to come off. [414]

***

During charge conferences, Daimler requested that the jury be instructed to consider apportionment of fault between Daimler and the codefendants who had settled before trial. Daimler contended that the settling co-defendants who caused the accident should bear some liability for Annette's death.

89

Plaintiffs responded that apportionment was inappropriate in the circumstances presented. They contended that, in crashworthiness cases such as the present one, where plaintiffs were seeking damages only for second-collision or enhanced injuries, i.e., injuries, such as Annette's death, which were not caused by the accident itself but were caused exclusively by the vehicle's design defect, there is no basis for apportionment of fault between the vehicle manufacturer and the parties who caused the accident. [416]

[This is an important distinction between *Boryszewski* and our case. In *Boryszewski*, plaintiff based liability on Daimler only for the second impact injuries. We, on the other hand, are holding Δ liable for both the rollover and crashworthiness injuries. Essentially, our case has no first/second impact distinction as to Δ. Thus, "injury apportionment" is irrelevant here.]

***

In *Waterson v. Gen. Motors Corp.*, 544 A.2d 357 (N.J. 1988), the plaintiff's car went out of control and crashed into a utility pole as the result of a defective axle. At the time of the accident she was not wearing a seat belt. The issue on appeal was the extent to which the plaintiff's failure to wear a seat belt affected her right to recover damages for the personal injuries she suffered as a result of the accident.

The Court held the jury could consider the plaintiff's comparative fault in not wearing a seat belt. If the jury were to find the plaintiff negligent, then the damage award should be reduced to fairly reflect her percentage of fault. [419] [citations omitted]

[The focus of apportionment is on the divisibility of first and second impact (enhanced) injuries ... the cause of the injury, not the accident itself.]

***

90

Although, as we have already observed, the facts before us are not directly on point with those in any of the apportionment cases we have discussed, it is essentially undisputed that one or more of the settling defendants (Burke, Gazzani Motors, and Mobil Oil) were responsible for the accident itself, i.e., the first collision. No suggestion is raised that Annette was liable for either the first collision or the second. In other respects, however, liability for Annette's death was clearly in dispute. Plaintiffs contended that the design defect in the Voyager's windshield header was the sole cause of her death. According to plaintiffs, Annette would not have died solely from the accident. Daimler, on the other hand, contended that the Voyager's roof system was reasonably safe and strong. Daimler maintained that the tire hit the Boryszewski's vehicle with such great force that, notwithstanding the roof system's adequate design, the roof collapsed, killing Annette. [423-4]

[Again, there was no collision between π and 3P. There was no impact with anything at all prior to the rollover.]

Recap of Distinguishing Factors

1. *Boryszewski* involved settling defendants who "undisputedly" caused the accident (first impact) and a non-settling defendant against whom the only claim wascrashworthiness (second, enhancing impact). As for the principle cases that court relied upon:

2. *Green* (cited in our brief) involved a collision between the defective vehicle and another vehicle (driver settled), and a subsequent crashworthiness claim;

3. *Waterson* dealt with an accident-causing defect (axle caused loss of control and impact with utility pole) and injury enhancement due to the plaintiff's failure to wear a seatbelt; and

4. *Poliseno v. General Motors Corp.*, 744 A.2d 679 (N.J. Super. A.D. 2000), involved a single-car accident in which the driver

hydroplaned while passing another vehicle. The plaintiff's sole claim against the manufacturer was a crashworthiness claim (defective door weld that allowed tree to invade driver cage).

Additional Thoughts

Two cases cited in *Green* bolster our position on the foreseeability issue.

In *Green v. Sterling Extruder Corp.*, 471 A.2d 15 (N.J. 1984), the court held that any degree of contributory negligence short of a willful act was unavailable as a defense in the case of a factory worker injured while using a defective machine for a reasonably foreseeable purpose. The catchy quotes are:

> Although the Court remains not of one mind on the issue that divided us in *Suter*, this appeal is hardly an appropriate vehicle for the rehashing of that question. We need not even count heads on it or display our ardor for, or aversion to, the respective contesting viewpoints, for it is abundantly clear to all of us that no matter where one stands on the *Suter* contributory fault question, plaintiff's conduct here amounted to no more than ordinary carelessness. No member of the Court would permit that kind of conduct to bar or reduce a worker's strict liability claim in the employment circumstances presented. [Id. at 19 ¶2]

> As one writer, commenting approvingly on *Bexiga*, has said, '[o]nce it is established that the defendant has a duty to protect persons from the consequences of their own foreseeable faulty conduct, it makes no sense to deny recovery because of the nature of the plaintiff's conduct.' [Id. at 20]

[quoting Patricia Marschall, "An Obvious Wrong Does Not Make a Right: Manufacturer's Liability for Patently Dangerous Products," 48 N.Y.U. L.Rev. 1065, 1088 (1973)]

In *Ramos v. Silent Hoist & Crane Co.*, 607 A.2d 667 (N.J. Super. A.D. 1992), the court utilized the following quote from Marschall: "Contributory negligence would serve to excuse the very conduct that gives rise to strict liability on the part of the manufacturer." [Id. at 674]

The upshot is that 3P's conduct on the date of the accident was certainly as foreseeable to Δ as a factory worker's "ordinary carelessness" was to the manufacturers in these cases.

This is where I put my propositions to the test. And this is where some attorneys lose their way, so listen close. You and I both know that not every statement of law will perfectly match what we want to tell the court. Many times we find ourselves mired in the murky, miasmal muck of inference, where we must be vigilant lest we stretch a syllogism past its breaking point. If a case gets you no farther than point A, don't push it to point B (more on this later).

Regardless of the merits of their client's case, hourly-fee attorneys (typically, but not always, employed on the defense side) follow a cardinal directive – generate fees by any means possible to squeeze every last penny out of the controversy. Thus, if you sue a sizable corporation, you can count on having to field some awfully harebrained motions. In the Florida case I mentioned earlier, one of the defendant's typical fusillade of pretrial motions was aimed at barring evidence of its global net worth from our punitive damages case. As this defendant posed it, the issue was whether evidence of its "financial condition bears any relevance to the issue of punitive damages after the United States Supreme Court's recent decision in *State Farm v. Campbell*, 123 S.Ct. 1513 (2003)." The defendant claimed that the *Campbell* decision barred such evidence as unconstitutional.

Having dealt with punitive damages issues in several States, I knew in my gut that this proposition was ludicrous. Sure enough, a quick review of the case confirmed it. The gist of *Campbell* is that a defendant's wealth can not be used *post trial* to justify an unconstitutionally large punitive award. Nowhere in that opinion did the Court hold that considering a defendant's wealth in determining a punitive award *at the trial level* is unconstitutional or irrelevant. In my response, I simply offered the court a straightforward treatment of *Campbell* and a few other pertinent Supreme Court cases. Our judge in that case is as cool as they come. Here is what he had to say to the defense lawyer at the subsequent hearing:[71]

0005

6   THE COURT: Okay. That's fine. There

7   is an issue, another motion, basically, that

8   says, "Well, we don't want you all or, Judge,

9   we don't want the plaintiff to introduce

10   evidence of the defendant's net worth," and

11   you cite as authority for that proposition,

12   the Campbell case, the Supreme Court case.

13   Do you all want to, let's say, withdraw

14   that motion?

15   MS. LUMISH: No. No, your Honor.

16   THE COURT: Don't you think perhaps that

17   motion is a little frivolous, if not

18   insulting, as well?

0006

4   THE COURT: Do you believe that the

5   Campbell case actually stands for that

6   proposition?

***

---

[71] Transcript of proceedings October 17, 2005, 11th Judicial Circuit, Miami-Dade County, Case No. 99-9450-CA-01

94

22   THE COURT: Are you telling me that if a

23   judge were to impose a sanction, a

24   punitive – a punitive award, let's say

25   against me, of $10,000, it would be of the

0007

1   same effect as imposing that $10,000 award of

2   punitive damages against Bill Gates?

3   I would venture to say that I do not

4   have the same financial wherewithal.

0008

1   Now, the net worth can come into play

2   if, for example, we were claiming that it was

3   a bankrupting award. Then we would need to

4   put in our net worth, and the case law is

5   clear on that. But unless and until that

6   occurs –

7   THE COURT: How would the jury know

8   whether it's a bankrupting award or not, if

9   they don't know what the net worth of the

10   individual or company to be sanctioned is?

0011

14   So, I might suggest that for the moment,

15   that your Honor just preclude the plaintiff

16   from introducing this in opening until we

17   have the opportunity to address it more fully

18   during the course of the trial.

19   THE COURT: No. Motion for – to

20   preclude the plaintiff from introducing

21   evidence of net worth is denied.

During a discovery dispute in an Arkansas case, the defendant alleged certain documents called "suspension orders" were privileged.

To support this assertion, the defendant dumped on the trial court a number of orders from trial courts in other States ruling that the same class of documents was privileged, arguing:

> As set forth above, other state and federal courts have consistently held that the Attorney-Client privilege and work product doctrine are applicable to Suspension Orders [text omitted]. Compelling production of Suspension Orders here would abrogate the privilege that exists and that has been upheld in other courts across the country. An order compelling production would have immediate and serious extra-territorial ramifications as documents and information that have been determined to be privileged in other jurisdictions would now be compromised, rendering those protections effectively meaningless.

From previous hearings I knew that, given sufficient motivation, our Arkansas judge was apt to launch into a spirited tirade at the drop of a hat. I wanted to rev him up like a revival camp preacher:

> ### Defendant's "Comity" Argument Is both Inconsistent and Offensive
>
> On pages 9-11 of its brief, Defendant cites cases from other jurisdictions such as Idaho, Georgia and Minnesota, in which courts found suspension orders to be privileged. In summarizing one such case, Defendant conveniently omits the fact that, before granting privilege to one block of suspension orders, the court denied privilege as to another block (compare Defendant's cite to *Guzman* at p. 11 with Exhibit A hereto, p. 19, ll. 21-5). Then, on page 16, Defendant contends that the aforementioned rulings are "consistent" among State and federal courts. Not only is this representation dead wrong, but Defendant's counsel knew as much when he signed the brief. Ms. Williams attaches as Exhibit C a virtually identical brief on the same issues filed one week earlier by Defendant in the pending case of [case name omitted]. On page

19 of that brief, Defendant cites the case of [case name omitted], in which the court ruled that one of Defendant's suspension orders *was not* privileged. For the Court's convenience, Ms. Williams attaches the order from that case (Exhibit D), as well as the Special Master's report on which it was based (Exhibit E). The ethical implications from that omission aside, Ms. Williams invites the Court to pay particular attention to what Defendant says about the *Helm* case (emphasis added):

> Clearly, Judge Manners [sic.] ruling was to resolve issues in that case and not any other. In similar fashion, his ruling in [case name omitted] was not intended to operate extraterritorially or be cited as authority to override or abrogate Defendant's attorney-client and work-product protections in other jurisdictions. **Indeed, this would violate the United States Constitution.**

It is not enough for Defendant to mislead this Court by claiming courts across the country consistently rule in favor of privilege. It is not enough for Defendant to make its comity argument with a straight face despite the patent inconsistency illustrated in its own brief. Defendant then has the temerity to pervert case law to support the following assertion: If this Court finds suspension orders are not privileged *in this particular case in Jefferson County, Arkansas,* that decision will effectively overrule contrary decisions of both State and federal courts in other, unrelated cases; therefore, *to keep things nice and tidy,* this Court has no choice but to surrender its constitutional sovereignty and *fall in line* with other courts.

***

When preparing her *Memorandum* on this issue, Ms. Williams was well aware of decisions from other States that supported her position. She did not mention these cases because, quite frankly, she did not wish to insult the Court's intelligence by littering her brief with rulings which (like the cases cited on pages 9-11 of Defendant's brief) (a) have absolutely no binding effect (b) on this Court (c) in this particular case. The fact that courts across the nation *differ* on this issue only reinforces this Court's discretion and responsibility to decide this issue under the peculiar circumstances of this case, and according to the *applicable* statutory and case law cited in Ms. Williams' *Memorandum.*

Finally, Defendant contends on page 17 of its brief: "To rule otherwise [i.e., to rule that suspension orders are not privileged in this case] will effectively render meaningless the rulings in all of these other courts." To support this assertion, Defendant paints a picture of Ms. Williams' counsel trotting the globe and posting suspension orders on every street corner they find. This suggestion ignores the fundamental reality that an order of this Court does not magically nullify protective orders entered in other jurisdictions. Thus, were this Court to order production of suspension orders in this case, the attorney in Georgia would still be barred from using them as evidence in the Georgia case. Furthermore, Ms. Williams' counsel resent the implication that they would encourage another attorney to violate such an order.

When I was in law school, some friends and I would often convene at a pool hall named *Old Blue's*. Most of the time, it was obvious that I had flunked geometry in high school – I could not sink a ball that was kissing a pocket. But on a rare occasion I would run the table. There was no trick to it. It was merely the mythical law of averages at work. Like those uncommon evenings at *Old Blue's*, everything fell into place with the Arkansas judge as perfectly as if it had been scripted:[72]

---

[72] Transcript of proceedings May 11, 2007, Circuit Court of Jefferson County, Arkansas, 11th Judicial District, West, 1st Division, Case No. CV-2003-627-1

Let's just be clear that when reading the brief, when I got to this one it really bothered me the way that that was argued. It really troubled me tremendously because it appeared that somebody was attempting to beguile the Court because we make a big old issue, and that's not an issue at all. Comity is not an issue in this case.[73]

We got the big picture that this would destroy every prior ruling in the United States. I don't buy that for one single second, and I don't like being insulted that way to even suggest that that is the case. You make a person want to present a test case. If that's the argument, you make a person want to see if that's truly the argument. I don't believe it for a moment. And that's the way I am being pushed by many of these arguments that are just completely out of it.[74]

And why do we spend a lot of time talking about that when there are real serious issues to be addressed? I don't understand. That's why I was wanting explained how would this invalidate comity. I still don't understand.[75]

[I]t makes me suspect somebody is blowing smoke, and I don't appreciate folks blowing smoke in my courtroom ....[76]

When my hunting/gathering is complete and I have a workable outline for my brief, I then delve into my opponent's authority. As we saw earlier, it is not beyond even a judge to misapprehend a

---

[73] Id., p. 49, ll. 5-11
[74] Id., p. 49, l. 24 to p. 50, l. 8
[75] Id., p. 51, ll. 2-7
[76] Id., ll. 19-21

published opinion. So the first thing I check for is accuracy. Be it a blatant misquote or a subtle misconstruction, I can use it to expose the vulnerability of my adversary's position. This brings me to one last piece of advice on research. Don't manipulate a direct quote to lend support to your proposition that it clearly does not. No matter how artfully you rationalize it, it remains a lie.

The Mexican rollover cases I referred to earlier were only two of 20 or more against the same manufacturers. In one of those cases, the Tennessee Court of Appeals had found that Mexican courts were available to the plaintiffs; therefore, it granted Defendants' motion to dismiss. The plaintiffs then tried to file their case in Mexico, but the Mexican court declined to exercise jurisdiction because the defendants were not domiciled in Mexico. Having thus proven that the courts of Mexico were not available to them, the plaintiffs refiled their claims in Tennessee.

The defendants promptly moved to dismiss on grounds of collateral estoppel and *res judicata*. Their argument was that the way Mexican courts interpreted Mexican law was irrelevant because a U.S. appellate court had already ruled and, right or wrong, that ruling should stand in the interest of *finality*. To support this assertion, they set forth the following quote from *Warwick v. Underwood* (40 Tenn. 238, 241 – Tenn. 1859):

> It is not material on this point whether the finding was *right or not* in the former suit. That cannot be questioned any more [sic.] between the same parties or their privies. *Right or wrong* the question was finally closed … This rule [of finality] is not alone for the benefit of the parties litigant, to put an end to strife and contention between them, and produce certainty as to individual rights, but it is also intended to give dignity and respect to judicial proceedings and relieve society from the expense and annoyance of interminable litigation about the same matter.

Keep in mind that the defendants are arguing for the finality of a pretrial ruling on jurisdiction, not a final judgment on the merits of a case. Now let's take a look at what the *Warwick* court actually said. I have emphasized in bold type the language the defendants conveniently omitted:

> It is not material on this point whether the finding **of the jury** was right or not in the former suit. That cannot be questioned any more [sic.] between the same parties or their privies. Right or wrong the question was finally closed, **unless a new trial had been obtained in the same suit.** This rule is not alone for the benefit of the parties litigant, to put an end to strife and contention between them, and produce certainty as to individual rights, but it is also intended to give dignity and respect to judicial proceedings, and relieve society from the expense and annoyance of interminable litigation about the same matter.

So we see how the omission of this phrase and that transfigures the meaning of a statement. There is no surer way to destroy one's credibility with a court. In my day, this sort of dishonesty would have been grounds for disciplinary action as early as the sixth grade. Hence, I consider the following reprimand from the Massachusetts Bar quite lenient:

Public Reprimand No. 2011-1

[Name Redacted]
Order (public reprimand) entered by the Board on February, 3, 2011

Summary

The respondent … was admitted to the Bar of the Commonwealth on December 13, 1999. He had no prior discipline.

Beginning in 2006, the respondent represented a window company in litigation with a homeowner concerning the installation of replacement windows. After a district court trial in July 2007, the court entered a judgment for the window company on the contract, and a judgment on the homeowner's counterclaim for breach of contract with double damages and attorney's fees under M.G.L. c. 93A. The specific facts found to warrant c. 93A damages were the company's unauthorized charge on the homeowner's credit card and a collection telephone call made to the homeowner's husband while hospitalized.

Upon consideration, the trial court rescinded the C. 93A damages and attorney's fees on the sole basis that the homeowner had failed to serve a c. 93A demand letter on the window company detailingthe unfair and deceptive acts that warranted c. 93A relief. The homeowner appealed to the Appellate Division of the District Court from the decision rescinding the C. 93A damages.

The respondent filed the window company's brief and a supplementary appendix in August 2008. In the statement of facts section, the respondent falsely stated: "For purposes of the appeal, the plaintiff will rely upon and adopt the findings of fact set forth in the trial judge's Amended Decision and Order. Those findings are as follows ...." There followed nearly three pages of single-spaced and indented text purporting to recite the trial court's findings of fact. In introducing and formatting the statement of facts in this fashion, the respondent intended to state and imply that the statement included a full verbatim copy of the trial court's findings. However, the respondent's recitation of facts did not include all of the trial court's findings. Among other things, the respondent intentionally left out all reference to the hospital telephone call, and references to the credit card charge as "unauthorized," without the use of ellipses or other indication of editing.

After a hearing before the Appellate Division of the District Court

102

on November 7, 2008, the court issued an opinion. The court agreed that c. 93A, §9(3), exempts counterclaims from the requirement of filing a demand letter, but upheld the lower court's decision to rescind double damages because the window company did not have sufficient notice of the basis of the c. 93A claim.

The court further found that the respondent engaged in "as brazen a piece of misrepresentation as we have ever seen," by deleting "certain words, phrases and sentences without use of an ellipsis, or any other indication of editing." The court imposed double costs and awarded appellate attorney's fees to the homeowner.

The respondent's conduct in falsely representing that the statement of facts was a complete presentation of the findings of the lower court violated Mass. R. Prof. C. 8.4(c), (d) and (h).

In mitigation, the respondent had never filed a brief on appeal before this. The deletions from the facts of the unauthorized credit card charge and the telephone call to the client's hospitalized husband seeking payment were intended as argument. In further mitigation, the respondent frequently referred to the unauthorized credit card charge and the telephone call to the client's hospitalized husband in the statement of the case and the argument section of his brief. The court recognized the disparity in the facts and there was no harm.

This matter came on before the Board on a stipulation of facts and disciplinary violations and a joint recommendation for discipline by public reprimand. The Board accepted the parties' recommendation and imposed a public reprimand.

Brief Structure

There is nothing mysterious about the format of a brief. It follows the basic essay outline, which in turn was based on the classical story structure that took shape when our ancestors drew pictures on the walls of caves. The three elements are:

1. **Introduction** – "Here is what you should do, Judge, and these are the five reasons you should do it."
2. **Body** – Expand on the five reasons.
3. **Conclusion** – "Here is why the five reasons we just talked about compel you to do what I ask."

Our appellate courts follow this recipe with only slight variations. The Oklahoma Supreme Court requires: (a) Title Page (b) Index (c) Summary of Record (d) Argument and (e) Conclusion and Prayer for Relief. The essential elements in Texas are a bit more elaborate:

1. Title Page
2. Identification of Parties and Counsel
3. Table of Contents
4. Statement of the Case
5. Issues Presented
6. Statement of Facts
7. Summary of the Argument
8. Argument
9. Prayer

Items 1-4, like Oklahoma's (a) & (b), are merely housekeeping matters. Items 5-7 are three distinct components of your Introduction. Item 8 is the Body and Item 9 is the Conclusion.

Your average appellate judge paid (and/or sacrificed) a truckload of money and kissed a trainload of ass to be rescued from the trenches of trial work; therefore, the last things he wants to do are work and be rushed. Therefore, appellate rules regarding the form and content of briefs have evolved with an eye toward concision and, the higher up the food chain you clamber, the broader the range of excuses a court will have to dismiss your appeal without addressing its merits.

For example, intermediate federal or State courts use only objective criteria to decide whether to reject a brief. The most common criterion is exceeding the page limitation. The U.S. Supreme Court, by contrast, uses far more versatile, subjective standards:

U.S. Sup. Ct. Rule 10

Review on a writ of certiorari is not a matter of right, but of judicial discretion. A petition for a writ of certiorari will be granted only for compelling reasons. The following, although neither controlling nor fully measuring the Court's discretion, indicate the character of the reasons the Court considers:

(a) a United States court of appeals has entered a decision in conflict with the decision of another United States court of appeals on the same important matter; has decided an important federal question in a way that conflicts with a decision by a state court of last resort; or has so far departed from the accepted and usual course of judicial proceedings, or sanctioned such a departure by a lower court, as to call for an exercise of this Court's supervisory power;

(b) a state court of last resort has decided an important federal question in a way that conflicts with the decision of another state court of last resort or of a United States court of appeals;

(c) a state court or a United States court of appeals has decided an important question of federal law that has not been, but should be, settled by this Court, or has decided an important federal question in a way that conflicts with relevant decisions of this Court.

A petition for a writ of certiorari is rarely granted when the asserted error consists of erroneous factual findings or the misapplication of a properly stated rule of law.

U.S. Sup. Ct. Rule 24(6)

A brief shall be concise, logically arranged with proper headings, and free of irrelevant, immaterial, or scandalous matter. The Court may disregard or strike a brief that does not comply with this paragraph.

Because appellate courts have such scant tolerance for superfluity, the best way to whet your aptitude for brevity is to write your trial briefs with appellate rules in mind. And nowhere will this skill come in handier than in your Introduction. While there is no precise ratio to determine the length of your introductory statement, common sense should tell you that *most of the time* it should be considerably shorter than the Body. It is, after all, a preview. Though appellate courts require it, too many lawyers at the trial level omit a statement of facts unless they're presenting or countering a motion for summary adjudication. But it is always best to lead with the facts, because oftentimes that statement of facts will prove to be far more impactful than any rhetoric you could conjure up. Here is an example from an Oklahoma case:

Statement of Facts – Oklahoma Court of Appeals

On July 26, 2003, Eric Thomas was driving his sister, Sarah Jones and her 2-year-old son, Eli Jones, to Crested Butte in a [make/model of SUV redacted], which Mrs. Jones had bought just two days earlier. While traveling at a reasonable highway speed in the westbound lane of U.S. Highway 64/87 in Raton, New Mexico, the SUV suddenly crossed the centerline and was struck by a 2000 Ford F-350 long bed pickup, which was towing a fifth-wheel trailer. The tremendous force of the collision caused the SUV to reverse course and roll over, and the pickup to burst into flames, resulting in the deaths of all three occupants of the SUV, as well as the those in the pickup.

Appellants and Intervenor-Appellants ("Appellants") asserted various claims against (a) Manufacturer (b) Dealer 1, which sold the SUV to Mr. and Mrs. Jones, and (c) Dealer 2, which last serviced the SUV.

At trial Appellants proved that, at 24,000 miles (March 2003), a mechanic at Dealer 2 replaced the outer bearings on the right front wheel of the SUV because they were pitted. He also noted that the bearings on the left front wheel were loose, but he did not use a dial indicator to ascertain the amount of looseness. Though he did not replace the left front bearings, he wrote on the work order that he had done so. Thus, when the original owner of the SUV asked specifically if the left front bearings had been replaced, Dealer 2 assured her they had been. No one at Dealer 1 or Dealer 2 advised the original owner to bring the SUV in for a 30,000-mile checkup, at which time either dealership would have routinely checked all wheel bearings. When Mr. Jones and his wife went to Dealer 1 to purchase a pre-owned vehicle on July 24, 2003, the SUV was sitting almost directly beneath a banner that advertised "Quality Checked," and the salesman assured them the SUV was in "mint condition." A "Quality Checked" vehicle undergoes a comprehensive, 115-point inspection that is performed only by Manufacturer-certified mechanics.

Even though Mr. and Mrs. Jones bought the most expensive warranty-extension package available, the only type of inspection they got was a so-called "multipoint" inspection: whoever was available (certified or not) performed an "eyeball" check of fluid levels, belts and hoses.

The tapered roller bearing in the left front wheel of the subject SUV was invented by Henry Timken over a century ago, and The Timken Company has been producing them ever since. The General Manager of Quality and Technical Standards for The Timken Company testified: (a) bearing failure can adversely affect the performance of the wheel, as well as the effectiveness of the brakes (b) a dial indicator should be used to check bearings for unusual wear (c) bearings should not get loose under normal conditions and (d) improperly setting the bearings at the factory will lead topremature damage at 24,000 miles. This testimony (a) confirmed the opinions of Appellants' experts on these subjects and (b) corroborated fact testimony of employees for Dealer 1 and Dealer 2.

Among other things, Appellants also proved: (a) in 1998, Manufacturer's Critical Concern Review Group was aware of a wheel bearing failure rate of 25% (b) prior to this accident, customers had made no less than 2,742 separate warranty complaints for failed bearings in Manufacturer's light trucks and (c) this accident was precipitated by a pre-collision fatigue failure of the left front wheel bearings, which caused the SUV to veer left uncontrollably.

Experts on both sides of the case agreed that: (a) the 3:1 weight ratio between the vehicles, which resulted in the F-350 shoving the SUV back 29 feet, rendered this an extremely violent collision (b) the metal used in wheel bearings is the hardest metal used in a motor vehicle (c) the **right** front wheel bore the brunt of the near-direct impact with the F-350, thereby suffering a massive amount of damage (d) by contrast, the **left** front wheel suffered such little impact damage that, except for the bearings, it remained drivable (e) **the right front wheel bearings were not even cracked by this**

savage impact, let alone broken and (f) **neither the combined personal experience of these experts nor the decades of scientific testing performed by Manufacturer and other automotive entities produced a single real-world instance of wheel bearings being broken by a vehicular collision.**

In fact, the entire case turned upon this vast incongruity between the forces that acted upon the right and left front wheels, a disparity that was quite apparent to any casual observer.In an attempt to divert the jurors from such obvious facts, Appellees argued that the bearings in the left front wheel fractured, not at the point of impact between the SUV and the F-350 (where the laws of physics dictate that the forces were at their most violent), but when it hit the ground (not pavement, but dirt and grass) during the rollover (at which point most of the energy of the initial collision had dissipated). So untenable was this position that it caused Appellees' expert on metallurgy to: (a) reverse his position on the possible causes of *brinell* marks after Appellants' expert had performed a simple demonstration on rebuttal (b) stumble all over himself when asked to explain his theories in light of contradictory physical evidence (c) defy the metallurgical findings of The Timken Company itself and (d) disregard the procedures Timken recommends for investigating bearing failures.

When the jurors concentrated solely upon the evidence presented at trial, they leaned in Appellants' favor. It was only after [the Foreman and two other jurors] tainted deliberations with extra-record testimony that they swung toward Appellees and delivered a defense verdict. Appellants filed their Motion for New Trial on September 30, 2005, but the trial court denied that motion.

The brisk delivery you just read was the result of over a month of toil, during which I revised the brief at least 20 times, and near the end of which I received invaluable input from no less than 6 sharp legal minds. Not only did we scrap words and phrases; we abandoned entire issues whose weaknesses we feared would divert the court's focus from stronger ones. After editing until it hurt, I snipped away just a little more. Countless *little darlings* (to be discussed later) were sacrificed that summer. When time came to send the original to the printer, the entire brief was 17 pages under the limit. Now observe how that statement of facts was further concentered for the next higher court:

Statement of Facts – Oklahoma Supreme Court

On July 26, 2003, Eric Thomas was driving his sister, Sarah Jones, and her 2-year-old son, Eli Jones, to Colorado in a [make/model of SUV redacted] when the left front wheel became loose, causing the SUV to veer into the opposing lane and collide head-on with a Ford F-350 pickup truck. All drivers and occupants perished.

At trial, Petitioners asserted that the accident was precipitated by a fatigue failure in the left front wheel bearings; Respondents claimed the bearings were fractured by impacts with the ground during the series of rollovers the SUV underwent after its initial impact with the F-350.

The experts agreed: (a) this was an extremely violent collision (b) the metal used in wheel bearings is the hardest metal used in a motor vehicle (c) the right front wheel bore the brunt of the near-direct impact with the F-350, thereby suffering a massive amount of damage (d) the left front wheel suffered such little impact damage that, except for the bearings, it remained drivable (e) the right front wheel bearings were not even cracked by this savage impact, let alone broken, and (f) neither the combined personal experience of these experts nor the decades of scientific testing performed by Respondents and other automotive entities had produced a single real-world instance of wheel bearings being shattered by a vehicular collision.

The key to resolving the controversy was to understand what happens when bearings fail (e.g., what damage they cause, what marks they leave, etc.). The housing that contains the bearings at

---

issue is called a "race." The race in the left front wheel of the SUV bore a 180-degree crack on both sides. Petitioners' metallurgy expert testified that such a symmetrical crack can only be caused by the gradual process of fatigue failure in the bearings. Respondents' expert was unable to rebut this evidence; though he performed multiple drop-tower tests on identical bearing assemblies, he was unable to produce a crack on both sides of the race with localized impacts.

During deliberations, a majority of the jurors favored a verdict for Petitioners until the Foreman grabbed a nearby soft-drink can and twisted it on his arm to show a symmetrical, 180-degree mark. The Foreman (an airplane mechanic) then conducted a mini-seminar on force vectors to convince his subordinate jurors of something Respondents' expert (an engineer with a Ph.D. in Theoretical and Applied Mechanics since 1979) had failed to prove – that the only way the subject bearings could have fractured was by impact. As a result, the verdict was materially altered.

I'll return to matters of length in a moment. The general guideline of treating your introductory statement as a preview will serve you well (a) most of the time at the trial level and (b) all of the time at the appellate. But there is no bright-line Introduction/Body proportion. Depending upon the subject matter or time constraints, you may find that a single sentence suffices as your opening:

> Defendant's argument fails because it ignores the
> plain meaning of both the facts and the pertinent law.

In another situation, you may find the facts so pivotal that they deserve the lion's share of your presentation. In one of the many briefs I have written for our Mexican clients, the procedural facts which underlay the legal issue at hand were so compelling that I devoted 4 pages to those facts, skipped the argument altogether and closed with a 1-page conclusion.

It is no accident that the Introduction and Conclusion often look

111

similar. The persuasive argument has been refined over the centuries to take the reader on a circular path. From speechwriters to musicians, every professional communicator follows this paradigm because it reflects the natural progression of the human intellect from (a) curiosity to (b) exploration to (c) resolution. Imagine that your judge is a museum patron and you are the curator. At the entrance, you draw her in with tantalizing previews of what's inside (Introduction). Hungry for more, the judge buys your ticket (i.e., she is willing to consider your argument). You then take her on a guided tour (Body). The tour ends exactly where it began – at the entrance where, based on the spectacular job you did during the tour, you entreat the judge to leave a donation before she departs (Conclusion).

Many times I find that my Conclusion summarizes the argument so well that it should replace the Introduction. On these occasions, however, I am forced to admit that the original Conclusion lacked the requisite *oomph* (otherwise known as the *deal closer* or *kill shot*). Other times I will build my brief backwards from the Conclusion, a technique I borrowed from distinguished attorney and author Vincent Bugliosi:

> In other words, I work backward from my summation, the exact reverse of what is normally recommended. Since final summation has to be based on the evidence at the trial, virtually all of my questions at the trial, and most of my tactics and techniques, are aimed at enabling me to make arguments I've already determined I want to make. (*Outrage* – W.W. Norton & Company, Inc. 1996 – p. 148)

We must not forget that, though they are similar in function, the Introduction and Conclusion are not interchangeable. In his discussion of "the model," Professor Trimble deftly expands on the classic triad by breaking the Introduction down into (1) "A well-defined thesis or position" and (2) "A clear plan of attack." To the Body he ascribes (3) "Solid evidence" and (4) "Strong continuity of argument." Finally, he characterizes the Conclusion as (5) "A persuasive closing appeal." (*Writing with Style*, p. 40)

One of the most annoying things to do to a judge is to merely repeat the Introduction with stilted, boilerplate language such as: "For the above reasons, this Court should grant Plaintiff's request for relief." Granted, some appellate courts are such sticklers for terseness that they leave you no room for anything else. But when in doubt, you will best serve your client by choosing the impassioned over the blasé. In the Introduction, you drew the judge a map whose signposts facilitated his trek through your argument. At journey's end, the last thing he wants to do is rehash every twist and turn. He deserves a reward for his hard work – some intellectual refreshment, as it were. People risk life and limb to climb mountains so they can gaze upon the world from the summit. Likewise, your Conclusion should give the judge a panoramic perspective on your argument. At this juncture it isn't necessary to reproduce a list of every point you have made. Like treetops in a forest, one or two will usually outshine the rest. These elemental assertions will present themselves when you ask: *What does it all mean?*

The Conclusion is a great place to use your keenest analogy. And it often proves a fine spot for your little darlings.

Little what?

One of my 1989 cubbyhole-officemates, poet Billy Mack Gammill,[77] identified the *little darling* as one of the writer's worst enemies. The little darling is a phrase, line or paragraph which (a) is so good (in his mind, anyway) that the author can't part with it but (b) doesn't fit the subject matter or flow of the particular piece he is composing. Anyone who has come up with a particularly inspired turn of phrase understands how excruciating it is to delete such a jewel. *After all, I may never be that brilliant again.* Mr. Gammill's solution is failsafe: *Don't obliterate it; just stick it in a drawer for later use.* Following Billy Mack's lead, as you edit your brief you simply create a list titled *Little Darlings, Miscellany* or what have

---

[77] Author of *Prune* (Copper Canyon Press 1979, reprinted by Triangle Man 1980).

you. When you run across something that seems out of place, cut it and paste it into your running collection of outtakes. Later, when you're popping brain cells to craft a dazzling conclusion, you may find the very stick of dynamite you need in that list. Here is the pith of our Conclusion to the appellate brief I referred to earlier:

Conclusion – Oklahoma Court of Appeals – Brief in Chief

Appellants were forced to begin this trial at a severe disadvantage caused by Appellee's oppressive discovery tactics, combined with the trial court's dereliction of its duty to adequately sanction Appellee for those tactics. Many of the trial court's rulings on jury instructions exacerbated Appellants' predicament by confusing the jurors on matters of law regarding the issue of defect, which lay at the heart of Appellants' case. [text omitted] Despite this steady barrage of harmful error, when the jurors first sat down to deliberate, the factual evidence adduced at trial still favored Appellants. But then something went terribly wrong.

By the time the trial court tendered this case to the jury, over 470 pleadings had been filed, 72 depositions had been taken and 30 witnesses, 9 of whom were experts, had testified during 3½ weeks of trial. No less than 8 law firms had expended thousands of hours, and hundreds of thousands of dollars, in the pursuit of justice. This was all for naught, because three jurors violated their oaths by interjecting extraneous information in the form of unsworn, unqualified and biased expert opinion which (a) was not introduced at trial and (b) in some instances actually contradicted expert trial testimony.

Both statutory and case law support the granting of a new trial in this case, based upon jury misconduct alone. When this misconduct is combined with the additional points of reversible error set out above, public policy compels it.

And here is the Conclusion from our Reply Brief in the same appeal:

Conclusion – Oklahoma Court of Appeals – Reply Brief

Both common sense and the laws of physics dictate that, if it is possible to shatter inner bearings in a vehicular impact, then the inner bearings in the right wheel should have been pulverized in the subject accident. Not only did Appellees' experts fail to explain why the right inner bearings were in fine working order after this violent impact; they could not offer the jury a single real-world instance of wheel bearings being broken by a vehicular collision. Post trial testimony shows that the jurors were following common sense and physics until the Foreman devised a new theory (a) which contradicted evidence and testimony presented at trial and (b) about which Appellants were denied an opportunity to cross-examine him.

Appellants never asked for a perfect trial; only a fair one. They received neither. Appellants ask this Court to grant them a new trial so they can try to achieve the latter.

The Length of Your Brief

Back around the time my Uncle Warren was fighting in World War II, Sir Winston L.S. Churchill quipped: "The length of this document defends it well against the risk of its being read."

Because we are obsessed with covering all contingencies, lawyers are notorious for expressing a single thought with one hundred unnecessary words. So afraid are we that our point will be missed that we drive it home in ten redundant ways (Exhibit A). Even the most ruthless self-editors among us are appalled now and then to find that we have mindlessly repeated ourselves within a 2-page span. In this respect we can identify with the recovering substance abuser – always on the mend but never completely cured. Like the alcoholic walking past a bar, we generally find our greatest temptation in the bombast of our opponent's brief.

I can not kick this carcass often enough. If you need to renounce religion or start believing in something, drink more coffee or switch to dirty martinis, do whatever you must ... but *do not let the length of your opponent's brief dictate that of your response.* I know this is counterintuitive in modern American culture, but in the sphere of letters you need not rebut a *Hummer* with yet another *Hummer.* In my experience, the attorney who devotes ten pages to an issue that merits only two is, more often than not, trying to befuddle the court. In that event, your task is to refocus the court, not by parading your gift for pomposity but by demonstrating such confidence in your position that you aren't afraid to shut up when you've said all that needs to be said. Hearkening back to Sr. Ortega:

> The stupendous reality that is language cannot be understood unless we begin by observing that speech consists above all in silences. (*Man and People*, p. 246)

Two pleadings are used to obscene excess in today's courts – the *Daubert*[78] motion and the motion *in limine*. The typical corporate litigant will file a barrage of these motions as close to the trial date as the scheduling order will allow in an attempt to (a) eviscerate his adversary's case (b) overwhelm the opposing attorney with paperwork and thus divert him from trial preparations (c) confuse the judge by burying her under a mountain of rhetoric and (d) lay the groundwork for a mistrial argument in the event the jury turns hostile. This strategy is often referred to as *the case about the case.* In the first multiple fatality case I was involved with, I swallowed one such defendant's bait. When I dropped a five-pound response brief on his desk one afternoon, the judge grimaced.

"Do you actually expect me to read all of that?"

Three years later, the defendants in another case hit me with 26 of these motions totaling over 200 pages, *exclusive of exhibits.* The total page count for my *combined* response was only 59. But its brevity did

---

[78] *Daubert v. Merrell Dow Pharmaceuticals, Inc.* (509 U.S. 579 – 1993)

not diminish its impact. On reading it, one of our experts went out of his way to thank me for the passion with which I had defended him.

Do not underestimate the power of the white space. If, as you read through your latest draft, a faint inner voice asks if you have said enough, try reciting this mantra: *Don't say more, say better.* If your brief isn't communicating, you can be sure it isn't due to a lack of verbiage. Chances are, the point you're trying to make lies hidden within the pages you hold in your hand – your task is to keep whittling until it emerges.

How to Build Your Statement of Facts

Were you to ask 10 attorneys what their initial reaction is when presented with a summary judgment motion, I suspect 9 of them would reply, "Where do I begin?" Like the old adage about a circle, it doesn't really matter so long as you break the job down into three manageable pieces: (1) the decisional criterion (2) substantive law and (3) material facts. I always tackle the research (tasks 1 and 2) first because (a) it is usually less time-consuming and (b) it often determines what facts (task 3) I choose from the evidence at hand. Having tackled research in a previous section, let us turn to that prickly aspect of the brief which too often receives short shrift.

The overwhelming authority instructs that the fact statement is typically the backbone of any argument for or against summary relief. Yet most attorneys pay far too little attention to the fact statement, primarily because constructing one can be such an ordeal. But it need not be so daunting an endeavor. The secret lies in the perspective from which you approach it. Before diving in, take a step back and consider the ways in which your workload has already been ameliorated:

- In trying to prove a negative to the court (lack of evidence), your antagonist has provided you a loose template by identifying specific issues, or categories of proof, into which all you need do is plug positive facts (but, as I will explain in the next section, you

117

must not allow your opponent to dictate the order in which you present those facts);

- Case and/or statutory authority have provided you with the applicable burden of proof for your particular type of case, further refining that template; and

- The documentary evidence, expert reports and witness testimony have vastly narrowed the possible universe of facts from which you must draw.

Because it constitutes the bulk of the evidence in my practice, let us train our focus on the deposition. (I presume your court reporter has provided you with electronic copies of all depositions in a workable format such as ASCII, MS *Word*, Corel *WordPerfect*, or *E-Transcript* from which all aforesaid formats may be derived. If all you have is PDF, call that reporter pronto and demand ASCII at the very least. Then make a note to never retain that numbskull again.)

The first time I read a deposition, I highlight significant portions of testimony in a color that is at once (a) sufficiently stark to grab my attention but (b) not too harsh on the eyes. (After you have been in practice for long enough, you will be able to anticipate what issues are likely to be contested in subsequent motion practice; therefore, time permitting, you will typically complete this task long before a summary application is ever filed.) Next, I copy/paste the highlighted excerpts into a separate document, then close the original deposition. Because my new document will also serve as a supportive exhibit (depending, of course, upon those prickly jurisdictional rules), I save it as "Response to Motion for Summary Judgment – Exhibit A." I then open or create the "Response to Motion for Summary Judgment" and begin inserting my summaries of facts from Exhibit A. As I utilize each snippet in the Statement of Facts, I delete its highlighting in Exhibit A – in this way, I avoid both duplicating and omitting facts:

[Case Style Omitted]

0055

1   Q. Ms. Watts, before we took a break we were

2   talking about what happened out there that day. Let

3   me – let's see, before we talk about where it happened

4   with the photograph, let me ask you a little background.

5   You're coming up onto the entrance ramp when this occurs,

6   aren't you, ma'am?

7   A. Yes.

8   Q. Okay. And do you remember what gear you were

9   in or how fast you were going either one?

10   A. Never switched gears.

11   Q. Okay. So you would have been in low gear?

12   A. Never switched gears.

13   Q. Okay. And do you remember how far back from

14   the emergency vehicle you first saw the wrecker?

15   A. As soon as you was coming down the hill.

16   Q. Okay. So before you ever got to where it was

17   at, you could see it and see the lights; is that correct?

18   A. Yes.

19   Q. Okay. So there's no question you knew it was

20   there; is that right?

21   A. I seen the flashing lights on the tow truck.

22   Q. What was your training – when you were

23   training to be a driver or at Southern Cal, what was your

24   training about emergency vehicles like that? What were

25   you taught to do?

0079

1   A. Yes.

2   Q. Okay. Now, what I want to do is ask you

3   something that may seem obvious, but I need it in the

4   record, ma'am. There wasn't anything obstructing your

5   vision of that emergency vehicle, was there?

6   A. No.

7   Q. There wasn't any trees or posts or nothing like

8   that; is that correct?

9   A. No.

10   Q. Okay. Nothing obstructing your vision of your

11   trailer either? Your mirrors were all working, all of

12   your lights were working; is that correct?

13   A. Yes.

14   Q. Okay. And you were certainly going slow enough

15   that if you had seen something you could have stopped; is

16   that fair?

17   A. Yes.

Deposition 2

[Case Style Omitted]

0034

1   A. No, it's not stupid. I need to just --

2   Q. Is there any question the mirrors were

3   operating that allowed --

4   A. Okay.

5   Q. -- you to see the trailer?

6   A. Yes, sir, it was, the mirrors, right.

7   Q. And the mirrors that were on this particular

8   tractor were mirrors that allowed you to see all the way
9   to the rear of the trailer --
10   A. Yes, sir.
11   Q. -- is that correct?
12   A. Yes.
13   Q. Because they are far enough out for you to see?
14   A. Yes, they are.
15   Q. Did those mirrors have any of those little
16   concave mirrors on them that helped you with a wider
17   view?
18   A. Yes.
19   Q. Do you remember was it one of those that's
20   integrated into the mirror or the concave or was it one
21   of those stick-ons?
22   A. It was -- the mirror didn't have one underneath
23   there.
24   Q. Okay. Integrated into it?
25   A. Okay. Integrated.
0035
1   Q. Okay. And so the jury understands that there's
2   different kinds, aren't there? Some of them are a big
3   mirror or and maybe the bottom half or bottom third of it
4   would be concave. That's the kind you had, wasn't it?
5   A. Okay.
6   Q. And others, sometimes they stick one on?
7   A. Right. We didn't have a stick on.
8   Q. Okay. You had one built into it?
9   A. Built in, right.
10   Q. Okay. And the purpose of that is it gives you
11   a wider view of the back, doesn't it?

12   A. Yes.

13   Q. Because it's concave, it gives you more range

14   so to speak?

15   A. Yes.

16   Q. Is that a fair way to say it?

17   A. Fair way to say it.

18   Q. Okay. And there's no question in your mind on

19   the night of this accident that you could -- driving that

20   rig, the way it was set up, you could see that trailer,

21   couldn't you?

22   A. Yes.

23   Q. Now, tell me, in other words, if you will,

24   let's just start you and Sharon stopped at the Pilot

25   there, didn't you?

0038

1   didn't want her to get in the right lane, it's because

2   she's coming across here --

3   A. Right.

4   Q. -- and you want to make sure she's in this

5   westbound lane; is that correct?

6   A. Yes, sir.

7   Q. Now, let's show the jury what we're talking

8   about here on this film. She's coming across from the

9   Pilot over here, and you wanted to make sure, as she

10   comes across, she stays in this inside lane going

11   westbound; is that correct?

12   A. Yes, sir.

13   Q. Now, that wrecker was sitting right down in

14   here, wasn't it, just in advance of that curve?

15   A. Somewhere between there and the curve.

16   Q. And it was off the right-hand side of the road,

17   wasn't it? The wrecker was sitting right over here?

18   A. It was sitting in the road.

19   Q. Okay. Was it on the shoulder or on the road?

20   A. It was in the road.

21   Q. And there's no question you could see the

22   lights flashing; is that fair?

23   A. Yes.

24   Q. That's the first thing that got your attention,

25   wasn't it, was the lights flashing?

0039

1   A. Yes, it was.

2   Q. Now, were you trained, when you were trained as

3   a trucker, that when an emergency vehicle is sitting

4   there with lights flashing be extra careful?

5   A. Yes, sir.

6   Q. Were you trained to stop and observe and make

7   sure that --

8   A. Yes, sir.

9   Q. Okay. And did she stop that night?

10   A. We just didn't just come to a stop, stop, but

11   we stopped enough to see what was going on.

12   Q. Okay. So she didn't completely stop, but she

13   slowed down?

14   A. What do you mean slow down? We didn't actually

have speed no way.

15   have speed no way.

12   Q. Okay. So she didn't completely stop, but she

13   slowed down?

14   A. What do you mean slow down? We didn't actually

15   have speed no way.

16   Q. Okay. You were going very slow?

17   A. Very slow.

18   Q. Okay. But she never actually rolled to a
19   complete stop?
20   A. Not a complete stop, no, sir.
21   Q. Okay. And when the lights were flashing, you
22   apparently saw that, and that's what you alerted you to
23   get up and look and see what's going on?
24   A. Yes.
25   Q. And no question you could see the wrecker
0040
1   sitting there and you could see the car behind it; is
2   that correct?
3   A. No car behind it.
4   Q. You couldn't see the car behind it?
5   A. No, sir, I did not.
6   Q. But you could see the wrecker?
7   A. Yes, sir.
8   Q. Which way was the wrecker -- was it facing
9   toward you or away from you?
10   A. Away from us.
11   Q. Okay. So the cab of the wrecker would have
12   been forward?
13   A. Right.
14   Q. You would have been looking at the back of it;
15   is that right?
16   A. Yes, sir.
17   Q. Did you see the brake lights on the wrecker?
18   A. No lights, just the top lights.
19   Q. Just the top lights flashing?
20   A. Yes, sir.
21   Q. Okay. And no question you could tell where it
22   was at?
23   A. What you mean by where it's at?

24   Q. There's plenty of light at that intersection
25   even at night, isn't there?

Exhibit A

0055

16   Q. Okay. So before you ever got to where it was
17 at, you could see it and see the lights; is that correct?
18   A. Yes.
19   Q. Okay. So there's no question you knew it was
20 there; is that right?
21   A. I seen the flashing lights on the tow truck.

0079

2   Q. Okay. Now, what I want to do is ask you
3 something that may seem obvious, but I need it in the
4 record, ma'am. There wasn't anything obstructing your
5 vision of that emergency vehicle, was there?
6   A. No.
7   Q. There wasn't any trees or posts or nothing like
8 that; is that correct?
9   A. No.
10   Q. Okay. Nothing obstructing your vision of your
11 trailer either? Your mirrors were all working, all of
12 your lights were working; is that correct?
13   A. Yes.

Exhibit B

0034

2   Q. Is there any question the mirrors were
3 operating that allowed –

125

4   A. Okay.

5   Q. – you to see the trailer?

6   A. Yes, sir, it was, the mirrors, right.

7   Q. And the mirrors that were on this particular

8   tractor were mirrors that allowed you to see all the way

9   to the rear of the trailer –

10   A. Yes, sir.

11   Q. – is that correct?

12   A. Yes.

13   Q. Because they are far enough out for you to see?

14   A. Yes, they are.

0035

18   Q. Okay. And there's no question in your mind on

19   the night of this accident that you could – driving that

20   rig, the way it was set up, you could see that trailer,

21   couldn't you?

22   A. Yes.

0038

17   wasn't it? The wrecker was sitting right over here?

18   A. It was sitting in the road.

19   Q. Okay. Was it on the shoulder or on the road?

20   A. It was in the road.

21   Q. And there's no question you could see the

22   lights flashing; is that fair?

23   A. Yes.

24   Q. That's the first thing that got your attention,

25   wasn't it, was the lights flashing?

0039

1   A. Yes, it was.

***

```
25    Q. And no question you could see the wrecker
0040
1     sitting there and you could see the car behind it; is
2     that correct?
3         A. No car behind it.
4         Q. You couldn't see the car behind it?
5         A. No, sir, I did not.
6         Q. But you could see the wrecker?
7         A. Yes, sir.
8         Q. Which way was the wrecker – was it facing
9     toward you or away from you?
10        A. Away from us.
11        Q. Okay. So the cab of the wrecker would have
12    been forward?
13        A. Right.
14        Q. You would have been looking at the back of it;
15    is that right?
16        A. Yes, sir.
```

Statement of Material Facts

5.   At all times material to the collision, nothing obstructed
     Defendants' view of the wrecker or the trailer they were
     pulling (Exhibit A, 79/2-13; Exhibit B, 34/2-14 and
     35/18-22).

Exhibit A

```
0055
16        Q. Okay. So before you ever got to where it was
17    at, you could see it and see the lights; is that correct?
18        A. Yes.
19        Q. Okay. So there's no question you knew it was
```

20   there; is that right?

21   A. I seen the flashing lights on the tow truck.

0079

2   Q. Okay. Now, what I want to do is ask you

3   something that may seem obvious, but I need it in the

4   record, ma'am. There wasn't anything obstructing your

5   vision of that emergency vehicle, was there?

6   A. No.

7   Q. There wasn't any trees or posts or nothing like

8   that; is that correct?

9   A. No.

10   Q. Okay. Nothing obstructing your vision of your

11   trailer either? Your mirrors were all working, all of

12   your lights were working; is that correct?

13   A. Yes.

Exhibit B

0034

2   Q. Is there any question the mirrors were

3   operating that allowed –

4   A. Okay.

5   Q. – you to see the trailer?

6   A. Yes, sir, it was, the mirrors, right.

7   Q. And the mirrors that were on this particular

8   tractor were mirrors that allowed you to see all the way

9   to the rear of the trailer –

10   A. Yes, sir.

11   Q. – is that correct?

12   A. Yes.

13   Q. Because they are far enough out for you to see?

14   A. Yes, they are.

0035

18   Q. Okay. And there's no question in your mind on
19   the night of this accident that you could – driving that
20   rig, the way it was set up, you could see that trailer,
21   couldn't you?
22   A. Yes.

0038

17   wasn't it? The wrecker was sitting right over here?
18   A. It was sitting in the road.
19   Q. Okay. Was it on the shoulder or on the road?
20   A. It was in the road.
21   Q. And there's no question you could see the
22   lights flashing; is that fair?
23   A. Yes.
24   Q. That's the first thing that got your attention,
25   wasn't it, was the lights flashing?
0039
1   A. Yes, it was.

***

25   Q. And no question you could see the wrecker
0040
1   sitting there and you could see the car behind it; is
2   that correct?
3   A. No car behind it.
4   Q. You couldn't see the car behind it?
5   A. No, sir, I did not.
6   Q. But you could see the wrecker?
7   A. Yes, sir.
8   Q. Which way was the wrecker – was it facing

9	toward you or away from you?
10	A. Away from us.
11	Q. Okay. So the cab of the wrecker would have
12	been forward?
13	A. Right.
14	Q. You would have been looking at the back of it;
15	is that right?
16	A. Yes, sir.

Statement of Material Facts

5.   At all times material to the collision, nothing obstructed Defendants' view of the wrecker or the trailer they were pulling (Exhibit A, 79/2-13; Exhibit B, 34/2-14 and 35/18-22).

6.   Both Defendants admit that they saw the wrecker's emergency lights as they approached it from the rear (Exhibit A, 55/16-21; Exhibit B, 38/17 to 39/1 and 39/25 to 40/16).

Exhibit A

0055

16	Q. Okay. So before you ever got to where it was
17	at, you could see it and see the lights; is that correct?
18	A. Yes.
19	Q. Okay. So there's no question you knew it was
20	there; is that right?
21	A. I seen the flashing lights on the tow truck.

0079
2   Q. Okay. Now, what I want to do is ask you
3   something that may seem obvious, but I need it in the
4   record, ma'am. There wasn't anything obstructing your
5   vision of that emergency vehicle, was there?
6   A. No.
7   Q. There wasn't any trees or posts or nothing like
8   that; is that correct?
9   A. No.
10   Q. Okay. Nothing obstructing your vision of your
11 trailer either? Your mirrors were all working, all of
12 your lights were working; is that correct?
13   A. Yes.

Exhibit B

0034
2   Q. Is there any question the mirrors were
3   operating that allowed –
4   A. Okay.
5   Q. – you to see the trailer?
6   A. Yes, sir, it was, the mirrors, right.
7   Q. And the mirrors that were on this particular
8   tractor were mirrors that allowed you to see all the way
9   to the rear of the trailer –
10   A. Yes, sir.
11   Q. – is that correct?
12   A. Yes.
13   Q. Because they are far enough out for you to see?
14   A. Yes, they are.

0035

18   Q. Okay. And there's no question in your mind on
19 the night of this accident that you could – driving that
20 rig, the way it was set up, you could see that trailer,
21 couldn't you?
22   A. Yes.

0038

17 wasn't it? The wrecker was sitting right over here?
18   A. It was sitting in the road.
19   Q. Okay. Was it on the shoulder or on the road?
20   A. It was in the road.
21   Q. And there's no question you could see the
22 lights flashing; is that fair?
23   A. Yes.
24   Q. That's the first thing that got your attention,
25 wasn't it, was the lights flashing?
0039
1   A. Yes, it was.

***

25   Q. And no question you could see the wrecker
0040
1 sitting there and you could see the car behind it; is
2 that correct?
3   A. No car behind it.
4   Q. You couldn't see the car behind it?
5   A. No, sir, I did not.
6   Q. But you could see the wrecker?
7   A. Yes, sir.
8   Q. Which way was the wrecker – was it facing

```
9      toward you or away from you?
10         A. Away from us.
11         Q. Okay. So the cab of the wrecker would have
12     been forward?
13         A. Right.
14         Q. You would have been looking at the back of it;
15     is that right?
16         A. Yes, sir.
```

Another approach I find useful is to build a rough outline of my deposition highlights, categorized according to either the burden of proof or the movant's areas of attack. Under each heading, I merely designate the deposition and a bare-bones summary of the testimony:

MSJ Response SOF Outline

Alternative Designs

- Medical Expert, Exhibit F: 60/3-14 (integrated seatbelts prevent excursion); 109/22-110/24 (if we keep his butt in the seat, he walks away)

Accident Sequence/Injury Causation

- Reconstructionist, Exhibit I: 12/7-12 (initial speed 19-29 mph); 12/15-18 (speed at trip was 14-16 mph); 45/12-46/4 (from trip to rest, vehicle rolled 20 feet staying close to the ground – in other words there was no bouncing or dropping)
- Medical Expert, Exhibit F: 10/24-11/16 (it took at least 800 pounds of force to cause Driver's injury); 15/17-16/7 (Driver's seated height places him at less than the 50th percentile for males); 32/11-20 (roof crush only 1.7 inches); 50/21-52/16 (to receive his injuries, Driver had to travel 5" just to contact the roof and an additional 4" to compress his spine); 54/15-56/16 (it took only 30-70 milliseconds for this compressive force to cause injury); 94/7-23 (contact alone won't injure you – it takes extra excursion to allow body to compress neck); 103/4-17 (recline angle was 20 degrees, which is average)
- Driver, Exhibit H: 23/11-25 (he's no rookie, but was an OTR driver and knows how to handle a vehicle in hazardous conditions); 24/11-19 (driving 25 mph); 26/18/23 (took foot off gas and tried to steer out of skid, to no avail)

No Alcohol or Pain Meds

- EMT (no odor of alcohol or report thereof), Exhibit M

- Paramedic (no odor of alcohol or report thereof), Exhibit J, 37/22-39/23 & 46/23-47/20
- Trooper, Exhibit L, 18/10-19 & 31/12-32/15
- Wife, Exhibit K, 9/22-11/3 (rarely drank since back surgery 2005), 23/17-26/9 (no alcohol that day) & 29/10-21 (never took pain meds when thought might have to drive)
- Driver, Exhibit H: 126/24-127/24 (always careful with Dilaudid in bad weather; none that day), 128/16-129/4 (beer only in summertime; none that day)
- Daughter, Exhibit G, 91/23-5

Seatbelt Use

- Paramedic, Exhibit J, 25/22-26/11 (unsure where no-use info obtained) & 42/17-43/10 (no conversation with daughter)
- Trooper, Exhibit L, 16/22-17/10 & 19/21-21/19 (assumed no seatbelt use from injury alone, no conversation w/Tim)
- Wife, Exhibit K, 28 (never wore seatbelt improperly)
- Daughter, Exhibit G: 32/13-34/23 (after close call, Driver buckled his seatbelt); 49/21-50/18 (still upright in seat after roll); 51/3-14 (due to slack, Driver was lying on webbing though still buckled); 56/5-24 (she released the buckle herself, and his body shifted); 88/18-89/5 (normally, Driver had plenty headroom, but belt had allowed his head to touch roof and his back to come away from the seatback)
- Driver, Exhibit H: 40/23-43/2 (oriented in same seated driving position after crash, felt belt on body after crash, asked daughter to unbuckle it, when she did his body settled further against door); 60/3-61/7 (put belt on after curve)
- Medical Expert, Exhibit F: 17/21-18/3 (neck injury alone favors restrained over unrestrained); 86/1-87/25 (because load marks are rarely left in low-energy events such as rollovers, it is best to look to witness testimony, accident statistics, actual testing and the nature of the injury itself to

determine the likelihood of belt use); 104/12-105/7, 107/10-108/2 (the physics of the accident confirm restraint even though no witness marks)

Hazardous Condition of Road

- Paramedic, Exhibit J, 9/19-10/11 & 21/2-24
- Trooper, Exhibit L, 7/16-8/4

How to Organize Your Statement of Facts

As Christmas 2001 approached, a young pilot drove to Wisconsin to inspect a jet he would be flying for a new employer. The job entailed a significant bump in salary and relocation to southern California. Just minutes from his home in Indiana, a tire on his SUV failed. During the ensuing rollover he was ejected through the closed and latched sunroof, despite the fact that he was properly wearing his seatbelt. He perished at the scene, leaving behind a wife and son. An Indiana jury awarded the widow a 7-figure verdict which, of course, the defendants appealed. Their principle complaints were that (a) we had not proffered sufficient evidence of defect or safer alternative design and (b) we had irreversibly tainted the trial by performing an impermissible demonstration with a seatbelt component known as a "slider bar." The local counsel and I agreed this would be one of those rare occasions that called for a fact statement which (a) was longer than usual and (b) incorporated procedural matters. We spent the bulk of our time fashioning a 12-page statement which was so compelling that it required surprisingly little commentary in the Argument and Authority section. With our deadline still three weeks away, we had crafted one concise brief that responded to two separate defense briefs.

Alas, our local counsel's senior partner hired a local ringer[79] to "finalize" the response brief. As he explained it, the Indiana Ringer would simply add argument and authority on one or two issues. Mere pages into my review of his first draft, I discovered two alarming realities: (1) his intention from the outset was to restructure, not finalize and (2) the grammatical mistakes and misquotes meant that, as had happened in the Florida case, we were again at the mercy of a slipshod composer who relied on a *Dictaphone* and a paralegal with the linguistic acumen of an 8th grade cheerleader. Not only did the paralegal ignore my editorial comments; she had the temerity to send me a snippy email in which she complained that they were a hindrance. Her misspelling "hinderance" did not instill confidence. To make matters worse, *one day before the deadline,* the Indiana Ringer decided to separate the response into two briefs.

Among the many ways that hack butchered our brief,[80] the foremost was that he rearranged the fact statement "to follow the organization of the issues presented by Defendants." The end result was a disjointed jumble presented with all the passion of a Ben Stein monologue. But don't take my word for it; observe for yourself:

Our Sensible Approach

STATEMENT OF FACTS

Anthony D. Zorn was the quintessential self-made man. One of seven children from a broken home, he grew up in a trailer whose amenities included a creek for bathing and an outhouse. A gifted athlete, Mr. Zorn helped Clemson win the national championship during his freshman year. He spent four years in England playing

---

[79] David W. Stone, IV. My treatment of Mr. Stone is restricted solely to the unrivaled legal writing ineptitude he amply demonstrated in this particular case. As I have no frame of reference from which to do so, I express no opinion regarding his general performance as a legal advocate.
[80] Indiana Court of Appeals, Case No. 73A05-0710-CV-552 – *Brief of Appellee and Cross Appeal* – July 11, 2008

professional football for the Leeds Cougars, serving as linebacker, head coach and community/media representative. He also spearheaded a youth football league called Britain Crusaders, which sponsored annual bowl games and provided opportunities for British and American children to visit each other's country. Tony was so successful at these endeavors that, under his leadership, the popularity of American football surpassed that of soccer in Leeds. When he returned to the States, he continued to play semi-professional football while finishing college and serving as assistant strength coach for the Cincinnati Bengals. He also became a successful pilot, achieving a Captain rating on private jets.

It was during his time in England that he had a chance encounter with Mary. So immediate was the attraction, and so perfectly did their personalities coalesce, that their kinship could not have been better scripted by a romance novelist. Tony took Mary back to the States with him and they were married in 1991. Mary recalls the birth of their son, Christopher, the following year as "the best surprise I've ever had in my life." Nor was the occasion lost on Tony: "I've never seen a man cry like he did when Christopher was born." There is no dispute that Tony was a doting father, taking interest in every aspect of Christopher's life. Tony and Mary shared such a keen interest in children that they obtained certification and volunteered for the Court Appointed Special Advocate program. So tireless was Tony in his devotion to Mary that a friend twice described her as 100% dependent upon him: "What he wanted more than anything was for Mary just to be able to be his wife and be Christopher's mom and, and to live free of all that stuff. And so he took care of everything."

***

As Christmas 2001 approached, the future could not have looked brighter for the Zorn family. [text omitted] After an intensive interview and screening process, Tony had accepted an offer to captain jets for [name of company redacted], earning $85,000/yr plus benefits. The jury saw from Tony's 2000 and 2001 tax returns that this was a handsome increase in salary. Despite Appellants' attempt to cloud the issue, there is no doubt in the mind of the man who hired him that (a) a full reference check had been performed and (b) a contract of employment existed between [name of company redacted] and Tony as of December 12, 2001. This was a prestigious position with a solid firm. Tony and Mary promptly put their house on the market and just as quickly received an offer. Tony's excitement about this new chapter in their lives was summed up in a note he sent to his brother: "New year, new job, new home. In mid-January Mary, Christopher and I are moving to southern California, Palm Springs." Accompanying the note was a picture of the jet he would be flying for [name of company redacted] – the very jet he drove to Appleton, Wisconsin to inspect on the morning of December 19 … the last day his family would see him alive. His life expectancy was 37.1 years.

After meeting two company representatives in Appleton, Tony dropped them at the local airport at 8:00 p.m. The parties agreed that Tony would have had to leave around midnight CST to arrive at the accident scene by 9:00 a.m. EST. No one knows what Tony did with the four extra hours. All parties agreed that: (a) the particular seatbelt assembly in Tony's SUV on December 20, 2001 was the same seatbelt assembly Appellant 1 supplied to Appellant 2 for installation in this vehicle in October 1996 (b) Tony was properly wearing his seatbelt when this accident began and (c) he was ejected through the sunroof, which had been closed and latched prior to the accident. Neither Appellant offered any evidence that the subject sunroof, seatbelt assembly or restraint system were altered or abused in any way after leaving the factory, thus failing to meet their burden on the issue of comparative fault with regard to these components. It was undisputed that the purpose of a seatbelt is to keep the occupant in her seat, inside the vehicle, during a foreseeable accident. The central question for the jury was how a properly restrained driver could get thrown through a closed and latched sunroof.

The evidence showed that Tony's actions during the accident sequence were appropriate at all times. When his left tire failed, the SUV pulled to the left. Seeing that the shoulder was more forgiving than the median, Tony eased off the gas and made a gradual steer to the right. Because the angle of the morning sun concealed the drop-off on the far side of the bridge, Tony had no reason to panic or slam on the brakes as he approached the bridge. Though he did everything right, the SUV's inherent instability prevented it from going exactly where he wanted it to. As soon as the drop-off became visible Tony hit the brakes, but it was too late. In the words of reconstructionist Carl Oaks: "He just ran out of real estate." Contrary to Appellants' portrayal, the SUV did not vault into the air like a stunt car off a ramp: "And it did not … depart the ground until the ground began to fall away from it. The embankment actually fell away and then it became airborne." In relation to other highway-speed rollover accidents, this one was not severe; in fact, the greatest change in velocity was no more than 15 mph.

Neither Appellant offered its own reconstructionist to rebut Mr. Oaks' findings. However, during its cross-examination of Mr. Oaks, Appellant 1 introduced an undamaged, exemplar slider bar over Mrs. Zorn's objection. Appellant 1 then displayed the bent slider bar from Tony's vehicle and challenged Mr. Oaks to reproduce that bend on the exemplar with his bare hands:

Q. If I hand you Exhibit … 5, you try to bend that and can you try to bend that and kink it?

A. If you try to bend it this way, it's harder, but if you twist it, then you will, it violates that "L" configuration, and it will snap there much easier.

Q. Can you do that?

A. Can I do it?

Q. Yes.

A. Probably not with my hands.

Q. All right.

A. Maybe two years ago I could have, but...

Q. Can we agree, Mr. Oaks, that as a result of this accident, the slider bar in the Zorn car was severely deformed?

A. It was deformed. I don't know how to say severely. It was deformed, absolutely.

Q. Isn't it true, sir, that you have never seen a slider bar as deformed as this one?

A. I had not, no. Huh-uh.

Q. And I think you told us that you've investigated thousands of accidents?

A. Yes, sir, probably 700 to 1,400 rollovers, but you know, not that many cars have slider bars.

Q. Let me move to another topic.

Appellant 1 voiced no objection to the prospect of such a demonstration.

Both lay and expert testimony was conclusive that, had Tony stayed in his driver seat until the SUV came to rest, he would have survived. Impacts to the passenger side of the SUV actually raised the roof on the driver side, thereby increasing Tony's survival space. The driver window was intact, and nothing had intruded into the vehicle. Though Dr. Madigan speculated that Tony was bouncing like a pinball and getting beaten to a pulp inside the vehicle, she was forced to agree with Mrs. Zorn's experts that there simply was no physical evidence Tony had collided with any interior component hard enough to cause him injury. In fact, the only evidence of occupant contact to the interior was a quarter-sized scuff mark in the plastic trim above the driver window. This abrasion was so slight that, though Dr. Madigan claimed it was a "possible" location of the head strike that caused Tony's significant head and neck injuries, her own photographs disproved her claim. The jurors were allowed to see these facts firsthand during an on-site inspection of the vehicle.

Neither Appellant offered an expert to testify as to medical causation of injuries. Though Dr. Madigan attempted to render such opinions, the fact remains that she is not a licensed physician: her doctorate is in bioengineering, not medicine, and the few medical courses she attended were associated with her engineering program. She has never treated a patient in her life, and she has no intention of ever doing so. Therefore, the trial court was bound by Indiana law to preclude her from speculating in this area. Dr. Stillwell, a medical examiner with peerless credentials, firmly established that Tony's injuries occurred outside the vehicle: (a) it is "almost unheard of" for brain injuries such as Tony's to occur inside a vehicle in an accident such as this (b) it is "extremely rare" for a person to bruise his lungs as Tony did unless he is ejected and (c) the bruising and laceration deep inside Tony's kidney are most consistent with ejection. In addition to his considerable experience investigating automotive fatalities, Dr. Stillwell relied on a practical comparison of relative G-forces, a study funded by Appellant 2 itself and a scientific article authored by a General Motors engineer to illustrate the commonsense proposition that occupants who stay inside a vehicle during a rollover have a 90% chance of surviving. When asked whether someone can be ejected in a rollover while wearing a properly functioning seatbelt, Dr. Stillwell replied: "I have only seen that happen when there was a door opening, or in one particular case where the seatbelt cut the legs off the occupant ...."

Appellants failed to offer a crashworthiness expert to rebut the testimony of Daniel S. Griffin, Ph.D., P.E. Educated and trained by the automotive industry, Dr. Griffin worked in the 1990s for the largest specialty automotive fastener supplier in the United States, which supplied bolts and various other metal fasteners to the "Big 3" auto manufacturers. Dr. Griffin explained the specific duties Appellant 2 owed to Anthony Zorn: Because Appellant 2 was aware prior to manufacturing the subject SUV that (a) SUVs are rollover prone and (b) a poorly installed luxury item such as a sunroof can cause partial and total occupant ejection in rollovers, Appellant 2 should have performed rollover testing which would have alerted it to the weakness of the mounting brackets. Though his own extensive testing demonstrates that the glass in this sunroof should have failed before the mounting brackets did, the evidence in this case clearly shows that the brackets failed first. Dr. Griffin offered three of "a hundred different ways" Appellant 2 could have prevented this failure which, in 1997, were technologically and economically feasible.

So how did Tony get out of a buckled seatbelt? Appellant 1 claimed it was due to a bend in the slider bar; however, this deformation accounted for only two inches of slack. As none of his limbs was severed, the only conceivable explanation was spoolout. Edward M. Howell, P.E. – a mechanical engineer who has (a) studied the behavior of restraint systems in rollover accidents since 1989 and (b) published around 50 peer-reviewed articles – studied and measured the locations of the load marks on Tony's seatbelt. He then performed a surrogate study to confirm that those marks corresponded to Tony's physical dimensions. Among the various sources of knowledge and experience he drew on to interpret the load marks were crash tests run by Appellant 2 and rollover tests performed by NHTSA. The jury learned that spoolout is not some rogue litigation theory; it is a predictable response to rollover forces dictated by the laws of physics. From distinctive marks made as the belt passed through the latch plate, Mr. Howell calculated 13 inches of looseness in the lap belt. He used other visible marks on the seatbelt webbing, as well as basic physics and geometry, to explain that (a) it was physically impossible for the stalk and slider bar to bend in the direction they did while Tony occupied the driver seat and (b) the bend in Tony's slider bar could be produced with very little force. He also found unique web grabber marks at the retractor end of the belt indicating 17 inches of spoolout. Finally, other belt marks showed interaction with the opening for the sunroof, confirming his earlier spoolout measurements.

Contrary to Appellant 1's misrepresentation of the record, Mr. Howell testified quite clearly that the retractor itself is defective:

Q. Focus again on the ball-and-cup retractor and the pass-through tongue..., and we can agree, sir, can't we, that overall, ball-and-cup retractors and pass-through tongues have saved a lot of lives and they've prevented a lot of injuries?

A. Sure. Seatbelts are a good thing.

Q. In fact, you would agree that this is a pretty good seatbelt and seatbelt system for frontal crashes?

A. For frontal crashes, the system works reasonably well. The issue I have is with respect to rollovers, it's not a reliable system.

Q. Well, in fact, at your deposition, you clarified that you're not claiming that the seatbelt retractor itself is defective; you're claiming that the overall restraint system is defective as used in this SUV?

A. Well, you're taking that out of context. What we're talking about there, I believe, is with respect to the Federal Motor Vehicle Safety Standards 209. And with respect to whether or not this retractor locks at .7 G's in a planar or frontal mode or a side mode or those types, sorts of things, it's not my suggestion that it would fail to do that. I believe it does. On the other hand, 209 does not have a specific requirement that deals with rollovers. And when we then talk about how it performs in rollovers, this system in general does not perform well. It's not reliable. The retractor is not reliable. And I believe, therefore, it's defective, and that's what led to Mr. Zorn's rejection..., or ejection. I'm sorry.

MR. MACE: Your Honor, I move to strike as nonresponsive.

Mr. Howell also established the duty Appellants breached and proposed feasible alternative designs that would have saved Tony's life, including a cinching latch plate, integrated seatbelts and pretensioners:

A.   A pretensioner is designed to..., excuse me..., is designed to actually tighten up the belt to some extent right before the crash. In other words, right before the crash, if you're wearing your seatbelt, normally it may be sitting here on your chest, and what the pretensioner is designed to do is, there is a sensor designed to sense the crash force and to tighten up the belt. And there is one of two ways they will do that. They may pull down on the buckle so they actually pull the buckle down, and it's set up on a little cable mechanism, and it actually pulls the buckle literally down by several inches, and that tightens up the belt. You can envision how that could happen. If you have your seatbelt on and somebody pulled the buckle down three inches or four inches, obviously that would tighten up your seatbelt.

On the other end, they can have them on the other end as well, and [Defendant] has both, that would actually, instead of pulling the belt off the retractor spool, it will actually spool it back in and tighten it up that way.

So either way, the idea is the pretensioner is designed to tighten up the belt. Initially, prior..., right at the onset of the crash, and it keeps, then, the belt tension and the belt tight through the duration, and that's what it's designed to do.

Q.   Now, in this document, do they note that, in fact, Appellant 2 had pretensioners in usage in other passenger vehicles, in particular, in Europe more than the United States?

A. It notes specifically that Europe has a 95 percent usage rate of pretensioners in passenger cars versus only six percent in North America, yes.

Q. Did Appellant 2 have..., we'll get into the details of it later in the day..., but did they have before this vehicle was built that's the subject matter of this case, feasible, technologically feasible, economically feasible, pretensioner designs that they were using?

A. Oh, sure, they were in production.

Q. How long had they been out before this vehicle was built?

A. Various manufacturers began them in different times, but certainly the early 90s.

Appellant 1's seatbelt expert, George M. Vinson, contended that spoolout is a physical impossibility for the subject seatbelt design. Though he offered an alternative explanation for three of the web grabber marks, he did not bother to address the marks on the latch plate or, more importantly, those associated with the sunroof. He testified on direct that it would have taken far more than 1,300 pounds of force to bend a slider bar as much as the one in Tony's SUV was bent. He then confirmed on cross-examination that the seatbelt assembly must be able to withstand at least 5,000 pounds of combined force to comply with the General Product Acceptance Specification. He also agreed that the slider bar, which anchors one side of the seatbelt assembly, should be able to withstand the same force.

It was at this moment during cross-examination that Mrs. Zorn's counsel, a middle-aged gentleman of average strength, impeached Mr. Vinson's testimony: using only his hands, he bent an exemplar slider bar with ease, taking great care to bend it exactly where Tony's slider bar bent in the accident. With the trial court's permission, he handed the exemplar (hereinafter "demonstration bar") to the jury, along with the slider bar from the accident for comparison. He then asked:

Q. Now, sir, you would accept that when I bench with my boys, I probably don't bench more than about 200 at my size, would you?

A. I don't know.

Neither Appellant objected at this juncture, nor was any objection heard between the time the jurors began passing the slider bars around and the mid-morning break.

After the break, Appellant 1 asked only that (a) the demonstration bar be stricken from the record and (b) the jury be instructed to disregard it. Though Appellant 2's counsel requested no relief whatsoever, he placed a desultory alibi on the record:

[MR. CONROY:] And just for the record too, Judge, I..., and shame on me, because I didn't know this was coming, I was looking down taking notes whenever counsel did what he did, and I should have caught what he did. But it is what it is.

Mr. Vinson was also forced to admit on cross that (a) Appellant 1 and Appellant 2 work hand-in-hand to develop specific restraint systems for specific vehicles (b) Appellant 1 breached its independent duty to assure that the restraint components it supplied were appropriate to the SUV and (c) the particular restraint system in Tony's vehicle is unique to the SUV and its cousins, the SUV-A and SUV-B.

Appellants were then given ample opportunity to attack Mrs. Zorn's slider bar demonstration on the issue of similarity, after which (a) Appellant 1 renewed its motion to strike and instruct the jury but (b) Appellant 2 asked for nothing more than an instruction.

Recognizing the burden on counsel "to raise objections at the appropriate time," the trial court took the motion under advisement. When the examination of Mr. Vinson was over, the trial court (a) misconstrued in Appellants' favor its own order with regard to demonstrative evidence (b) emphasized again the fact that Appellants had waited far too long to object to the demonstration at issue and (c) promised a ruling on the oral Motion to Strike immediately after the impending lunch break. Just before the recess, Appellant 1's counsel hastened to adopt Mr. Conroy's alibi:

> [MR. MACE:] I also was busily writing notes, and I didn't even..., wasn't even aware of it happening until after it occurred.

On the whole, Mr. Vinson's efforts were lost on the jury, because his own client, Appellant 1, had debunked his premise a decade earlier. One piece of evidence Appellants failed to mention in their briefs was placed in the record early in the trial as Plaintiff's Exhibit 199. In this series of communications dated April and May 1996:

- Appellant 1 tells Appellant 2 that light trucks have a higher rollover-ejection rate than other passenger cars;

- Appellant 1 notes that ejection is the leading cause of fatalities in passenger vehicles;

- Appellant 1 admits that spoolout can and does occur in rollovers;
- Appellant 1 recommends pretensioners specifically to prevent spoolout; and

- Appellant 1 notes that 95% of the vehicles in Europe already utilize pretensioners.

Worrisome as Exhibit 199 was to both Appellants, the slider bar issue was particularly disastrous for Appellant 2 because Appellant 1 had absolutely nothing to do with its design, manufacture or assembly. During the lunch break, Appellant 2's counsel realized that his acquiescence in Appellant 1's slider bar diversion had backfired. It was only when court reconvened, hours after the performance of the slider bar demonstration, that Appellant 2 requested a mistrial. Coincidentally, no sooner had one of the two counsel representing Appellant 2 requested the mistrial than the other appropriated an alibi identical to that used earlier by his colleagues:

> MR. RIEGNER: Just for the record, Judge, I also was taking notes and neither of us knew what happened until it was over with.

Recognizing again the necessity of raising a timely objection, the trial court denied the motion for mistrial but granted the motion to strike, and admonished the jury to disregard the demonstration.

With regard to Appellant 1's complaints about Mrs. Zorn's closing argument: (a) Appellants did not object to the inadvertent reference to wealth and (b) the court promptly admonished the jury about the "us against them" and "send a message" comments, Mrs. Zorn's counsel apologized and clarified, and neither Appellant indicated it considered the court's admonishment inadequate. Finally, in their closing arguments: (a) Appellant 2 did not even address damages and (b) Appellant 1 stated: "As to damages, I'll talk briefly. There's no dispute." This all-or-nothing strategy offered the jurors no ceiling on damages in the event they found for Mrs. Zorn on liability.

The Indiana Ringer's Derelict Approach

STATEMENT OF THE FACTS

After an intensive interview and screening process, Tony had accepted an offer to captain jets for [company name redacted], earning $85,000/yr. plus benefits. His 2000 and 2001 tax returns were admitted and showed an increase in salary. There was no doubt in the mind of the man who hired him that a full reference check had been performed regarding Tony and a contract of employment existed between [company name redacted] and Tony as of December 12, 2001. This was a prestigious position with a solid firm. Tony and Mary promptly put their house on the market and quickly received an offer. Tony's excitement about this new chapter in their lives was summed up in a note he sent to his brother: "New year, new job, new home. In mid-January Mary, Christopher and I are moving to southern California, Palm Springs." Accompanying the note was a picture of the jet he would be flying for [company name redacted] – the very jet he drove to Appleton, Wisconsin to inspect on the morning of December 19, 2001, the last day his family would see him alive. His life expectancy was 37.1 years.

After meeting two company representatives in Appleton, Tony dropped them at the local airport at 8:00p.m. The parties agreed that Tony would have had to leave around midnight CST to arrive at the accident scene by 9:00a.m. EST. There was no evidence what he did during the extra four hours.

All parties agreed that the particular seatbelt assembly in Tony's SUV on December 20, 2001, was the same seatbelt assembly that Appellant 1 supplied to Appellant 2 for installation in this vehicle in October 1996. It was agreed that Tony was properly wearing his seatbelt when this accident began. It was agreed he was ejected through the sunroof, which was closed and latched prior to the accident. Neither defendant offered any evidence that the subject sun roof, seatbelt assembly or restraint system were altered or abused in any way after leaving the factory. It was undisputed that the purpose of a seatbelt is to keep the occupant in her seat, inside the vehicle, during a foreseeable accident.

The evidence of reconstructionist, Carl Oaks, was that Tony's actions during the accident sequence were appropriate at all times. When its left tire failed, the SUV pulled to the left. Tony eased off the gas and made a gradual steer to the right. Because the angle of the morning sun concealed the drop-off on the far side of the bridge, Tony had no reason to panic or slam on the brakes as he approached the bridge. Though he did everything right, the SUV's inherent instability prevented it from going exactly where he wanted it to. As soon as the drop-off became visible Tony hit the brakes, but it was too late: "He just ran out of real estate." The SUV "did not ... depart the ground until the ground began to fall away from it. When the embankment fell away the and then it became airborne." In relation to other highway-speed rollover accidents, this rollover was not severe; in fact, the highest change in velocity was no greater than 15 mph.

Neither defendant offered a reconstructionist to rebut Mr. Oaks' findings. During its cross-examination of Mr. Oaks, Appellant 1 introduced an undamaged, exemplar slider bar over Mrs. Zorn's objection. Appellant 1 then displayed the bent slider bar from Tony's vehicle and challenged Mr. Oaks to reproduce that bend on the exemplar with his bare hands. Appellant 2 voiced no objection to the prospect of such a demonstration.

Both lay and expert testimony was conclusive that, had Tony stayed in his driver seat until the SUV came to rest, he would have had more than a 90% survival chance. Impacts to the passenger side of the SUV actually raised the roof on the driver side, increasing Tony's survival space. The driver side window was intact, and nothing had intruded into the vehicle. Madigan agreed with Mrs. Zorn's experts that there simply was no physical evidence Tony had collided with any interior component hard enough to cause him injury. In fact, the only evidence of occupant contact to the interior was a quarter-sized scuff mark in the plastic trim above the driver window. This abrasion was so slight that her own photographs did not show the claimed impact point. The jurors were allowed to see these facts firsthand during an on-site inspection of the vehicle.

Neither defendant offered an expert to testify as to medical causation of injuries. Though. Madigan attempted to render such opinions, she is not a licensed physician. Her doctorate is in bioengineering, not medicine. She has never treated a patient in her life, and she has no intention of ever doing so.

Dr. Stillwell, a medical examiner with extensive credentials, established that Tony's injuries occurred outside the vehicle. He said it is "almost unheard of" for brain injuries such as Tony's to occur inside a vehicle in an accident such as this. He said it is "extremely rare" for a person to bruise his lungs as Tony did unless he is ejected alive. He said the bruising and laceration deep inside Tony's kidney are most consistent with ejection. In addition to his considerable experience investigating automotive fatalities, Dr. Stillwell relied on a practical comparison of relative G-forces, a study funded by Appellant 2 itself and a scientific article authored by a General Motors engineer to illustrate the common sense proposition that occupants who stay inside a vehicle during a rollover have a 90% chance of surviving. When asked whether someone can be ejected in a rollover while wearing a properly functioning seatbelt, Dr. Stillwell replied: "I have only seen that happen when there was a door opening, or in one particular case where the seatbelt cut the legs off the occupant ...."

Daniel S. Griffin, Ph.D., P.E. was educated and trained by the automotive industry. He worked in the 1990s for the largest specialty automotive fastener supplier in the United States, which supplied bolts and various other metal fasteners to [the "Big 3" auto manufacturers]. Dr. Griffin explained the specific duties [Appellant 1] owed to Anthony Zorn. Because Appellant 2 was aware prior to manufacturing the subject SUV that (a) SUVs are rollover prone and (b) a poorly installed luxury item such as a sunroof can cause partial and total occupant ejection in rollovers, Appellant 2 should have performed rollover testing which would have alerted it to the weakness of the mounting brackets. Though his own extensive testing demonstrated that the glass in this sunroof should have failed before the mounting brackets did, the evidence in this case clearly shows that the brackets failed first. Dr. Griffin offered three of "a hundred different ways" Appellant 2 could have prevented this failure which, in 1997, were technologically and economically feasible.

Appellant 1 claimed that Tony got out of the buckled restraint system because of the bending of the slider bar. This deformation accounted for only two inches of slack. Edward M. Howell, P.E. is a mechanical engineer who has (a) studied the behavior of restraint systems in rollover accidents since 1989 and (b) published around 50 peer-reviewed articles. He studied and measured the locations of the load marks on Tony's seatbelt. He then performed a surrogate study to confirm that those marks corresponded to Tony's physical dimensions. Among the various sources of knowledge and experience he drew on in interpreting the load marks were crash tests run by Appellant 2 and rollover tests performed by NHTSA. The evidence before the jury was that spool out is a predictable response to rollover forces dictated by the laws of physics. From distinctive marks made as the belt passed through the latch plate, Mr. Howell calculated 13 inches of looseness in the lap belt. He used other visible marks on the seatbelt webbing, as well as basic physics and geometry, to explain that it was physically impossible for the stalk and slider bar to bend in the direction they did while Tony occupied the driver seat and that the bend in Tony's slider bar could be produced with very little force. He also found unique web grabber marks at the retractor end of the belt indicating 17 inches of spool-out. Other belt marks showed interaction with the opening for the sun roof. This confirmed earlier spool-out measurements. Mr. Howell established the duty defendants breached, and proposedfeasible alternative designs including the use of pretensioner that would have saved Tony's life.

Appellant 1's seatbelt expert, George M. Vinson, contended that spool-out is a physical impossibility for the subject seatbelt design. He testified on direct that it would have taken far more than 1,300 pounds of force to bend a slider as much as the one in Tony's SUV was bent. On cross examination he conceded that the seatbelt assembly must be able to withstand at least 5,000 pounds of combined force to comply with the General Product Acceptance Specification. He also agreed that the slider bar, which anchors one side of the seatbelt assembly, should be able to withstand the same force.

Mrs. Zorn's counsel then bent an exemplar slider bar over his knee with ease, taking great care to bend it exactly where Tony's slider bar bent in the accident. With the trial court's permission, he handed the exemplar (hereinafter "demonstration bar") to the jury, along with the slider bar from the accident for comparison. Neither defendant objected, nor was any objection heard between the time the jurors began passing the slider bars around, and the mid-morning break.

After the break, Appellant 1 asked only that the demonstration bar be stricken from the record and the jury be instructed to disregard it. Appellant 2 made no objection and requested no relief.

Mr. Vinson admitted Appellant 1 and Appellant 2 work closely together in developing specific restraint systems for specific vehicles. He admitted the particular restraint system in Tony's vehicle is unique to the SUV and two other similar vehicles, the SUV and SUV.

Defendants were given an opportunity to attack the demonstration on the issue of similarity. Appellant 1 then renewed its motion to strike and instruct the jury. Appellant 2 asked for an instruction. The trial court took the motion under advisement. When the examination of Mr. Vinson was over the trial court emphasized that Appellants had waited far too long to object to the demonstration at issueand promised a ruling on the "Motion to Strike" immediately after the impending lunch break.

154

In a series of communications dated April and May 1996 and admitted as Exhibit 199, Appellant 1 told Appellant 2 that light trucks have a higher rollover-ejection rate than other passenger cars. It noted the still higher roll over fatality rate of SUVs. Appellant 1 noted that ejection is the leading cause of fatalities in passenger vehicles.

Appellant 1 admitted spool-out can and does occur in rollovers. Appellant 1 recommended pretensioners specifically to prevent spool-out and Appellant 1 noted that 95% of the vehicles in Europe already utilize pretensioners.

Appellant 1 had nothing to do with its design, manufacture or assembly of the slider bar. When court reconvened after lunch, Appellant 2 requested a mistrial. Recognizing again the necessity of raising a timely objection, the trial court denied the motion for mistrial but granted the motion to strike, and admonished the jury to disregard the demonstration.

With regard to Appellant 1's complaints about Mrs. Zorn's closing argument: (a) Appellants did not object to the inadvertent reference to wealth; and (b) the court promptly admonished the jury about the "us against them" and "send a message" comments, Mrs. Zorn's counsel apologized and clarified, and neither of Appellants indicated they felt the court's admonishment to be inadequate. Finally, in their closing arguments, Appellant 2 did not even address damages and Appellant 1 stated: "As to damages, I'll talk briefly. There's no dispute." This all-or-nothing strategy offered the jurors no guidance on damages in the event they found for Mrs. Zorn on liability.

Anthony D. Zorn was a self-made man. One of seven children from a broken home, he grew up in a trailer whose amenities included a creek for bathing and an outhouse. He was a gifted athlete. He spent four years in England playing professional football for the Leeds Cougars, serving as linebacker, head coach and community/media representative. He also spearheaded a youth football league called Britain Crusaders, which sponsored annual bowl games and provided opportunities for British and American children to visit each other's country. Tony was so successful at these endeavors that, under his leadership, the popularity of American football surpassed that of soccer in Leeds. When he returned to the States, he continued to play semi-professional football while finishing college and serving as assistant strength coach for the Cincinnati Bengals. He also became a successful pilot, achieving a Captain rating on private jets.

It was during his time in England that he had a chance encounter with Mary. So immediate was the attraction, and so perfectly did their personalities coalesce, that their kinship could not have been better scripted by a romance novelist. Tony took Mary back to the States with him and they were married in 1991. Mary recalls the birth of their son, Christopher, the following year as "the best surprise I've ever had in my life." Nor was the occasion lost on Tony: "I've never seen a man cry like he did when Christopher was born." There is no dispute that Tony was a doting father, taking interest in every aspect of Christopher's life. Tony and Mary shared such a keen interest in children that they obtained certification and volunteered for the Court Appointed Special Advocate program. So tireless was Tony in his devotion to Mary that a friend twice described her as 100% dependent upon him. "What he wanted more than anything was for Mary just to be able to be his wife and be Christopher's mom and, and, to live free of all that stuff. And so he took care of everything."

***

As Christmas 2001 approached, the future could not have looked brighter for the Zorn family. [text omitted]

No evidence expert or lay was presented as to any defect in the manufacture of the tire that failed or the reason for the failure.

Coming so late to the case, the Indiana Ringer's first instinct as an advocate should have been to defer to those of us who had slogged through the pretrial and trial phases. Nowhere was this more crucial than with the fact statement. Why? Because the fact statement is your sole opportunity to introduce your client and his claims to the court. *If you blow this first impression, you don't get a second chance. This is where you tell your client's story.* To allow your opponents to determine when that story begins, how it progresses or where it ends constitutes neglect of the basest order. While you obviously want to rebut certain factual omissions and distortions in the opposing brief, it is critical that you weave the rebuttal into your client's own timeline. Deemphasizing your opponent's chosen arrangement of facts is another of the many ways you turn his offensive strike against him.[81]

Though he agreed the Indiana Ringer's final briefs were hideous, our local counsel was confident we would carry the day. He was wrong. After the appeal had languished for two years,[82] the Indiana Court of Appeals reversed us. It would be unfair for me to blame the reversal solely on the Indiana Ringer. A cursory reading of the opinion[83] shows that the majority thumbed its nose at standards of review that have been in place for two centuries in order to serve its own political agenda. But that reality does not absolve the Indiana Ringer, and we did not let that charlatan anywhere near our Petition to Transfer,[84] which received a favorable ruling (936 N.E.2d 201, Ind. 2010).[85]

---

[81] Unfortunately, at the time of this writing I am aware of at least one appellate court which is of such a bush-league mindset as to require the appellee to follow the appellant's topics seriatim. In such a situation, of course, your duty to the client is to operate as best you can within the prohibitive rules. Even in this event, there is no excuse for not assembling those facts in a legible and cogent fashion.

[82] As a general rule, appellate courts move slower than snot running up a fencepost in subzero temperatures.

[83] 905 N.E.2d 418 (Ind. App. 2009)

[84] The Indiana Supreme Court's Petition to Transfer is the equivalent of a Petition for Certiorari.

[85] The Court mentions Mr. Stone as one of Plaintiff's counsel solely because he entered an appearance at the intermediate level.

Editing

A well written appellate brief typically requires 8-12 drafts, the first half devoted to figuring out what to say and the remainder devoted to determining how best to say it. There are two types of editing: content and form. Editing for content is a process that began during your research phase. When you edit for content, you ask questions such as:

Does this thought logically flow from the previous one?

Does this argument support my thesis or harpoon it?

Does this word fit?

For all the grief I give to the linguistic purists, I recognize that there is a time to focus on form. That time is now, when you are satisfied with the content of the brief and you want to make its presentation impeccable. I know, I know – you've got a docket a mile long, you don't have enough hours in a day to make the managing attorney happy … bitch, moan, grouse, whine. Life's tough all over. Let's say you formulate the most brilliant argument that has hit a judge's desk in her 40 years on the bench. If your brief is so cluttered with misspellings and nonsensical punctuation that she can't follow your reasoning, you'll fare no better than if you had filed a preschooler's crayon drawing.

In 2007 I agonized so over an appellate reply brief that I once awoke in the middle of the night fearing I had botched a citation. Despite numerous rewrites and careful editing by at least four pairs of ultracritical eyes, the brief we filed bore a duplicate word. I was so embarrassed that I could not focus on any other project until I had fired off a Notice of Correction. There are two lessons to be learned here. The first is that it is human nature to make such mistakes. Lesson 2 is that we should therefore be dogged in our efforts at proofreading and revision. I shudder to think how long my Notice of

Correction might have been had I filed the very first draft that had spilled from my fingertips.

I recently observed to a colleague that my living room is a museum of outdated technology. In the cabinet to the left of the mantle you'll find my vinyl LPs. In the cabinet to the right is my thousand-pound, 1970s vintage component stereo system that was designed to play those LPs, to which I added a cassette deck so I could listen to those LPs in my car, which I replaced with a CD changer when digitized music supplanted vinyl. Two feet from that cabinet sits the combination VHS/DVD player which was superseded a few years ago by the DVR that sits beside it. All of this gadgetry has now been rendered obsolete by an MP3/MP4 player roughly the size of a credit card and the weight of a man's wallet. The biggest drawback to this electronic revolution we're in the midst of is that accuracy too often takes a backseat to speed and convenience. If you don't believe me, take a look at the linguistic atrocities your average preadolescent commits every time she sends a text message to her "bff."

No matter how fast the world is moving outside your office, you owe your client and your judge a duty to slow down. The first and most significant step toward fulfilling this duty is to print a hardcopy of your brief. Hardly anyone today has just one application running on his computer at a time. As a result, when you compose and edit on your computer you have calendar alarms, email alerts and those innumerable little icons at the top of the screen dividing your attention. The effect of averting your eyes from that screen to a piece of paper is as stark as if you had shut a soundproof door on a Pearl Jam concert.

Having narrowed your focus to the printed page, you are far more apt to catch mindless mistakes. The most common of these mistakes is the omitted word. This, again, is an unfortunate result of technology. In days of antiquity, when a computer the size of a tractor-trailer could barely perform the simplest mathematical equations, one wrote rough drafts in longhand and plinked the final version on a mechanical typewriter. This laborious task forced our minds to plod along at half their normal speed. The advent of PCs, laptops and PDAs has so streamlined the compositional process that, as our fingers fly to keep pace with our unfettered thought processes, we actually "see" words in our briefs that aren't there. For example, though the sentence on the screen may read, "The alone support summary judgment in this matter," the human mind so effortlessly completes the sentence by supplying the missing word "facts" that the most imperious editor may not detect its omission after multiple on-screen reviews.

One editing technique I often find useful is to read one sentence, glance away from the page, read it again, then repeat this drill with each succeeding sentence. Another reason we often overlook mindless errors is that we get so caught up in the argument we're making that we tend to gloss over its building blocks (words and punctuation). Like the *kōan* of Zen Buddhism, this routine jostles your mind from its comfort zone (the flow of the argument), forcing it to concentrate on a bite-sized statement in its own exclusive context.

Another technique is to read your brief backwards. When I was introduced to this method in the late 1980s, the idea was to start at the end and work one's way to the opener one word at a time. This worked fine for pieces that were only a few pages long. If you edited 20- to 30-page briefs this way, however, you would eventually need mental therapy. I recommend taking it sentence by sentence, or even paragraph by paragraph. I freely admit that I have used this particular approach no more than twice in my entire legal career. It's merely a suggestion. You are certainly capable of devising your own procedure. Anything that redirects your attention from the argument to the presentation of that argument will suffice.

There is no panacean method for editing. It is a laborious and barbarous process. As with anything, the more you practice it the better at it you will become. Let's try it together. Let us revisit the eyesore produced by the Indiana Ringer. Keep in mind that the following excerpts come from a brief that has been printed, bound and filed with an appellate court.

The evidence of reconstructionist, Carl Oaks, was that Tony's actions during the accident sequence were appropriate at all times.

The foregoing statement suggests that our witness manufactured his own evidence. It is one thing to be a lazy writer; it is another altogether to imply that one's own expert did something unethical. The ringer goes on to quote Mr. Oaks:

> The SUV "did not … depart the ground until the ground began to fall away from it. When the embankment fell away and then it became airborne."

What's wrong with the final sentence? Correct – it is a fragment. But even worse, *it is not what Mr. Oaks said.* Had the Indiana Ringer simply stuck the transcript in front of his scarcely literate transcriber rather than channeling it through his *Dictaphone*, she would have known that what he really said was: "The embankment actually fell away and then it became airborne." How many mistakes can you find in the next passage?

> Current and controlling case aw requires that a general verdict be upheld if any theory supports the decision. In this case the verdict against Appellant 2 and Appellant 1 are supported by multiple theories.
>
> There was no evidence presented as to the cause of the failure of the car on the SUV. Absent such evidence there was no proper basis for the jury to apportion fault to the non-party manufacturer. The mere fact that a tire fails after it has been sued for some time does not support a conclusion of any defect in manufacture

The corrections are in brackets below:

> Current and controlling case [law] requires that a general verdict be upheld if any theory supports the decision. In this case the verdict against [Appellants] [is] supported by multiple theories.
>
> There was no evidence presented as to the cause of the failure of the [tire] on the SUV. Absent such evidence[,] there was no proper basis for the jury to apportion fault to the non-party tire manufacturer. The mere fact that a tire fails after it has been [used] for some time does not support a conclusion of any defect in manufacture[.]

Try this one:

> Appellant 1 had nothing to do with its design, manufacture or assembly of the slider bar.

Corrected version:

> Appellant 1 had nothing to do with [the] design, manufacture or assembly of the slider bar.

By presenting a final product with such artless blunders, this writer has told the appellate panel, "I don't care about this brief, so I invite you to treat my client like the dimwit that I am." Well, that's not fair. If I'm going to put words into the Indiana Ringer's mouth, I should at least try to emulate his style: "Dont care;, breathe treat. client ddivot*"

But uncovering such obtuse mistakes is child's play. What distinguishes the incisive legal writer from the impostor is the ability to improve upon what at first blush appears to be file-ready. This is the art of *refinement*. To illustrate this process, I will now contrast two drafts of our Petition to Transfer.

QUESTION PRESENTED ON TRANSFER

On review of a general verdict, does Indiana Constitution Art. 1, §20 permit the court to conduct a trial *de novo* (a) considering the evidence in a light *least* favorable to the verdict (b) weighing the evidence and (c) reversing the verdict even though the evidence *does not* lead to a single conclusion contrary thereto?

PETITION TO TRANSFER

Mary P. Zorn asks that this Court (a) transfer jurisdiction over this case from the Court of Appeals ("COA") (b) reverse the decision of the COA and (c) reinstate the jury's general verdict in her favor.

BACKGROUND AND PRIOR TREATMENT OF ISSUES ON TRANSFER

A.   Nature of the Case

Anthony D. Zorn was a devoted husband to Mary and a doting father to Christopher. As Christmas 2001 approached, he had secured a new job that would entail a move to California and a significant boost in salary. After inspecting the jet he would captain for his new employer, Tony had nearly completed his drive home from Wisconsin when his left front tire tread separated. Though Tony responded commensurate with his years of flight training, the [make/model of SUV redacted] fell off an embankment, rolling 3-4 times. Though properly belted, Tony was ejected and died at the scene.

B.   Trial Proceedings

Mrs. Zorn introduced a study funded by Appellant 2 and a

scientific article authored by a General Motors engineer to illustrate the commonsense proposition that occupants who stay inside a vehicle during a rollover have a 90% chance of surviving. Both lay and expert testimony was conclusive that, had Tony stayed in his driver seat until the SUV came to rest, he would have survived. Impacts to the passenger side of the SUV actually raised the roof on the driver side, increasing Tony's survival space. The driver window was intact, and nothing had intruded into the vehicle. Experts on both sides of the case agreed that there was no physical evidence Tony had collided with any interior component hard enough to cause him injury. The jurors were allowed to see these facts firsthand during an on-site inspection of the vehicle, and through photographs such as Plaintiff's Exhibit 32. When asked whether someone can be ejected in a rollover while wearing a properly functioning seatbelt, Mrs. Zorn's medical expert Dr. Stillwell replied: "I have only seen that happen when there was a door opening, or in one particular case where the seatbelt cut the legs off the occupant ...."

Despite the efforts of Appellants *and the COA* to exaggerate the forces of the accident, the evidence proved otherwise. Mrs. Zorn's reconstructionist, Carl Oaks, testified: (a) "And [the SUV] did not ... depart the ground until the ground began to fall away from it. The embankment actually fell away and then it became airborne."; (b) in relation to other highway-speed rollover accidents, this rollover was not severe; in fact, the greatest change in velocity was no more than 15 mph; and (c) the vehicle landed in soft mud. Again, these facts indicate that Tony would have survived the accident had he remained inside the vehicle. Neither defendant offered a reconstructionist to rebut Mr. Oaks.

Edward M. Howell, P.E. – a mechanical engineer who has (a) studied the behavior of restraint systems in rollover accidents since 1989 and (b) published around 50 peer-reviewed articles – determined the locations of the load marks on Tony's seatbelt. He then performed a surrogate study to confirm that those marks corresponded to Tony's physical dimensions. Among the various sources of knowledge and experience he drew on in interpreting the load marks were crash tests conducted by Appellant 2 and rollover tests performed by NHTSA. The jury learned that spool-out is not some rogue litigation theory; it is a predictable response to rollover forces dictated by the laws of physics. From distinctive marks made as the belt passed through the latch plate, Mr. Howell calculated 13 inches of looseness in the lap belt. He used other visible marks on the seatbelt webbing, as well as basic physics and geometry, to explain that (a) it was physically impossible for the stalk and slider bar to bend in the direction they did while Tony occupied the driver seat and (b) the bend in Tony's slider bar could be produced with very little force. He also found unique web grabber marks at the retractor end of the belt indicating 17 inches of spool-out. Finally, other belt marks showed interaction with the opening for the sunroof, confirming his earlier spool-out measurements.

Mr. Howell did not propose the pretensioner and cinching latch plate in tandem; rather, he proposed them, along with integrated seatbelts, as three separate alternative designs, each of which alone would have increased Tony's chances of surviving this accident.

Appellant 1's rebuttal witness on restraints, George M. Vinson, did not bother to address the marks on the latch plate or, more importantly, those associated with the sunroof. He admitted that (a) Appellant 1 had breached its independent duty to assure that the restraint components it supplied were appropriate to the SUV and (b) Appellant 2 had implemented pretensioners in its European models prior to 1996. He also testified that it would have taken far more than 1,300 pounds of force to bend a slider bar as much as the one in Tony's SUV was bent. He then confirmed on cross-examination that the seatbelt assembly must be able to withstand at least 5,000 pounds of combined force to comply with the General Product Acceptance Specification. He also agreed that the slider bar, which anchors one side of the seatbelt assembly, should be able to withstand the same force. To impeach Mr. Vinson's testimony

165

Mrs. Zorn's counsel, a middle-aged gentleman of average strength, used nothing but his bare hands to bend an exemplar slider bar with ease, taking care to bend it exactly where Tony's slider bar bent in the accident. Contrary to the historical revision of the COA, Mrs. Zorn never intended to broach the subject of the slider bar; Appellant 1 injected it into the proceedings *over Mrs. Zorn's objection.*

Mrs. Zorn also introduced Exhibits 17, 18 (Appellant 2 studies of pretensioners from 1992 & 1993) and 199 (a series of communications between Appellant 1 and Appellant 2 from 1996). These documents established:

- Appellant 1 supplied fully functional pretensioners for European vehicles in 1992;
- Several foreign manufacturers utilized pretensioners in their U.S.-marketed vehicles in 1992;
- Pretensioners were first installed in European vehicles in the early 1970s;
- The total cost of implementing pretensioners on Appellant 2's U.S. vehicles was projected to be $35.00 per vehicle;
- Appellant 1's research and recommendations address pretensioners and integrated seatbelts as separate though complimentary ways to minimize occupant ejection;
- Both Appellant 2 and Appellant 1 knew in 1996 that spoolout ("intermittent release of webbing") can occur during a rollover;
- 95% of the vehicles in Europe in 1996 used pretensioners;
- According to NHTSA, light trucks (a division of Appellant 2 which includes SUVs such as the subject SUV) are twice as likely to roll over as other vehicles;
- Light trucks also have twice the ejection rate as that of passenger vehicles;
- Pretensioners were proven effective in rollover testing performed in the U.S. in 1995.

Educated and trained by the automotive industry, Daniel S. Griffin Ph.D., P.E., worked in the 1990s for the largest specialty automotive fastener supplier in the U.S., which supplied bolts and various other metal fasteners to the "Big 3" auto manufacturers. The core of his engineering education involved the study of how materials such as glass and metal behave. This unique combination of formal education and practical experience keenly suited him to address the failure of the brackets to retain the sunroof in this accident. Though his own extensive testing demonstrates that the glass in this sunroof should have failed before the mounting brackets did, the evidence in this case shows that the brackets failed first. Dr. Griffin offered three of "a hundred different ways" Appellant 2 could have prevented this failure which, in 1997, were technologically and economically feasible. His first alternative design was simply to strengthen the brackets that secure the sunroof to the body frame. His second alternative design involved pins that interlock with the glass when it closes, and the third was to add a retainer lip to the glass that would catch the frame as it was pushed outward. None of these designs would add noticeable weight, and they would cost no more than one or two dollars per vehicle. Neither defendant offered a crashworthiness expert to rebut Dr. Griffin.

The jury reached its verdict after roughly 7 hours of deliberations. Appellants timely filed post trial motions, which the trial court denied.

C. Disposition on Appeal

In its unpublished opinion, the COA noted: (a) Appellants did not challenge the jury instructions (b) Anthony Zorn was "wearing a properly fastened seatbelt" at the time of the accident (c) the sunroof was closed and latched prior to the accident (d) there was no dispute that Appellants owed Tony a duty of care and (e) Tony's "seatbelt and vehicular structure did not restrain him throughout the collision."

The COA focused on "a single issue: whether the Estate presented sufficient evidence to establish its product negligence claim," later narrowing that focus even further: "The plaintiff must proffer a demonstrably better design that is feasible to implement in order to show that the defendant was negligent in selecting and implementing a design deemed to be inferior." The COA proceeded to weigh Mrs. Zorn's evidence, concluding:

(a) Mrs. Zorn's seatbelt expert lacked credibility because he had not produced any statistics or test results to prove his alternative design (mistakenly represented as a *combination* of a pretensioner *and* cinching latch plate) was superior to the existing design;

(b) Mrs. Zorn's crashworthiness expert lacked credibility because (1) he had not actually built a sunroof with stronger brackets to prove stronger brackets would have better resisted the forces of the accident and (2) though his foundational testing consisted of striking panes of glass with head forms to determine that the sunroof glass should have failed before the mounting brackets did, "the evidence here did not suggest that the sunroof dislodged due to a head strike"; and

(c) Mrs. Zorn's Exhibit 199 failed to prove anything about pretensioners because, as the COA interpreted that document, Appellant 1's testing and recommendations addressed pretensioners and integrated seatbelts as an inseparable unit and, by implication, the jury could not have considered them separately.

In her dissent Justice Riley reproached: "In order to reach its conclusion that the Estate failed this burden, the majority engages in a patent exercise of reweighing the evidence and Howell's credibility."

ARGUMENT

I.   The Standard of Review for a General Verdict

In *Ross v. Review Bd. of Indiana Employment Sec. Division* (182 N.E.2d 585 – Ind. 1962), this Court held:

> As long as there is any substantial ground upon which the decision of the lower tribunal may be sustained on appeal, the judgment will not be reversed. The reviewing court may examine the entire record to sustain the lower court's action. The court does not search the record to reverse, although it may do so in order to affirm. [Id. at 586]

More recently, this Court held in *Picadilly, Inc. v. Colvin* (519 N.E.2d 1217 – Ind. 1988):

> A general verdict will be sustained if the evidence is sufficient to sustain any theory of liability. [Id. at 1221]

Indiana courts have applied this presumption of the correctness of a jury's verdict for 150 years (*Dukes v. State* – 11 Ind. 557 – Ind. 1859). Nearly a century ago, this Court held:

> In determining the sufficiency of the evidence, this court is limited to a consideration of that most favorable to appellee, including such inferences favorable to appellee as might be fairly drawn by the jury. [*Southern Products Co. v. Franklin Coil Hoop Co.* – 106 N.E. 872, 873 – Ind. 1914]

In *Carbone v. Schwarte* (629 N.E.2d 1259, 1261 – Ind. App. 3 Dist. 1994), the court held:

> We must consider only the evidence and reasonable inferences favorable to the non-moving party; we may not weigh conflicting evidence or judge the credibility of witnesses because of the constitutional right under Article 1 §20 of the Indiana Constitution to have a jury perform the fact-finding functions.

When ruling on a post trial motion such as one for judgment on the evidence, the trial court enjoys broad discretion (*Luphahla v. Marion County Sheriff's Dept.* – 868 N.E.2d 1155, 1157 – Ind. App. 2007). Furthermore:

> Certainly, when the trial court has declined to intervene and has refused to set aside the verdict, an appellate tribunal is not permitted to do so unless the verdict is wholly unwarranted under the law and the evidence. [*Ingersoll-Rand Corp. v. Scott* – 557 N.E.2d 679, 684 – Ind. App. 2 Dist. 1990]

The courts of Indiana have described "unwarranted under the law and the evidence" in various ways:

> It is only where the evidence is without conflict and can lead to but one conclusion, and the trial court has reached an opposite conclusion, that the decision of the trial court will be set aside on the ground that it is contrary to law. [*Hinds v. McNair* – 129 N.E.2d 553, 559 – Ind. 1955]

> Reversal of the trial court is warranted only if the evidence which is not in conflict leads solely to a conclusion contrary to that reached by the jury.

[*Get-N-Go, Inc. v. Markins* – 544 N.E.2d 484, 486 – Ind. 1989]

A jury verdict within the contemplation of the instructions given is insulated from attack on appeal. [*Salcedo v. Toepp* – 696 N.E.2d 426, 434 – Ind. App. 1998]

II. The COA Ignores the Standard of Review by Viewing the Evidence in a Light *Least* Favorable to the Verdict

In the opening paragraph, the COA establishes where its sympathies lie when it adopts the dehumanizing moniker "the Estate" to refer to Mrs. Zorn. The COA proceeds to distort the facts in favor of Appellants by saying that the subject vehicle "launched approximately ten feet into the air" and emphasizing Appellants' defense that "Anthony's injuries resulted from the unusually severe nature of the crash." Though the fact is completely irrelevant to its analysis, the COA emphasizes Appellants' defense of compliance with governmental standards. Finally, the COA creates an impossible burden of proof for Mrs. Zorn by defining as the "crucial inquiry" whether Appellants failed to produce, not a safer design, but a "superior" one. Such blatant prejudice against a jury verdict (a) conflicts with decisions of both this Court and the Court of Appeals and (b) strays so far from well entrenched law that the departure may fairly be characterized as historical.

III. The COA Defies the Standard of Review by Weighing the Evidence and Assessing Witness Credibility

The most egregious example of the COA's incursion into the jury's constitutional domain is its mistreatment of expert Edward M. Howell, P.E. The discussion at pages 10-20 is more a *Daubert* attack than a dispassionate review of the evidence:

171

> Howell could not produce his own testing that
> replicated the actual conditions of the Zorn accident.
> He could not determine at what point in the sequence
> of the accident the release of Zorn's belt webbing
> would have occurred.

This observation ignores the facts that (a) it is impossible to recreate a rollover accident and (b) our inability to pinpoint exactly when the spoolout occurred does not erase the laws of physics that tell us it did occur. Thus, the COA places on Mr. Howell an impossible burden of certainty that this Court refuses to impose on expert testimony:

> [N]o threshold level of certainty or conclusiveness
> is required in an expert's opinion as a prerequisite
> to its admissibility. Assuming the subject matter is
> one which is appropriate for expert testimony and
> that a proper foundation has been laid, the expert's
> opinion or conclusion that, in the context of the
> facts before the witness, a particular proposition
> is "possible," "could have been," "probable," or
> "reasonably certain" all serve to assist the finder of
> fact in intelligently resolving the material factual
> questions. The degree of certainty in which an
> opinion or conclusion is expressed concerns the
> weight to be accorded the testimony, which is a
> matter for the jury to resolve. [*Noblesville Casting
> Div. of TRW, Inc. v. Prince* – 438 N.E.2d 722, 731 –
> Ind. 1982]

Implicit in the *Prince* holding is the logic that an expert need not "reinvent the wheel" for every new case. [*Meisberger v. State* – 640 N.E.2d 716, 720 – Ind. App. 1 Dist. 1994] Because Exhibits 17, 18 and 199 – admissible under Evid. R. 801(d)(2) – proved that

Appellants and other researchers had established the feasibility of pretensioners, any further testing Mr. Howell performed would have been inadmissible as cumulative.

Later in its opinion, the COA combines two separate alternative designs into one for the apparent purpose of using *Pries v. Honda Motor Co., Ltd.* (31 F.3d 543 – C.A.7 1994) to discredit Mr. Howell:

> The Estate claimed that [Appellant 2] was negligent because it did not select and utilize cinching latch plates and pretensioners. [text omitted] Whether a seatbelt assembly featuring a pretensioner and cinching latch plate as suggested by Howell would have enhanced restraint in the aggregate ... is a question left unanswered.

But Mr. Howell did not introduce these designs as one system. In fact, his testimony on pretensioners and cinching latch plates occurred *one week* apart. The COA discounts Exhibit 199 in the same manner, construing Appellant 1's conclusion (that less belt slack and higher belt angles reduce occupant ejections in rollovers) to mean that Appellant 1 did not test pretensioners and integrated seatbelts separately (implying that one won't work without the other). Yet nowhere on the face of that document does Appellant 1 even suggest such a thing. As with Mr. Howell's alternative designs, it was the jury's prerogative to weigh this evidence and determine its relevance to the issues at hand.

> Finally, the COA chastises Mr. Howell because he:

> ... did not have the benefit of any statistical study comparing the nature and number of injuries associated with the seatbelt assembly used in Zorn's vehicle to the "alternative" seatbelt assembly proposed by Howell with the two devices he suggested.

But the court rejected this very argument in *Jackson v. Warrum* (535 N.E.2d 1207 – Ind. App. 1 Dist. 1989):

> This rule conflicts with our products liability law which has never required the plaintiff to prove the negative fact of what the injury would have been with a safer product. [Id. at 1219]

The *Warrum* court observed that the plaintiff had presented evidence that (a) the low-entry design of the garbage truck cab at issue placed the driver dangerously close to the point of impact in head-on collisions and (b) a cab design in use by another contemporary manufacturer placed the driver 36" back from any potential point of impact (Id., p. 1220).

> Although this evidence did not establish the amount of injury that would have resulted in a hypothetical accident involving a safer or non-defective cab and chassis design, we indicated previously that the plaintiff was not required to prove this negative fact. Thus, evidence existed which arguably supported plaintiffs' enhanced injury product liability claim. [Id.]

In its headlong endeavor to rescind the jury's verdict, the COA has again run afoul of long-settled Indiana principles.

IV. The COA Turns the Standard of Review on its Head by Reversing the General Verdict Even Though the Evidence *Does Not* Lead to a Single Contrary Conclusion

The COA cavalierly dispatches Daniel S. Griffin, Ph.D., P.E. by fabricating a single contrary conclusion where none exists:

> Importantly, although Dr. Griffin testified about

174

fortifying a sunroof structure to withstand an occupant load, [text omitted] the evidence here did not suggest that the sunroof dislodged due to a head strike ....

For Mrs. Zorn's sunroof claim to fail on appeal, the evidence must preclude any possibility that the sunroof was dislodged in whole or in part by a head strike. Only two portions of testimony are probative on this issue. Carl Oaks:

> Q. And you also thought that the sunroof became dislodged in this first roll as well, correct?
>
> A. In my opinion, at least it was loosening. I don't know how much, to what extent, but the roof was distorting and it would at least become..., it wouldn't be in its normal configuration.
>
> Q. Well, I think you used the words "dislodged" in your deposition, didn't you?
>
> A. That would be, that would probably be the best word.

And Kevin Stillwell, M.D:

> Q. Fair enough. And I think you told us in your deposition that if we assume that this vehicle rolled over three times that, that in your opinion, Mr. Zorn would have been ejected through the..., completely through the sunroof and out of the vehicle after the second roll?
>
> A. Yes, sir.

From this evidence, the only conclusion one can draw with any certainty is that both the sunroof and Anthony Zorn had completely exited the vehicle before the third roll. Mr. Oaks does not opine that the sunroof had *completely* evacuated the portal of ejection prior to the second roll, nor does Dr. Stillwell rule out the possibility that Tony *started to exit* the vehicle during the first roll. Thus, the facts are capable of more than one inference and a reasonable juror could have found, as our jury did, that it was a head strike that caused the sunroof to fully vacate the portal.

So we see that the jury's verdict is sustainable on the sunroof claim alone, provided we resist the COA's attempts to rewrite legislative and decisional history. Most disconcerting is the fact that, in its mishandling of Mr. Howell and Dr. Griffin, the COA has not only usurped the office of the jury; it has implicitly declared that the trial court abused the broad discretion it enjoys as thirteenth juror, in direct contravention of the pronouncements in *Luphahla* (868 N.E.2d 1155) and *Ingersoll-Rand* (557 N.E.2d 679).

CONCLUSION

Mary and Christopher Zorn lost an irreplaceable soul on December 20, 2001 due to a minor tread mishap he would have survived had Appellants equipped his SUV with the same technology they had been outfitting European vehicles with for years prior to its design and manufacture. Laboriously Mrs. Zorn proved every element of her case. Though the jury's verdict could not bring Tony back to Mary and Christopher, it was a moral victory that assured them Appellants might not take another life in their voracious quest for profit at the expense of consumer safety. The only way to achieve the COA's result is to ignore the facts proved at trial. Though this is an unpublished opinion, the COA needs to be corrected immediately, because it has indicated a willingness to nullify jury verdicts on a whim, undermining a century and a half of Indiana law to further a political agenda. Therefore, Mrs. Zorn asks that transfer be granted and the verdict reinstated.

What you just read is what I call a *raw draft* – the kind you pen while your anger is still churning. In fact, my original intent was to demand an apology from the COA until (a) I ran across case law that suggested my client would by no means be the first to do so and (b) our local counsel warned that such histrionics tend to place the Indiana Supreme Court in a posture to defend the COA, which we certainly did not want to do.

Having beaten up on Steven Stark earlier, I will now give him credit for at least trying to impart good advice ... though he ultimately fails to pull it off. At page 147 of *Writing to Win*, he declares:

> 1. No briefs [sic.] should be written by a committee.
>
> At most, you want two authors with compatible styles writing a brief in close consultation with each other. You can use others for specific research projects ("What is the standard of review?") but when the drafting starts, a brief needs a unitary style.

Mr. Stark is correct in his conclusion that your brief needs a "unitary style." But his suggested formula is all wet. For one thing, if the author of a legal brief is unable to determine the standard of review on his own with very little effort, he should be fired (perhaps even disbarred). And for the reasons I discussed earlier, no trial or appellate brief should ever have more than one author. By the same token, that author would be a fool not to avail himself of trusted editors and kibitzers. *In this exclusive respect*, no appellate brief should be a solo effort.

So I circulated the above raw draft among (a) my employing attorneys who were also lead trial counsel (b) our local counsel who had provided invaluable contributions to our answer brief at the COA level (the one the Indiana Ringer consummately slaughtered) (c) two local appellate attorneys and (d) a former trial judge who had proved a reliable sounding board in a previous appeal. And then, my friend, the magic happened.

The next three weeks saw the draft undergo no less than 14 revisions. An appellate brief is only as good as the record that supports it. Thus, the lead trial attorneys had already made the foremost contribution by crafting an ironclad trial record. Our local counsel inserted facts I had overlooked, and kept me honest with matters of local form and tenor. From their considerable personal experience with the Indiana Supreme Court, the local appellate attorneys were quick to clue the rest of us in on the psychology of that court: while an ongoing feud between the courts would operate in our favor, we did not want to steal the upper court's thunder by being overly critical of the lower court. So I toned down the rhetoric a few extra notches.

When one of the locals suggested that I call the deceased "Capt. Zorn," I nearly fell out of my chair. *Of course! Though he's a private pilot, he has earned the Captain rating on jets.* After hundreds of pages of trial and appellate briefing, it took a fresh pair of eyeballs to see something so fundamental. A comparison of the Question Presented sections will illustrate the former judge's suggestion:

Draft One

> On review of a general verdict, does Indiana Constitution Art. 1, §20 permit the court to conduct a trial *de novo* (a) considering the evidence in a light *least* favorable to the verdict (b) weighing the evidence and (c) reversing the verdict even though the evidence *does not* lead to a single conclusion contrary thereto?

Final Draft

> When a trial court refuses to vacate a general verdict, does Indiana Constitution Art. 1, §20 permit the Court of Appeals to (a) disregard the broad discretion of the trial court (b) consider evidence in a light *least* favorable to the verdict (c) weigh evidence (d) assess experts' credibility and (e) reverse the verdict though the evidence *does not* lead to a single contrary conclusion?

Now compare the headings in the Argument section:

Draft One

I.   The Standard of Review for a General Verdict
II. The COA Ignores the Standard of Review by Viewing the Evidence in a Light *Least* Favorable to the Verdict
III. The COA Defies the Standard of Review by Weighing the Evidence and Assessing Witness Credibility
IV. The COA Turns the Standard of Review on its Head by Reversing the General Verdict Even Though the Evidence *Does Not* Lead to a Single Contrary Conclusion

Final Draft

I.   The COA Misconstrues the Issue on Appeal
II. The COA Contravenes Prior COA Decisions and Those of this Court by Viewing Evidence in a Light *Least* Favorable to the Verdict, Weighing Evidence, Assessing Witness Credibility and Imposing an Insurmountable Burden of Proof
III. The COA Violates the Standard of Review by Reversing the General Verdict Though the Evidence *Does Not* Lead to a Single Contrary Conclusion

From this alternate perspective, the COA had to clear some procedural hurdles before it could even dream of looking at the evidence: (1) the presumption of correctness that attached to the trial court's post trial rulings (2) the trial judge's broad discretion regarding admissibility of evidence and (3) the strong inference of correctness that attaches to jury verdicts.

Here are more comparisons (by no means exhaustive) to generally illustrate the editorial process.

Draft One

A.   Nature of the Case

Anthony D. Zorn was a devoted husband to Mary and a doting father to Christopher. As Christmas 2001 approached, he had secured a new job that would entail a move to California and a significant boost in salary. After inspecting the jet he would captain for his new employer, Tony had nearly completed his drive home from Wisconsin when his left front tire tread separated. Though Tony responded commensurate with his years of flight training, the [make/model of SUV redacted] fell off an embankment, rolling 3-4 times. Though properly belted, Tony was ejected and died at the scene.

Final Draft

A.   Nature of the Case

As Christmas 2001 approached, Anthony D. Zorn had secured a lucrative job that promised an exciting move for his family. After inspecting the jet he would fly for his new employer, Capt. Zorn had nearly completed his drive home when his left front tire tread separated. Though Capt. Zorn responded commensurate with his flight training and experience, the [make/model of SUV redacted] fell off an embankment, rolling 3-4 times. Capt. Zorn was ejected through the sunroof and died at the scene, leaving behind wife Mary and nine-year-old son Christopher. The rubber gasket of the sunroof was found wrapped around his lower torso. The SUV came to rest on its wheels, the driver's seatbelt still fastened.

Bear in mind that we had only 4,200 words to work with – for everything we added, we had to find something else to delete or consolidate. For example, in section B our local counsel wanted to remind the court as often as possible that the seatbelt had failed. By consolidating "Both lay and expert testimony" into "The testimony," I was able to make this addition without increasing the total number of words:

Draft One

Both lay and expert testimony was conclusive that, had Tony stayed in his driver seat until the SUV came to rest, he would have survived.

Final Draft

The testimony was conclusive that, had Capt. Zorn's seatbelt kept him in the driver seat until the SUV came to rest, he would have survived.

In the next paragraph of section B, I eliminated unnecessary verbiage and resisted beating up on the COA to excess:

Draft One

Despite the efforts of Appellants *and the COA* to exaggerate the forces of the accident, the evidence proved otherwise.

Final Draft

Despite Appellants' efforts to exaggerate the forces of the accident, the evidence proved otherwise.

Here are more examples of how conforming one's brief to an appellate court's limitation on length tends to expose both non-pivotal facts and loquacity:

Draft One

> Mr. Howell did not propose the pretensioner and cinching latch plate in tandem; rather, he proposed them, along with integrated seatbelts, as three separate alternative designs, each of which alone would have increased Tony's chances of surviving this accident.

Final Draft

> Mr. Howell submitted the pretensioner, cinching latch plate and integrated seatbelts as feasible alternative designs, each of which alone would have increased Capt. Zorn's chances of surviving this accident.

Draft One

> Appellant 1's rebuttal witness on restraints, George M. Vinson, did not bother to address the marks on the latch plate or, more importantly, those associated with the sunroof. He admitted that (a) Appellant 1 had breached its independent duty to assure that the restraint components it supplied were appropriate to the SUV and (b) Appellant 2 had implemented pretensioners in its European models prior to 1996. He also testified that it would have taken far more than 1,300 pounds of force to bend a slider bar as much as the one in Tony's SUV was bent. He then confirmed on cross-examination that the seatbelt assembly must be able to withstand at least 5,000 pounds of combined force to comply with the General Product Acceptance Specification. He also agreed that the slider bar, which anchors one side of the seatbelt assembly, should be able to withstand the same force. To impeach Mr. Vinson's testimony Mrs. Zorn's counsel, a middle-aged gentleman of average strength, used nothing but his bare hands to bend an exemplar slider bar with ease, taking care to bend it exactly where Tony's slider bar bent in the accident. Contrary to the historical revision of the COA, Mrs. Zorn never intended to broach the subject of the slider bar;

> Appellant 1 injected it into the proceedings *over Mrs. Zorn's objection.*

Final Draft

> Appellant 1's rebuttal witness on restraints, George M. Vinson, admitted that (a) Appellant 1 had breached its duty to assure that the restraint components it supplied were appropriate to the SUV and (b) Appellant 2 had implemented fully functioning pretensioners in its European models at least as early as 1994.

Draft One

> ### C.   Disposition on Appeal
>
> In its unpublished opinion, the COA noted: (a) Defendants did not challenge the jury instructions (b) Anthony Zorn was "wearing a properly fastened seatbelt" at the time of the accident (c) the sunroof was closed and latched prior to the accident (d) there was no dispute that Appellants owed Tony a duty of care and (e) Tony's "seatbelt and vehicular structure did not restrain him throughout the collision."
>
> The COA focused on "a single issue: whether the Estate presented sufficient evidence to establish its product negligence claim," later narrowing that focus even further: "The plaintiff must proffer a demonstrably better design that is feasible to implement in order to show that the defendant was negligent in selecting and implementing a design deemed to be inferior." The COA proceeded to weigh Mrs. Zorn's evidence, concluding:
>
> > (a)   Mrs. Zorn's seatbelt expert lacked credibility because he had not produced any statistics or test results to prove his alternative design (mistakenly represented as a *combination* of a pretensioner *and* cinching latch plate) was superior to the existing design;

(b)   Mrs. Zorn's crashworthiness expert lacked credibility because (1) he had not actually built a sunroof with stronger brackets to prove stronger brackets would have better resisted the forces of the accident and (2) though his foundational testing consisted of striking panes of glass with head forms to determine that the sunroof glass should have failed before the mounting brackets did, "the evidence here did not suggest that the sunroof dislodged due to a head strike"; and

(c)   Mrs. Zorn's Exhibit 199 failed to prove anything about pretensioners because, as the COA interpreted the document, Appellant 1's testing and recommendations addressed pretensioners and integrated seatbelts as an inseparable unit and, by implication, the jury could not have considered them separately.

In her dissent Justice Riley reproached: "In order to reach its conclusion that the Estate failed this burden, the majority engages in a patent exercise of reweighing the evidence and Howell's credibility."

Final Draft

C.   Disposition on Appeal

Appellant 1 filed a motion asking the trial court to correct errors, render judgment on the evidence, grant a new trial and amend the judgment. Appellant 2 filed a motion to correct errors. The trial court denied both. The COA reversed the jury verdict. In her dissent, Judge Riley reproached: "In order to reach its conclusion that the Estate failed this burden, the majority engages in a patent exercise of reweighing the evidence and Howell's credibility."

184

When you read the print-ready product, you will note similar refinements in the Argument and Conclusion sections, as well as further streamlining of citation format:

Final Draft

PETITION TO TRANSFER

Mary P. Zorn asks that this Court (a) transfer jurisdiction from the Court of Appeals ("COA") (b) reverse that court's decision and (c) reinstate the jury's verdict.

BACKGROUND AND PRIOR TREATMENT
OF ISSUES ON TRANSFER

A.   Nature of the Case

As Christmas 2001 approached, Anthony D. Zorn had secured a lucrative job that promised an exciting move for his family. After inspecting the jet he would fly for his new employer, Capt. Zorn had nearly completed his drive home when his left front tire tread separated. Though Capt. Zorn responded commensurate with his flight training and experience, the [make/model of SUV redacted] fell off an embankment, rolling 3-4 times. Capt. Zorn was ejected through the sunroof and died at the scene, leaving behind wife Mary and nine-year-old son Christopher. The rubber gasket of the sunroof was found wrapped around his lower torso. The SUV came to rest on its wheels, the driver's seatbelt still fastened.

B.   Trial Proceedings

The following facts support the jury's verdict in this Product Liability action.

Mrs. Zorn introduced a study funded by Appellant 2 and a scientific article authored by a General Motors engineer to prove the commonsense proposition that occupants who stay inside a vehicle during a rollover have a 90% chance of surviving. The testimony was conclusive that, had Capt. Zorn's seatbelt kept him in the driver seat until the SUV came to rest, he would have survived. Impacts to the passenger side of the SUV raised the roof on the driver side like a tent, augmenting Capt. Zorn's survival space. The driver window remained intact, and nothing intruded into the vehicle. All experts agreed there was no physical evidence Capt. Zorn had collided with any interior component hard enough to cause him injury. The jurors saw these facts firsthand during an on-site inspection of the vehicle. When asked whether someone can be ejected in a rollover while wearing a properly functioning seatbelt, Mrs. Zorn's medical expert Kevin Stillwell, M.D. replied that he had only seen that happen when a door opened, or in one particular case where the seatbelt had amputated the occupant's legs.

Despite Appellants' efforts to exaggerate the forces of the accident, the evidence proved otherwise. Mrs. Zorn's reconstructionist, Carl Oaks, testified: (a) the SUV did not "depart the ground until the ground began to fall away from it. The embankment actually fell away and then it became airborne" (b) in relation to other highway-speed rollover accidents, Capt. Zorn's was not severe; in fact, the greatest change in velocity was no more than 15 mph and (c) the rolls occurred in grass and soft mud. *Neither Appellant offered a reconstructionist to rebut Mr. Oaks.*

The central question was how a properly belted driver could get thrown through a closed and latched sunroof. Edward M. Howell, P.E. – a mechanical engineer who has (a) studied the behavior of restraint systems in rollover accidents since 1989 and (b) published around 50 peer-reviewed articles – has never seen full ejection occur without belt failure. He physically identified the locations of the dispositive load marks on Capt. Zorn's seatbelt. He then performed a surrogate study to confirm that those marks corresponded to Capt. Zorn's physical dimensions. Among the various sources of knowledge he drew upon to interpret the load marks were crash were crash tests conducted by Appellant 2 and rollover tests performed by the National Highway Traffic Safety Administration ("NHTSA"). From both his testimony and Appellants' own documents, the jury learned that spoolout is a predictable response to rollover forces dictated by the laws of physics. From distinctive marks made as the belt passed through the latch plate, Mr. Howell calculated 13 inches of looseness in the lap belt. He also found unique web grabber marks at the retractor end indicating 17 inches of spoolout, providing ample slack to allow Capt. Zorn to slip free the belt's hold. Finally, other belt marks showed interaction with the opening for the sunroof, confirming his earlier spoolout measurements. Mr. Howell submitted the pretensioner, cinching latch plate and integrated seatbelts as feasible alternative designs, each of which alone would have increased Capt. Zorn's chances of surviving this accident.

Mrs. Zorn also introduced Exhibit 199 – a series of communications between Appellants from 1996. An admission of party opponents under I.R.E. 801(d)(2), this document established:

- According to NHTSA, light trucks (a division of Appellant 2 which includes the subject SUV) are twice as likely to roll as other vehicles;
- Light trucks also have twice the ejection rate as that of passenger vehicles;
- Ejection is the leading cause of fatalities in passenger vehicles;
- SUVs exceed all other light trucks in fatality percentage;
- Appellant 1 recommends pretensioners to prevent spoolout ("intermittent release of webbing");
- Both Appellants knew in 1996 that spoolout can occur during a rollover;
- 95% of the vehicles in Europe in 1996 used pretensioners; and
- U.S. testing in 1995 proved pretensioners dramatically minimize occupant ejection in rollovers.

Mr. Howell confirmed these facts, and testified further that various manufacturers routinely used pretensioners in the early 1990s.

Appellant 1's rebuttal witness on restraints, George M. Vinson, admitted (a) Appellant 1 had breached its duty to assure that the restraint components it supplied were appropriate to the SUV and (b) *Appellant 2 had implemented fully functioning pretensioners in its European models at least as early as 1994.*

Educated and trained by the automotive industry, Daniel S. Griffin, Ph.D., P.E. worked in the 1990s for the largest specialty automotive fastener supplier in the U.S., which supplied bolts and various other metal fasteners to the "Big 3" auto manufacturers. The core of his engineering education involved the study of how materials such as glass and metal behave under stress. This unique combination of advanced education and practical experience keenly suited him to address the failure of the brackets to retain the sunroof in this accident. He testified categorically that this rollover accident was foreseeable to Appellants. Though Dr. Griffin's extensive testing demonstrates that the glass in this sunroof should have failed before the metal mounting brackets did, the evidence shows that the brackets failed first. But for the failure of the sunroof brackets, Capt. Zorn would not have had a portal of ejection which led to the fatal injuries he sustained outside the vehicle. Dr. Griffin offered three of "a hundred different ways" Appellant 2 could have prevented this failure which were technologically and economically feasible long before 1997. His first alternative design was to simply strengthen the brackets that secure the glass to the frame. His second solution involved pins that interlock with the glass when it closes, and the third was to add a retainer lip to the glass that would catch the frame as it was pushed outward. None of these designs would add noticeable weight, and they would cost no more than two dollars per vehicle. *Neither defendant offered a crashworthiness expert to rebut Dr. Griffin.*

After deliberating for roughly 7 hours, the jury awarded Mrs. Zorn a general verdict of $25,000,000, apportioning $1,250,000 to Appellant 1 and $7,750,000 to Appellant 2.

C.   Disposition on Appeal

Appellant 1 filed a motion asking the trial court to correct errors, render judgment on the evidence, grant a new trial and amend the judgment. Appellant 2 filed a motion to correct errors. The trial court denied both. The COA reversed the jury verdict. In her dissent, Judge Riley reproached: "In order to reach its conclusion that the Estate failed this burden, the majority engages in a patent exercise of reweighing the evidence and Howell's credibility."

ARGUMENT

I.   The COA Misconstrues the Issue on Appeal

"We find dispositive a single issue: whether the Estate presented sufficient evidence to establish its product negligence claim." But that is not the issue an appellate court is allowed to address in this instance. Before the COA could even consider weighing the evidence, it was required to find that the trial judge, who heard and saw the entire trial firsthand, abused his discretion. The trial court's post trial rulings carry a strong presumption of correctness (*Ingersoll-Rand v. Scott* – 557 N.E.2d 679, 683 – Ind. App.1990 – Transfer Denied). In *Paragon FamilyRestaurant v. Bartolini* (799 N.E.2d 1048, 1055-6 – Ind. 2003), this Court held:

> When, as in this case, the trial court declines to
> intervene and refuses to set aside the jury verdict, it is
> not the province of an appellate court to do so unless

189

to do so unless the verdict is wholly unwarranted under the law and the evidence. (Quotation merged, citation omitted.)[87]

More recently, this Court held in *Raess v. Doescher* (883 N.E.2d 790, 793 – Ind. 2008):

> Upon appellate review of a trial court ruling on [a motion for judgment on the evidence], the reviewing court must consider only the evidence and reasonable inferences most favorable to the nonmoving party.

Likewise, the trial court's rulings on the admissibility of evidence are "afforded great deference on appeal." (*Link v. State* – 648 N.E.2d 709, 711 – Ind. App. 3 Dist. 1995)

Yet the COA assigns no error to the trial judge's rulings on either the post trial motions or the evidence. Furthermore, the COA (a) acknowledges that Appellants did not challenge the jury instructions and (b) asserts that the trial court's jury charge on burden of proof was "in accordance with" Indiana law. Having made these two findings, the COA had no authority to inquire any further (*Salcedo v. Toepp* – 696 N.E.2d 426, 433 – Ind. App. 1998):

---

[86] In the official *Bartolini* opinion, the last 12 words were in quotation marks. Likewise with the final 14 of *Doescher*. A fundamental principle of appellate interpretation is that when a court quotes a previous case favorably, it adopts that language as its own. Hence, when one cites the latter case as authority, acknowledging the former is unduly repetitive unless it is a particularly noteworthy opinion. In this event, quotation marks become superfluous, and they may be omitted without adulterating the meaning or impact of the cited language. It is arguable that the notation "quotation merged, citation omitted" is redundant. While I err on the side of caution for the present time, I dropped the notation from *Doescher* in this instance so that you may consider how much sleeker the passage comes across once we free it of extraneous clutter.

A jury verdict within the contemplation of the instructions given is insulated from attack on appeal.

Should we assume for the sake of argument that the above mandates do not exist, the reviewing court still may not reach the sufficiency of the evidence without clearing another Constitutional hurdle (*Nudd v. Burrows* – 91 U.S. 426, 439 – 1875):

Questions of law are to be determined by the court; questions of fact, by the jury. The authority of the jury as to the latter is as absolute as the authority of the court with respect to the former.

This is because the jury is in a "superior position to appraise and weigh the evidence." (*Zenith Radio Corp. v. Hazeltine Research, Inc.* – 395 U.S. 100, 123 – 1969) In *Ross v. Review Bd. of Indiana Employment Sec. Division* (182 N.E.2d 585, 586 – Ind. 1962), this Court held (emphasis added):

As long as there is any substantial ground upon which the decision of the lower tribunal may be sustained on appeal, the judgment will not be reversed. The reviewing court may examine the entire record to sustain the lower court's action. **The court does not search the record to reverse, although it may do so in order to affirm.** [Likewise, *Picadilly, Inc. v. Colvin* – 519 N.E.2d 1217, 1221 – Ind. 1988: "A general verdict will be sustained if the evidence is sufficient to sustain any theory of liability."]

Indiana courts have presumed the correctness of a jury's verdict for 150 years (*Dukes v. State* – 11 Ind. 557 – 1859).

Therefore, *assuming only for the sake of argument* that the trial court abused its discretion in ruling on the post trial motions, Mrs. Zorn submits that the sole issue the COA should have addressed is:

When we (a) view the evidence in a light most favorable to the verdict (b) indulge in all inferences supportive of the verdict and (c) disregard all evidence and inferences contrary thereto, does that evidence sustain any theory of liability? (*Southern Products Co. v. Franklin Coil Hoop Co.* – 106 N.E. 872, 873 – Ind. 1914; *Carbone v. Schwarte* – 629 N.E.2d 1259, 1261 – Ind. App. 3 Dist. 1994)

Under *Ford Motor Co. v. Rushford* (868 N.E.2d 806, 810 – Ind. 2007), Mrs. Zorn's burden was to prove (1) a duty owed (2) a breach of that duty and (3) injury proximately caused thereby. The COA recognizes Appellants owed a duty to Capt. Zorn. The COA concedes: (a) Capt. Zorn was "wearing a properly fastened seatbelt" during the accident (b) the sunroof was closed and latched prior to the accident and (c) Capt. Zorn's "seatbelt and vehicular structure did not restrain him throughout the collision." Mrs. Zorn (a) established that Capt. Zorn would have survived had he been contained in the vehicle and (b) offered the jury no less than 6 feasible and effective alternative designs, one of which Appellant 1 was installing in European vehicles years before Capt. Zorn's SUV was designed and manufactured. On these facts alone, the COA should have affirmed the verdict without further inquiry. Every path the COA took from this point forward led it further astray the deep-rooted principles set down by this Court.

II. The COA Contravenes Prior COA Decisions and Those of this Court by Viewing Evidence in a Light *Least* Favorable to the Verdict, Weighing Evidence, Assessing Witness Credibility and Imposing an Insurmountable Burden of Proof [App. R. 57(H)(1)(2)(6)]

Having misstated the issue on appeal, the COA proceeds to consider evidence favorable to Appellants by, among other things:

- Emphasizing Appellants' defense that the crash was "unusually severe," while ignoring unrefuted testimony that the forces of the accident were relatively minor;
- Highlighting Appellants' contentions that (a) marks found on the seatbelt webbing represented normal wear and (b) spoolout is scientifically impossible, even though Appellant 1 itself admits otherwise in Exhibit 199; and
- Underscoring Appellants' defense of compliance with inapplicable government standards.

The only expert challenged under I.R.E. 702 was Mr. Howell. The trial court's decision that his testimony was reliable may be vacated only for an abuse of its broad discretion (*Sears, Roebuck and Co. v. Manuilov* – 742 N.E.2d 453, 459 – Ind. 2001). Nor may the reviewing court substitute its own judgment therefor (*Burnett v. State* – 815 N.E.2d 201, 204 – Ind. App. 2004). Though the COA does not even address this claim of error, its treatment of Mr. Howell constitutes a *Daubert* attack rather than a dispassionate review of the evidence. For instance, the COA argues:

Howell could not produce his own testing that replicated the actual conditions of the Zorn accident. He could not determine at what point in the sequence of the accident the release of Zorn's belt webbing would have occurred.

This observation ignores the facts that (a) it is impossible to precisely recreate a rollover accident and (b) our inability to pinpoint exactly when spoolout occurred does not abolish the laws of physics that tell us it happened. Thus, the COA places on Mr. Howell an impossible burden of absolute certainty which this Court refuses to impose (*Noblesville Casting Div. of TRW, Inc. v. Prince* – 438 N.E.2d 722, 731 – Ind. 1982):

[N]o threshold level of certainty or conclusiveness

is required in an expert's opinion as a prerequisite to its admissibility. Assuming the subject matter is one which is appropriate for expert testimony and that a proper foundation has been laid, the expert's opinion or conclusion that, in the context of the facts before the witness, a particular proposition is "possible," "could have been," "probable," or "reasonably certain" all serve to assist the finder of fact in intelligently resolving the material factual questions. The degree of certainty in which an opinion or conclusion is expressed concerns the weight to be accorded the testimony, which is a matter for the jury to resolve.

Implicit in the *Prince* holding is the simple logic that an expert need not "reinvent the wheel" for every new case; he may base his opinions on the work of other experts (*Meisberger v. State* – 640 N.E.2d 716, 719 – Ind. App. 1 Dist. 1994). Because Exhibit 199 proved Appellants and other researchers had established thatpretensioners both are feasible and improve safety in the aggregate, any further testing Mr. Howell performed would have been cumulative.

The COA proceeds to weigh Mr. Howell's testimony, combining two separate alternative designs into one to garner support from *Pries v. Honda Motor Co., Ltd.* (31 F.3d 543 – C.A.7 1994), a case which is factually irrelevant:

> The Estate claimed that Appellant 2 was negligent because it did not select and utilize cinching latch plates and pretensioners. [text omitted] Whether a seatbelt assembly featuring a pretensioner and cinching latch plate as suggested by Howell would have enhanced restraint in the aggregate ... is a question left unanswered.

But Mr. Howell did not introduce these designs in tandem. In fact, his testimony on pretensioners and cinching latch plates occurred *one week apart*. The COA discounts Plaintiff's Exhibit 199 in the same manner, misconstruing Appellant 1's conclusion (less belt slack and higher belt angles reduce occupant ejections in rollovers) to imply that pretensioners won't work without integrated seatbelts. Yet the document does not even suggest such a finding – a cursory reading shows that it addresses pretensioners and integrated seatbelts as distinctly separate features. As with Mr. Howell's alternative designs, it was the jury's exclusive prerogative to determine the weight and relevance of this evidence.

Finally, the COA chastises (a) Mr. Howell because he "did not have the benefit of any statistical study comparing the nature and number of injuries associated with theseatbelt assembly used in Zorn's vehicle to the 'alternative' seatbelt assembly proposed by Howell with the two devices he suggested" and (b) Dr. Griffin because he "did not actually build an alternative structure and testit." But this very standard was rejected in *Jackson v. Warrum* (535 N.E.2d 1207, 1219 – Ind. App. 1 Dist. 1989):

> This rule conflicts with our product liability law which has never required the plaintiff to prove the negative fact of what the injury would have been with a safer product.

The *Warrum* court observed that the plaintiff had presented evidence that (a) the low-entry design of the truck cab at issue placed the driver dangerously close to the point of impact in head-on collisions and (b) a cab design in use by another contemporary manufacturer placed the driver 36" back from any potential point of impact (Id., 1220).

> Although this evidence did not establish the amount of injury that would have resulted in a hypothetical

accident involving a safer or non-defective cab and chassis design, we indicated previously that the plaintiff was not required to prove this negative fact. Thus, evidence existed which arguably supported plaintiffs' enhanced injury product liability claim. (Id.)

Any of these examples standing alone compels a reversal of the COA. Each demonstrates a substitution of the reviewer's assessment of facts for that of the jury, depriving Mrs. Zorn of her Constitutional right to have a jury determine those facts (IN Const. Art. 1, §20; U.S. Const., 7th and 14th Amendments). Such disregard for a jury verdict (a) conflicts with decisions of both this Court and the COA and (b) constitutes an unprecedented departure from well entrenched law.

III. The COA Violates the Standard of Review by Reversing the General Verdict Though the Evidence *Does Not* Lead to a Single Contrary Conclusion

In *Get-N-Go, Inc. v. Markins* (544 N.E.2d 484, 486 – Ind. 1989), this Court held:

> Reversal of the trial court is warranted only if the evidence which is not in conflict leads solely to a conclusion contrary to that reached by the jury.

The COA states that, though Dr. Griffin's testing consisted of striking panes of glass with head forms to determine that the sunroof glass should have failed before the mounting brackets did, "the evidence here did not suggest that the sunroof dislodged due to a head strike." But this statement misrepresents the evidence. For the COA's assertion to stand, the evidence must preclude any possibility that the sunroof was dislodged in whole or in part by a head strike. Only two portions of testimony are probative on this issue. Carl Oaks:

> Q. And you also thought that the sunroof became dislodged in this first roll as well, correct?
>
> A. In my opinion, at least it was loosening. I don't know how much, to what extent, but the roof was distorting and it would at least become..., it wouldn't be in its normal configuration.
>
> Q. Well, I think you used the words "dislodged" in your deposition, didn't you?
>
> A. That would be, that would probably be the best word.

And Dr. Stillwell:

> Q. Fair enough. And I think you told us in your deposition that if we assume that this vehicle rolled over three times that, that in your opinion, Mr. Zorn would have been ejected through the..., completely through the sunroof and out of the vehicle after the second roll?
>
> A. Yes, sir.

From this evidence, the only conclusion one can draw with certainty is that both the sunroof and Capt. Zorn had completely exited the vehicle *before the third roll*. Mr. Oaks does not opine that the sunroof had *completely* evacuated the portal of ejection prior to the second roll, nor does Dr. Stillwell rule out the possibility that Capt. Zorn *started to exit* the vehicle during the first roll. The jury saw pictures from Dr. Griffin's testing that clearly showed the brackets failing prematurely.

Thus, the facts are capable of more than one inference, and a reasonable juror could have found that it was Capt. Zorn's head that caused the sunroof to fully vacate the portal. Even if we suspend the operation of every pertinent standard of review and allow an appellate court to test the sufficiency of Mrs. Zorn's evidence, the jury's verdict is sustainable on the sunroof claim alone under Indiana's longstanding, black-letter precepts of law.

CONCLUSION

A devoted husband and doting father was killed on December 20, 2001 due to a simple tread separation he would have survived had Appellants equipped his SUV with the same technology they had been outfitting European vehicles with for years prior to its design and manufacture. Laboriously, Mrs. Zorn proved every element of her case, as required by *Miller v. Todd* (551 N.E.2d 1139, 1141 – Ind. 1990). On its face, this Opinion: (a) disregards salient facts which support the verdict (b) relieves Appellants of their heavy burdens on appeal (c) evinces a deliberate search of the record for facts unfavorable to the verdict (d) weighs conflicting evidence and (e) rates the credibility of Mrs. Zorn's experts. The COA's determination that Mrs. Zorn's evidence was lacking is belied by (a) the sheer length of its factual discussion alone and (b) the fact that the ruling of the tripartite appellate panel was not unanimous.

In nullifying the jury verdict, the COA (a) contravenes standards of review that have been established in Indiana for 150 years and (b) undermines two centuries of U.S. Supreme Court precedent (*Respublica v. Lacaze* – 2 U.S. 118, 121-2 – U.S. 1791). Therefore, Mrs. Zorn asks that transfer be granted and the verdict reinstated.

Miscellaneous Tips and Stylistic Comments

When I was a young attorney, I tried to bluff my way through a job interview by claiming to have *conducted* numerous depositions though I had only *defended* one or two. As the panel of interviewers eyed me skeptically, one of them probed deeper.

"Let's not misunderstand each other. We need someone who can hit the ground running, because this firm takes a proactive approach to discovery. You'll be taking a lot of depositions. Will you be comfortable with that?"

My response will go down in history as one of the most boneheaded comments a rookie lawyer has ever made.

"Absolutely. After all, there's only one kind of deposition."

Just as there are numerous angles from which to examine a witness, each brief you write should be tailored to fit the peculiar circumstances (both substantive and procedural) surrounding the case. In this section I will give you examples of the variety of approaches one may take to writing a brief.

A New Approach to a Tired Subject

I mentioned the *Daubert* motion earlier. I've combated a number of attorneys who abuse this type of motion so habitually, I would wager that when they have sex they chant *Kumho, baby, Kumho!*[87] Product liability litigation has become so expert-dependent that one or two successful *Daubert* motions can destroy a plaintiff's case. Thus, lawyers typically feel the need to recite the history of the world in response. By doing so, however, they further obscure the fact that the *Daubert* motion was originally intended to be the exception rather than the rule. The trick defendants typically use is to (a) attack an expert's *opinions* under the guise of *methodology* and (b) apply a stricter standard for qualifications than is warranted. When I read one such set of motions, I wearied of the usual "sky is falling" approach. I

---

[87] *Kumho Tire Co., Ltd. v. Carmichael* (526 U.S. 137 – 1999) is often cited in tandem with *Daubert*.

199

decided it was high time somebody set the record straight. So, rather than drag the Court back through the winding detours Defendants had drawn to overcomplicate the query, I used my opener to clear the canvas for the court, applying the analysis in strict accordance with applicable law, and detouring only where necessary to rebut particularly pointed attacks.

Daubert Response – Western District of Oklahoma

STATEMENT OF PERTINENT AUTHORITY

In its notes to the 2000 Amendment to Fed. R. Evid. 702, the Advisory Committee observes (quotations merged, citations omitted): "A review of the caselaw after *Daubert* shows that the rejection of expert testimony is the exception rather than the rule. *Daubert* did not work a seachange over federal evidence law, and the trial court's role as gatekeeper is not intended to serve as a replacement for the adversary system." The Committee further cautions that the rule "is not intended to provide an excuse for the automatic challenge to the testimony of every expert." This holding reflects a growing impatience on the part of trial and appellate jurists with litigants who pervert the original intent of Rule 702 by deforming the guideposts of *Daubert* into clubs.

In *Daubert v. Merrell Dow Pharmaceuticals, Inc.* (509 U.S. 579, 595 – 1993), the court held (emphasis added):

> The inquiry envisioned by Rule 702 is, we emphasize, a flexible one. *** The focus, of course, must be solely on principles and methodology, **not on the conclusions that they generate**.

The court in *Nemir v. Mitsubishi Motor Sales of America, Inc.* (6 Fed. Appx. 266, 270 – C.A.6 2001), stressed that this flexibility is especially applicable when the test is applied to the testimony of an engineer. Furthermore (Id. at 275; quotation merged, citation omitted):

In evaluating an expert witness, *Daubert* and Rule 702 require only that the expert testimony be derived from inferences based on a scientific method and that those inferences be derived from the facts of the case at hand ... not that they know the answers to all the questions a case presents – even to the most fundamental questions.

In other words, no expert is required to eliminate a limitless universe of alternatives. The central intent of Rule 702 as interpreted by *Daubert* is, in the words of the *Nemir* court, "simply to afford the Court limited control over extreme and unreliable" expert testimony (Id., fn. 35).

In *Gopalratnam v. Hewlett-Packard Co.* (877 F.3d 771 – C.A.7 2017) (quotation merged, citations omitted), the court expanded on the *Daubert* interdiction against the misapplication of Rules 702 and 703:

The district court's role as gatekeeper does not render the district court the trier of all facts relating to expert testimony. The jury must still be allowed to play its essential role as the arbiter of the weight and credibility of expert testimony. Rather, Rule 702's reliability elements require the district judge to determine only that the expert is providing testimony that is based on a correct application of a reliable *methodology* and that the expert considered sufficient data to employ the methodology. This examination does not ordinarily extend to the reliability of the *conclusions* those methods produce – that is, whether the conclusions are unimpeachable. In other words, an expert may provide expert testimony based on a valid and properly applied methodology and still offer a conclusion that is subject to doubt. It is the role of the jury to weigh these sources of doubt. (Id. at 780-1)

> The district court usurps the role of the jury, and
> therefore abuses its discretion, if it unduly scrutinizes
> the quality of the expert's data and conclusions
> rather than the reliability of the methodology the
> expert employed. (Id. at 781)

Among the pithier restatements of this precept are: (a) an expert may not be excluded because his counterpart is more persuasive than he (*Rink v. Cheminova, Inc.* – 400 F.3d 1286, 1293 fn. 7 – C.A.11 2005); (b) the district court should not "choose one set of facts over another" (*McCloud ex rel. Hall v. Goodyear Dunlop Tires North America, Ltd.* – 479 F.Supp.2d 882, 893 – C.D. Ill. 2007); and (c) the trial court's "role under *Daubert* is that of gatekeeper, not that of armed guard." (*Ruiz-Troche v. Pepsi Cola of Puerto Rico Bottling Co.*, 161 F.3d 77, 86 – C.A.1 1998)

It cannot be overstated that the federal circuits *unanimously* agree with the canon that the reliability/admissibility of expert testimony must be evaluated on a case-by-case basis (*Ford v. Nationwide Mut. Fire Ins. Co.* – 62 F. App'x 6, 9 – C.A.1 2003; *Amorgianos v. Nat'l R.R. Passenger Corp.* – 303 F.3d 256, 266 – C.A.2 2002; *Petruzzi's IGA Supermarkets, Inc. v. Darling-Delaware Co.* – 998 F.2d 1224, 1238 – C.A.3 1993; *AVX Corp. v. United States* – 518 F. App'x 130, 135 – C.A.4 2013; *Pipitone v. Biomatrix, Inc.* – 288 F.3d 239, 245 – C.A.5 2002; *United States v. Smithers* – 212 F.3d 306, 320 – C.A.6 2000; *C.W. ex rel. Wood v. Textron, Inc.* – 807 F.3d 827, 835 – C.A.7 2015; *Olson v. Ford Motor Co.* – 481 F.3d 619, 628 – C.A.8 2007; *United States v. Sanchez-Birruetta* – 128 F. App'x 571, 572–73 – C.A.9 2005; *Lippe v. Howard* – 287 F. Supp. 3d 1271, 1278 – W.D. Okla. 2018; *Calta v. N. Am. Arms, Inc.* – 2007 WL 4800641, at *3 – M.D. Fla. 2007 – Not Reported; *Heller v. D.C.* – 952 F. Supp. 2d 133, 140 – D. D.C. 2013; *Murfam Farms, LLC ex rel. Murphy v. United States* – 2008 WL 7706607, at *1 – Fed. Cl. 2008 – Not Reported). Therefore, fact-specific outcomes in other cases are immaterial to this Court's analysis.

An expert's testimony is admissible if it is (a) based on a reliable foundation and (b) relevant (*Krik v. Exxon Mobil Corp.* – 870 F.3d 669, 674 – C.A.7 2017). A lack of "supporting studies is not, in itself, fatal to the admissibility" of expert testimony (*Jahn v. Equine Services, PSC* – 233 F.3d 382, fn. 8 – C.A.6 2000). A lack of "absolute certainty goes to the weight of [an expert's] testimony," not its admissibility (*Stutzman v. CRST, Inc.* – 997 F.2d 291, 296 – C.A.7 1993). Courts should afford experts wide latitude in their opinions, including opinions not based on firsthand knowledge. As the court in *Gopalratnam* (877 F.3d 771 at 789) noted:

> It is common in technical fields for an expert to base an opinion in part on what a different expert believeson the basis of expert knowledge not possessed by the first expert. *** Such a scenario is explicitly contemplated by the Rules of Evidence.

The *Gopalratnam* court cited Rule 703, noting its alternative requisite that an expert may base an opinion on facts or data he has either "been made aware of" or "personally observed." Plaintiffs would note that Rule 702 bears the same disjunctive connector: "A witness who is qualified as an expert by knowledge, skill, experience, training, or education may testify ...." In other words, there is not just one accepted avenue to expertise; there are many. As the Advisory Committee illustrates:

> Nothing in this amendment is intended to suggest that experience alone – or experience in conjunction with other knowledge, skill, training or education – may not provide a sufficient foundation for expert testimony. To the contrary, the text of Rule 702 expressly contemplates that an expert may be qualified on the basis of experience. In certain fields,

experience is the predominant, if not sole, basis for
a great deal of reliable expert testimony.

Hence, contrary to the typical complaint of products liability
defendants, an expert need not conduct an independent, case-
specific test for every opinion or alternative design he tenders.
For example, in *Montgomery v. Mitsubishi Motors Corp.* (448
F. Supp. 2d 619, 629 – E.D. Pa. 2006), an expert's design defect
opinion in an automobile rollover case was admissible, despite
his having performed no case-specific testing, where it was based
on his experience and qualifications in the automotive industry,
including his knowledge of the testing conducted on the vehicle
during its design phase. And in *Great N. Ins. Co. v. BMW of N.
Am. LLC* (84 F. Supp. 3d 630, 642 – S.D. Ohio 2015) – a products
liability case concerning an automobile fire alleged to have been
caused by a defective design leading to debris build-up – an expert
witness was allowed to testify even though he was not specific
about which openings allegedly allowed in debris, and did not
identify any other fires in similar vehicles attributable to the alleged
defect, conduct testing or analysis to determine whether all vehicles
were similarly defective, or test his alternative design's strength,
structural integrity, aerodynamic properties, or airflow properties
because, among other things (a) the design issues were simple
and (b) the expert followed the scientific method in forming his
conclusions. The court adopted the following quote from *Kumho
Tire Co., Ltd. v. Carmichael* (526 U.S. 137, 148-9 – 1999):

> Experts of all kinds tie observations to conclusions
> through the use of what Judge Learned Hand
> called "general truths derived from ... specialized
> experience." Hand, *Historical and Practical
> Considerations Regarding Expert Testimony*, 15 Harv.
> L.Rev. 40, 54 (1901). And whether the specific expert
> testimony focuses upon specialized observations,

the specialized translation of those observations into theory, a specialized theory itself, or the application of such a theory in a particular case, the expert's testimony often will rest "upon an experience confessedly foreign in kind to [the jury's] own." *Ibid.*

Nor does federal law require an expert to return to the drawing board and conduct a formal, documented analysis in the event he clarifies or amends his opinion. To the contrary, adapting one's conclusions to fit an ever-evolving data field lies at the heart of the scientific method. This truism is reflected by the court's rejoinder in *Erickson v. Baxter Healthcare, Inc.* (151 F. Supp. 2d 952, 968 – N.D. Ill. 2001):

> The defendants also suggest that Dr. Mosley's change in opinion based on new records makes all of his opinions unreliable, but this is frivolous. The failure to cite scholarly articles does not render his opinions unreliable in light of his experience in this field; one would hope that a trained epidemiological expert need not consult a journal to discuss the symptoms of hepatitis or HIV.

In *Kumho* (526 U.S. 137 at 152-3), the Court clarified that the trial court has discretion to altogether dispense with the *Daubert* inquiry (termed an "unnecessary reliability" proceeding) in a case where the expert's methods are so conventional that they are "properly taken for granted ...." Also, the Court enjoys broad discretion in determining the reliability of expert testimony. This latitude is so generous that an appellate panel will not overturn the Court's decision unless it has "a definite and firm conviction that the trial court has made a clear error of judgment or exceeded the bounds of permissible choice." (*Attorney General of Oklahoma v. Tyson Foods, Inc.* – 565 F.3d 769, 779 – C.A.10 Okla. 2009 – quotations and citations omitted)

Standing Your Ground with the Court

Few relationships are more delicate than that between an attorney and the judge whose status conference that attorney failed to attend. In one of our cases, not only did our firm fail to docket such a date, so did our associate counsel in Missouri and our local counsel in Texas. By the time we realized it (a) the conference was set to begin in a mere 20 minutes and (b) none of us, including our local counsel, was within a hundred miles of the courthouse. I called the judge's chambers immediately, but my call was shunted to voice mail. I followed up with an urgent, apologetic email to the judge's clerk.

The following day, the judge issued a scathing order in which she (a) proclaimed that we had no excuse for missing the conference (despite the fact that she had not bothered to ask if we had one) and (b) directed the defendants to submit an application for attorney fees as sanctions. Each defendant claimed in its affidavit that it required not 1 but 2 attorneys to spend 4 hours apiece preparing for the 15-minute housekeeping powwow, resulting in a total combined request for $8,850.

The attitude of my employing attorneys was nonchalant: "We'll pay it if it's fair." But it galled me that the defendants would so transparently seek to capitalize on the situation. The surest way to pare down the defendants' award was to tell the judge to do her job in such a way that we came off as messengers, not insisters or complainers. I also felt it was important to show this judge we would not be cowed by her overreaction to an isolated mistake for which we had volunteered more than one sincere apology:

Response to Attorney Fee Request – USDC, Northern District of Texas, Dallas Division

The lodestar method for calculating attorney fees was most recently articulated in *Mendoza v. Regis Corp.* (2008 WL 245176 – W.D. Tex. 2008 – Slip Op.):

The lodestar is computed by multiplying the number of hours *reasonably* expended by the prevailing hourly rate for similar work in the community. The lodestar is then adjusted depending on the circumstances of the case and the respective weight of twelve factors set forth in *Johnson v. Georgia Highway Express, Inc.* as applied to the case. (Id. at 2; footnote omitted; emphasis added)

It was explained in *Akron Center for Reproductive Health v. City of Akron* (604 F. Supp. 1275 – N.D. Ohio 1985) that it is the District Court's duty to assess reasonableness within the framework of the specific proceeding on which the requested fees are based (Id. at 1287). In so doing, the Court should draw upon its own past experience with that type of proceeding (Id. at 1288). One of the various factors that comprise this evaluation is whether efforts were needlessly duplicated (Id.). As the court admonished in *Johnson v. Georgia Highway Express, Inc.* (488 F.2d 714, 717 – C.A.5 1974):

The trial judge should weigh the hours claimed against his own knowledge, experience, and expertise of the time required to complete similar activities. If more than one attorney is involved, the possibility of duplication of effort along with the proper utilization of time should be scrutinized. The time of two or three lawyers in a courtroom or conference when one would do may obviously be discounted.

Therefore, Plaintiffs shall timely pay whatever amount the Court, in its discretion, deems reasonable.

Because I matter-of-factly reminded the judge that her duty was not contingent upon whether she loved or hated a particular litigant, she discounted each defendant's award by over 50%.

Analogy and Source Selection

Let's face it – the vast majority of legal briefs are tedious and boring. This is primarily due to the misconception that the only supportive materials which belong in a brief are statutes, case law and legal treatises. This restrictive view ignores a wealth of forensic tools offered by the world at large. The writer communicates by drawing on ideas and images that he and his reader understand. Some of the most common sources of this shared experience are television, theatre, music and literature. Granted, you need precedent to *support* your thesis. But when you're looking for the best way to *persuade* a judge, all non-legal sources are fair game.

A defendant in an Ohio case filed an *in limine* motion aimed at excluding a number of our fact witnesses. The defendant argued that the nature of their testimony required support from an expert witness. Not only were these witnesses pivotal to our case; their testimony would paint a nasty picture of this defendant at trial. For my response, I borrowed from a 1997 film:

Response to Motion to Exclude – Hamilton County, Ohio

Every other piece of testimony offered by these four witnesses is nothing more than a statement of fact. For example, Mr. Roberts observed that there was no valve stem in the left front tire. Either it is there or it is not. Messrs. Hall and Smiley will testify from their personal experience in management positions that [Dealer] had a policy of not replacing valve stems during tire replacements. Only a [Dealer] employee could make such a determination. Thus, their testimony certainly falls within the "skilled witness" category described in *Cansler v. Mills*.[1] Finally, no one is better qualified to testify as to what services were or were not actually performed on the vehicle than the technician himself. If we rounded up every faculty member and top graduate of MIT for the last 50 years and combined all of that brain power, not even the resulting Ultimate

---

Expert would be better equipped than Mr. Kurtz to testify as to (a) whether he replaced the valve stems or (b) how fully he inflated the replacement tires.

As Plaintiff reflects on the ostensible premise of [Dealer's] motion, she is reminded of a scene from *Liar, Liar*.[2] In that film, attorney Fletcher Reede has been rendered temporarily incapable of lying by his son's birthday wish. At a divorce trial, opposing counsel plays an audiotape of his client committing adultery, to which Reede complains:

> **Fletcher**: Your honor, I object!
> **Judge**: Why?
> **Fletcher**: Because it's devastating to my case!

Fundamental to our rules of procedure and evidence is the ability to distinguish between fact and fantasy. Plaintiff did not create the facts of this case. Plaintiff can no more change the facts than she can stop the sun from rising. No matter how vehemently [Dealer] tries to mischaracterize it, fact testimony remains fact testimony. If that fact testimony suggests a [Dealer] employee negligently installed the decedent's tires, it is within the exclusive province of the jury to draw a fitting conclusion. Plaintiff has faith that the good people of Ohio are capable of doing so on these issues without being spoonfed by a $500/hr brain-trust.

---

[1] 765 N.E.2d 698 (Ind. App. 2002)
[2] 1997, Universal Studios

Another misbelief is that the only facts relevant to one's argument are the facts of the underlying case. To the contrary, you should make use of any fact, wherever it may be found, that best serves your position. Product liability defendants will try anything and everything to preclude a punitive claim. I once found myself responding to a summary judgment motion on that issue. The gist of the argument was that our claim for punitive damages should be dismissed because: (a) the acts and omissions of the defendant occurred at its corporate headquarters in the State of Michigan and (b) the State of Michigan does not recognize a punitive cause of action. Having seen the same argument a dozen times before, I knew the centerpiece of my response would be the fact that the majority of products this defendant manufactures are sold outside the State of Michigan. While the statement alone made intuitive sense, I wanted to turn it into a podium pounder by illustrating it with concrete figures. It took me very little time to discover a website that offers a State-by-State listing of factory-authorized automobile dealerships. I then surfed to another invaluable public-access source – the defendant's annual report, which I found at the defendant's very own URL. The numbers I derived from these sites served as the opener to my statement of undisputed facts.

**Response to Motion for Summary Judgment on
Punitive Damages – Hamilton County, Ohio**

Unlike most private citizens, a business entity can establish a residence in any State of the U.S. by simply incorporating and christening an office as "headquarters." The bulk of Manufacturer's argument in favor of applying Michigan law is that Manufacturer's relevant conduct occurred almost exclusively in the State of Michigan. One seminal fact this argument overlooks is that the overwhelming majority of vehicles Manufacturer designs and produces are sold outside the borders of Michigan. Manufacturer has a total of 9,480 dealerships throughout the United States (Exhibit 1a), a scant 99 of which are in the State of Michigan (Exhibit 1b). This means that Manufacturer's Michigan dealerships make up only .01% of Manufacturer's nationwide presence. It is also notable that Manufacturer has 103 dealerships in the State of Ohio where this fatal accident occurred (Exhibit 2a) and 67 dealerships in the State of Indiana where the subject vehicle was purchased (Exhibit 2b). Presently 45 States, plus the District of Columbia, endorse

---

210

> punitive damages in product liability and/or negligence actions. Asking this Court to apply the substantive law of Michigan in this case is tantamount to imposing the will of a 10% minority upon the majority. Such a concept evokes socio-political ideologies Mr. Collins would rather not mention in a modern American proceeding.

Analogy is perhaps the most effective weapon in a communicator's arsenal. With analogy we bring the abstract to life by tethering it to a concrete image. As with persuasive source material, the variety of analogies one may employ is limited only by his creativity. When selecting an analogy, however, you must keep your audience in the forefront of your mind. For example, I once proposed the following in a summary judgment motion:

> Plaintiffs submit that for Manufacturer to say this scenario is not reasonably foreseeable is to assert that the wind never blows in Oklahoma.

Though the analogy made perfect sense to me, it was lost on our judge in New Jersey. At the subsequent hearing the judge, who has a nettlesome habit of reading motions aloud into the record, actually paused to ask, "I don't know, does the wind blow in Oklahoma?"

A year later I was having a better day when, in a motion to exclude expert testimony, the defendant complained that our expert did not produce certain source materials at his deposition. What the defendant conveniently ignored were the facts that these materials (a) were far too voluminous for one human being to carry and (b) are freely accessible to the public at a U.S. government website:

> Mr. Collins submits that penalizing Dr. Griffin for not "producing" these databases at a deposition is akin to striking his testimony that the sky is blue merely because he didn't stick a chunk of "sky" in his briefcase.

Sometimes we find our best material in the documents produced

211

by our opponent. Crucial to your average defective motor vehicle case is evidence that proves a manufacturer had notice of a defect prior to the victim's injury or death. To establish the length of time a manufacturer is chargeable with this knowledge, plaintiffs often look to previous models of that particular vehicle. Thus, we use terms such as "image car," "predecessor vehicle" and "family of vehicles" to illustrate the reality that no one vehicle is designed and manufactured in a vacuum. As you might guess, manufacturers are none too happy for juries to hear this evidence. Their typical argument is that successive vehicle models are not "substantially similar" to each other; therefore, any comparison among them would confuse the jury.

Because our firm tends to lock horns with the same manufacturers again and again, I can for the most part recycle previous responses on this subject. But I am always on a quest for a better way to express what I've already said. As I revamped one such response, I ran across a memo obtained in discovery that I had not seen before. I found the language in this memo so enthralling that I spent the entire morning playing with the image it evoked (the excerpt below is an amalgamation of a brief written for an Ohio case and a refinement thereof performed 3 years later for one in Tennessee).

Response to Motion *in Limine*

Manufacturers do not *reinvent the wheel* when they design a new vehicle model. To the contrary, each new version of a particular model builds upon its predecessor. As Defendant's own counsel has admitted in open court: "no new vehicle program starts out as a blank piece of paper." To fully appreciate this point, one must understand that, in vehicle manufacturing parlance, the word "new" does not mean what reasonably intelligent, English speaking humanbeings think it means. When Manufacturer built the first generation E-SUV, 45% of its parts were carried over from the B-SUV into the 4-door and 82% found their way into the 2-door (Exhibit B, top page; *Buell-Wilson*, 73 Cal.Rptr.3d 277 at 294).

Despite this, Manufacturer has claimed in case after case that the E-SUV was no less than a revolutionary departure from its predecessor, as if Manufacturer had wiped the slate clean and built a "new" vehicle from the ground up (much like its present argument with the G-SUV). Looking again at the top page of Exhibit B:

> The 45/55 split of existing non-new versus new is about midway between the proposed all-new program guidelines of 20-30% carryover parts and the proposed major change program guidelines of 60-65% carry-over content.

So, if one were to develop a Manufacturer-to-English dictionary, we would find the following translations:

Manufacturer-Speak	English
Major Change	Minor Change
Non-New	Old
New	45% Old
All-New	30% Old

The reality is that, in the ongoing development of the E-SUV family: (a) the G-SUV is merely the result of variations made in the F-SUV which (b) was developed from the D-SUV which (c) evolved from the C-SUV which (d) was the four-door rendition of the B-SUV which (e) was a derivative of the A-pickup.

In the Oklahoma appeal I discussed earlier, the highest State court denied certiorari. While crafting my argument to the U.S. Supreme Court, it occurred to me that I needed to find a hook – a relatively new and intriguing issue that tied in with our case. The fact that the foreman had manufactured his own evidence in the jury room would not be good enough, I feared, because of the overwhelming reticence of appellate courts to intrude upon jury deliberations. It was

213

obvious to anyone who read the post trial transcript that the foreman bore a secret agenda from the beginning of the trial – to secure a defense verdict. When I discussed the case with other attorneys, I would often hear the term "stealth juror." My research into the phrase led me to a little paperback book between whose covers I found the very roadmap our foreman had followed. I made it the centerpiece of my opening argument.

Petition for Certiorari – United States Supreme Court

REASONS TO GRANT THIS PETITION

I.   The Constitutional Right to a Fair and Impartial Jury Is under Assault by Agenda-Driven Jurors

The right to have one's claims tried by a fair and impartial factfinder has been called "one of the pillars of due process." [*ESSO Standard Oil Co. (Puerto Rico) v. Mujica Cotto* – 327 F.Supp.2d 110, 130 – D. Puerto Rico 2004 (affirmed 389 F.3d 212)] This right applies with equal force in civil trials (*Marshall v. Jerrico, Inc.* – 446 U.S. 238, 242-3 – C.A.10 1980).

In *Skaggs v. Otis Elevator Co.* (164 F.3d 511 – C.A.10 Okla. 1998), the court held:

> Although the Seventh Amendment does not contain language identical to that found in the Sixth Amendment … the right to a jury trial in a civil case would be illusory unless it encompassed the right to an impartial jury. (Id., 514-15)

> The denial of trial by an impartial jury is also the denial of due process.... (Id.; quotation merged; citation omitted)

It is a longstanding rule of law that, if a juror would ignore jury

---

instructions or evidence in favor of her own agenda, she is unfit for duty. Thus, in *Morgan v. Illinois* (504 U.S. 719, 738 – 1992), this Court held that a juror who was prepared to impose the death penalty without considering mitigating factors was removable for cause.Likewise, the court in *U.S. v. Wilson* (493 F.Supp.2d 415, 421 – E.D.N.Y. 2006) declared removable for cause a juror whose bias in favor of political minorities "indicates that he is unduly influenced by popular culture and stereotypes." And in *U.S. v.Parker* (133 F.3d 322, 327 – C.A.5 1998), the court affirmed the removal of a juror who admitted that a family member's recent criminal conviction would cloud his view of the evidence.

In 2002, Trent Hammerstein wrote a book titled "Stealth Juror – The Ultimate Defense Against [sic.] Bad Laws and Government Tyranny" (Paladin Press) in which he openly encourages his readers to (a) lie during *voir dire* to get themselves impaneled and then, during deliberations (b) ignore the evidence and jury charges in favor of their own agendas. Suffusing the book is an almost rabid suspicion of trial judges based primarily on their role in excluding inadmissible evidence. Though the author's stated concern is limited to criminal defendants, one needs no imagination to discern the impact stealth jurors inspired by the following battle cries are having on civil trials:

> Technically, lying on a voir dire form is a felony.
> [text omitted]
> In my opinion, in some cases you have a moral and ethical right to lie …. (Id., p. 51)

> So at the beginning of the trial, when you are forced to take an oath to obey the judge's instructions (which he really doesn't have the right or power to give), just nod, mouth the words you're told to, and mentally cross your fingers, because the judge will almost always make you promise to obey his instructions,

even over your own conscience or feelings. (Id., pp. 56-7)

The first thing to do in the jury room is try to get yourself elected foreman, forewoman, foreperson or whatever they call it. (Id., p. 74)

[The judge's jury instructions] are generally invalid and improper no matter how many judges say they aren't because the jury, not the judge, is the final arbiter of guilt or innocence. (Id., p. 75)

Finally, some subject headings in his chapter titled "What You Can Do to Fix the System Even if You're Never on a Jury" are "Establish Citizen Oversight Panels to Control Judges," "Drastically Reduce the Power of Judges" and "Strictly Limit the Voir Dire Process."

The "stealth juror" movement has gained such ground that it prompted Dan Abrams (host of *Abrams Report*) to address it on April 2, 2004. In a segment titled "Runaway Jury," Phillip Anthony, a jury consultant with VisionQuest, referred to the O.J. Simpson murder trial as a watershed event for jury behavior: "The lightbulb went on for a lot of folks that if they ended up being selected as a juror, it could be an opportunity to engage in some form of social engineering." Later in the piece, he added: "Usually, they've experienced something personally that causes them to want to put forward their agenda."

Whether we label them "stealth" or "activist," jurors who ignore jury instructions and evidence in favor of their own agendas are anathema to fundamental due process. Because such jurors are schooled by the above referenced book – and web sites such as www.fija.org – in ways to evade detection, often the only way to uncover them is to (a) analyze the effect they had on a verdict after that verdict has been delivered by (b) delving into the objective facts of what was said and done behind the closed door to the jury room.

Here are some of the more lighthearted examples of creativity from the bench. In *Alfaro v. Dow Chemical* (751 S.W.2d 208, 217 – Tex. App. Hous. 1 Dist. 1988), Justice Duggan wrote:

> Unless litigants are afforded some relief in cases where a trial in Texas would be grossly unfair, it is not far-fetched to imagine that the following ditty might become the number one hit song in Yugoslavia by 1990:
> I cain't prove no Texas Nexus.
> I got hurt near home in Zren-Ja-Neen.
> Still I filed my suit in Texas.
> They ain't got no *forum non conveen* [sic].
>
> (With apologies to George Strait and the author of "All My Exes Live in Texas," and with credit to lyricist/ briefing attorney Kate Hall of this Court.)
>
> I respectfully dissent.

And it appears Justice Easterbrook is well read (*Bammerlin v. Navistar Intern. Transp. Corp.* – 30 F.3d 898, 902 – C.A.7 1994):

> Sherlock Holmes observed that "when you have eliminated the impossible, whatever remains, however improbable, must be the truth." A. Conan Doyle, *The Sign of Four*, ch. 6. Courts need not disdain a method that both engineers and detectives find useful.

Judge Sam Sparks has learned to channel his anger through poetry:

IN THE UNITED STATES DISTRICT COURT FOR THE WESTERN DISTRICT OF TEXAS AUSTIN DIVISION

KEYSTONE MEDIA INTERNATIONAL, LLC,
Plaintiff,

-vs-   **Case No. A-06-594-SS**

DAVID B. HANCOCK,
Defendant.

ORDER

BE IT REMEMBERED on the 25th day of April 2007 the Court reviewed the file in the above-styled cause, and specifically the defendant Hancock's Motion for Protection filed April 23, 2001, and after reading it a second time to make sure it was not a practical joke, the Court enters the following:

Stallions can drink water from a creek without a ripple;
The lawyers in this case must have a bottle with a nipple.

Babies learn to walk by scooting and falling;
These lawyers practice law by simply mauling

Each other and the judge, but this must end soon
(Maybe facing off with six-shooters at noon?)

Surely lawyers who practice in federal court can take
A deposition without a judge's order, for goodness sake.

First, the argument about taking the deposition at all,
And now this – establishing their experience to be small.

> So, let me tell you both and be abundantly clear:
> If you can't work this without me, I will be near.
>
> There will be a hearing with pablum to eat
> And a very cool cell where you can meet.
>
> AND WORK OUT YOUR INFANTILE PROBLEM WITH THE DEPOSITION.
>
> IT IS ORDERED that the Motion to Dismiss is DISMISSED.
>
> SIGNED this the 25th day of April 2007.
>
> S/Sam Sparks
> United States District Judge

Finally, in the Mexican cases I've discussed, Judge Brothers opened his concluding thoughts in a long awaited order with a quote from a timeless Beatles tune:

> ### CONCLUSION
>
> *The long and winding road that leads to your door*
> *Will never disappear ...*
> *Don't keep me waiting here,*
> *Lead me to your door ...*
>
> It has been a "long and winding road" through a procedural morass leading these cases to this point. There is no just reason to make these parties wait any longer for the doors of this Court to be opened to finally allow trials on the actual merits.

Closing Thoughts and Pet Peeves

Margins

Presentation is every bit as crucial as substance. And, with a myriad of word processing tools at our fingertips, there is no excuse for a sloppy end product. Compare the following *before* and *after* examples:

Example A:
The Mediocre Brief

PLAINTIFFS' RESPONSE TO DEFENDANT'S MOTION IN LIMINE TO EXCLUDE TESTIMONY OF PLAINTIFFS' EXPERT DR. THIBEDEAU

Plaintiffs ask that this motion be overruled because, in its attempt to bar Dr. Thibedeau's admissible testimony, Defendant has deliberately misquoted case law and misrepresented his testimony.

I. Dr. Thibedeau's Opinion on the Inadequacy of the Rollover Warning Is Based on Investigation and Psychological Testing Spanning 40 Years

Dr. Thibedeau earned his Ph.D. in psychology in 1961, Exh. A, 1, and held numerous staff positions until his semi-retirement in 2002, Id., 2. He is board certified in Human Factors, he has earned a variety of professional awards and his teaching in recent years has focused on Human Factors/Memory and System Reliability and Safety, Id., 3. Among his research grant and contract areas are: "Ability of humans to keep track of changing events"; "Human memory and the identification process"; "An evaluation of the design and effectiveness of automobile facilitators (instructions, warnings and labels)"; and "Development of a manual for use in automobile facilitator (instructions, warnings and labels) design

---

and evaluation," Id., 4-5. Of his 350 publications, symposia and technical reports, Id., 6-28, he has devoted 3 full-length books to Human Factors and Warnings, Id., 6. This gentleman has devoted virtually his entire professional life to the study of how human beings respond to emergencies and warnings, Exh. B: 11/1 to 13/7; 26/2-5; 42/21 to 43/24.

Example B:
The Impeccable Brief

PLAINTIFFS' RESPONSE TO DEFENDANT'S MOTION *IN LIMINE* TO EXCLUDE TESTIMONY OF PLAINTIFFS' EXPERT DR. THIBEDEAU

Plaintiffs ask that this motion be overruled because, in its attempt to bar Dr. Thibedeau's admissible testimony, Defendant has deliberately misquoted case law and misrepresented that testimony.

I. Dr. Thibedeau's Opinion on the Inadequacy of the Rollover Warning Is Based on Investigation and Psychological Testing Spanning 40 Years

Dr. Thibedeau earned his Ph.D. in psychology in 1961 (Exh. A, 1), and held numerous staff positions until his semi-retirement in 2002 (Id., 2). He is board certified in Human Factors, he has earned a variety of professional awards, and his teaching in recent years has focused on Human Factors/Memory and System Reliability and Safety (Id., 3). Among his research grant and contract areas are:

- "Ability of humans to keep track of changing events";
- "Human memory and the identification process";
- "An evaluation of the design and effectiveness of automobile facilitators (instructions, warnings and labels)"; and

- "Development of a manual for use in automobile facilitator (instructions, warnings and labels) design and evaluation" (Id., 4-5).

Of his 350 publications, symposia and technical reports (Id., 6-28) he has devoted 3 full-length books to Human Factors and Warnings (Id., 6). This gentleman has devoted virtually his entire professional life to the study of how human beings respond to emergencies and warnings (Exh. B: 11/1 to 13/7; 26/2-5; 42/21 to 43/24). Recently, a significant portion of this study has focused on [Defendant's SUV] (Exh. B, 48/15 to 49/13), specifically: (a) the adequacy of the warning Defendant provides to alert passengers to the unique rollover propensity of the [SUV] and (b) the human factors implications (i.e., driver reaction) related to the [SUV]'s legendary instability (Exh. B: 50/7-16; 82/2 to 83/10; 84/11 to 86/4; 161/14 to 162/4; 167/8-13; 172/10 to 173/25).

I've seen briefs that look far worse than Example A. In fact, I know of one knucklehead who not only filed such a brief with an appellate court – *he actually numbered the pages of his appendix by hand.*[88] Anyway, it took this author less than 10 minutes to transform Exhibit A into Exhibit B by, among other things:

a) Deleting the underscore because it is unnecessary clutter – the bold print is sufficient to accentuate the title,

b) Setting off subtitle I by hanging the left margin by 5 points,

c) Enclosing the record cites in parentheses,

d) Setting off the expert's areas of research in a bulleted list, indented on the left *and right* margins by 5 points, and

e) Fully justifying the body text.

---

[88] You guessed correctly – the Indiana Ringer.

I wish to emphasize that last point. There are some writers and judges who resist full justification. The most common defense of left justification is that full justification too often skews the spacing between words. Granted, it ofttimes does. But which is the lesser evil? I prefer to sacrifice uniform spacing because, in my opinion, left justification makes the brief look ragged and amateurish. Because the analytical mind craves symmetry, full justification and mirrored margins will always be hallmarks of professionalism.

That Infernal Underscore

Some years ago I shared a laugh with a colleague at the fact that, though we once celebrated the thermal-paper fax machine as a technological milestone, today we get testy with court reporters if an electronic transcript does not appear in our e-box within 24 hours of a deposition. While the internet is a vast and invaluable font of information, it contains a few pitfalls for today's legal writer. One such hazard is the hyperlink.

Though it has taken its sweet time (thanks in large part to Trolls and Yapping Chihuahuas), the legal writing establishment has begun to catch up to technology. In the early 1990s, it was common practice to use the cumbersome underscore to indicate the case name in a citation, despite the fact that a growing number of word processing programs had the capability to italicize. The ascendancy of the personal computer brought the subtler form of italics into the mainstream. Recently, however, I've seen an alarming resurgence of underscoring. Why? Because case names and statutes are hyperlinked on the internet, and hyperlinks are underlined. Though, in the foregoing pages, we have seen our share of lawyers who are not so scrupulous, a majority of practitioners do understand the need to preserve the integrity of a direct quote. Thus, most attorneys (especially those who are inexperienced with the law, writing or both) presume that the author of the opinion meant for the underscoring to be there. But the problem with this reasoning is that, in the digital era, judges and their clerks cut/copy/paste just as often as they compose. With respect to case names, therefore, it is more likely than not that the original formatting was permanently overwritten for internet consumption 10 to 10,000 cycles ago. To compound the problem, many times the original citation was italicized; thus, the feckless copier/paster reproduces an atrocity that is doubly emphasized. Add to this the fact that the most popular legal research programs highlight search terms and you end up with a behemoth that is underscored, italicized *and* in bold type. This is another of the myriad situations in which the legal writer is called upon to THINK.

The accuracy of a direct quote inheres in its substantive meaning. As with rules of grammar, a hierarchy of importance comes into play. We have seen how the omission of just a single phrase can turn the meaning of a passage on its head. Thus, it is essential that we (a) reproduce each word accurately and in its original sequence (a task that is practically guaranteed by the copy/paste function) and (b) alert the reader whenever we add or omit words. If the original contains an elemental grammatical error, such as a comma where a period should be, we indicate it with the abbreviation "[sic.]" which means "the author of the quote screwed it up, not I." Or we might supply a missing word: "the of the matter" becomes "the [fact] of the matter." Our concern here is to at once (a) preserve the original meaning and (b) make it as understandable as we can for our reader.

On the other hand, there are aspects of a quote that have no impact on its meaning. For example, if the original author misspells a nonessential word such as "thier," it is juvenile to suggest that I have tainted his intended meaning by correcting this minor error in form without alerting my reader (unless, of course, the original author used the misspelling to illustrate a broader point). Likewise, I may clean up expendable punctuation to clarify the passage for the reader, thus elucidating the author's meaning. And so it is with the case name. Borrowing from an earlier example, in my research I run across the following quote from *Mendoza v. Regis Corp.* (2008 WL 245176 at 2 – W.D. Tex. 2008 – Not Reported):

> The lodestar is computed by multiplying the number of hours *reasonably* expended by the prevailing hourly rate for similar work in the community. The lodestar is then adjusted depending on the circumstances of the case and the respective weight of twelve factors set forth in ***Johnson v. Georgia Highway Express, Inc.*** as applied to the case.

Even if the author of this quote had committed the original to pen and paper, I don't have the time to try and track it down to ascertain whether she meant to use one, two or all three forms of excess emphasis (the third being the internet-blue font which is not reflected above). Regardless of original intent, a citation is not a declarative statement; therefore, logic dictates that this redundant emphasis is not substantive. So, by dropping the underscore and bold typefaces, and changing the font color to black, I have not adulterated the intended meaning in the slightest.

Consolidate until You Can Consolidate No More ... Then Consolidate Once Again

We've discussed how the citation interrupts the flow of an argument. But we also understand the folly of dumping important information into the gutter. Thus, the conscientious communicator is always on the prowl for ways to make his citation format as unobtrusive as possible. You have already seen my method of combining all of this collateral information and setting it off in brackets or parentheses:

[Id.[89] at 2; emphasis added; citations & footnotes omitted]

(Id. at 2; emphasis added; citations & footnotes omitted)

But we mustn't get so carried away with our commentary that we lose all sense of reason. In countless briefs and published opinions I have seen the notation "emphasis in original." This is redundant. When I read a direct quote, my logical assumption is that every substantive indicator of meaning within the quotation marks (or the indented margins of the block quote) was in the original *unless I am told otherwise*. Therefore, if the writer did not alter the quote, I find it insulting to have to read such a disclaimer.

Another subtlety too few lawyers and judges understand is that the "packaging" of the citation is not set in stone. For instance, the jurisdiction and date do not always require their own little parenthetical cubbyhole. Consider the following statement:

> Such claims must be weighed carefully to protect the free flow of information between attorney and client (*State v. Rankin*, 465 So.2d 679 (La. 1985)) and the notes and mental processes of attorneys.

Most writers think nothing of placing parentheses within parentheses. But it is because the citation itself interrupts the flow of the statement that we have set it off in parentheses to begin with. The painstaking writer asks, *Why clutter the statement with a second set of parentheses?* Hence, a more streamlined presentation:

---

[89] There is some confusion over whether the notation "Id." should be italicized. Because "Id." is an abbreviation of the Latin "idem," many follow the traditional rule which holds that foreign words should be italicized. But as we saw with the plural forms memoranda and criteria, determining when a foreign term has been so completely assimilated into English that it is no longer considered foreign (at which point the italics become superfluous) is a dicey endeavor. Don't waste your time wrangling about it. Ignore the caterwauling of the Yapping Chihuahuas and use whichever form you find most pragmatic.

Such claims must be weighed carefully to protect the free flow of information between attorney and client (*State v. Rankin*, 465 So.2d 679, La. 1985) and the notes and mental processes of attorneys.

Such claims must be weighed carefully to protect the free flow of information between attorney and client (*State v. Rankin* – 465 So.2d 679 – La. 1985) and the notes and mental processes of attorneys.

Save the Flattery for Your Mother or Parole Officer – It Has No Place in a Courtroom

I once found myself in the curious position of editing an appellate response that was written by a relatively young lawyer in Missouri but would be argued by a lawyer in Tennessee who had been in practice for over 40 years. The first mistake the young lawyer made was to send the first draft to the older attorney before giving me a chance to work it over. So annoyed was the elder lawyer at the brief's excessive references to the appellate panel as "This Honorable Court" that he gave the poor kid quite a dressing down. I enjoyed quite a chuckle just days later, when the Tennessee lawyer unwittingly exposed himself as a hypocrite: as he argued a motion to the trial court, his compulsion to preface his every other utterance with the hackneyed phrase, "May it please the court" both portrayed him as a stuttering boob and rendered his argument barely intelligible.

Fawning sobriquets like "This Honorable Court" and "May it please the court" serve only to (a) feed the gargantuan ego of the Curmudgeon and (b) disgust the more moderate ego of the conscientious jurist. In either case, the flatterer does nothing but demean himself in the eyes of the decisionmaker, because such stock phrases are facially inauthentic. The current trend is to capitalize "court" only when referring to (a) the instant tribunal (b) the court of last resort in a State and (c) the U.S. Supreme Court. These conventions will change periodically with the tides of human preference. Remember, the office is a distinct entity from the officeholder. The former commands homage; the latter no more or less courtesy than you afford a colleague. Dispense altogether with bootlicking words such as "Honorable" when directly addressing any court.[90] When in doubt, choose subtlety. If you fail to capitalize "court" where a judge thinks you should, human nature guarantees two alternative outcomes: (1) the Curmudgeon will have found 300 reasons to hate your guts beforehand, so it won't matter, or (2) the emotionally balanced judge (a) will most likely not even notice (b) may find it refreshing or (c) might go so far as to applaud your sapience.

Equally nettlesome is the rampant overuse of the adverb "respectfully." When I was a budding lawyer, I watched a judge abruptly suspend his busy motion docket to chastise a colleague of mine for this practice. Here is the gravamen of that judge's advice:

"Every time you preface a comment with 'respectfully' or 'with all due respect,' I think you're about to spew venom. When no venom-spewing ensues, I become quite annoyed at the fact that my blood pressure just shot up ten points in response to a false alarm. It would be pretty naïve of me to presume that you did not think your opponent was full of bull. So, every time you sugarcoat a point of disagreement, you are treating me with *dis*respect. As long as your tone and demeanor show respect, there is no need for you to profess it. So do us all a favor and save the warning signals for when you're about to get really nasty."

A more sinister form of gratuitous flattery is self-deprecation. In a viciously contested trial in Montana against two manufacturers and a used car dealership on behalf of a brain-damaged quadriplegic, the defendants won a mistrial, then filed motions for sanctions against our trial attorneys. In their briefs, the defendants identified 18 separate "offenses" as exclusive causes of the mistrial. I dove into

---

[90] After all, you can't account for where this yahoo has been, or what he's done, in his private time; hence, it is irresponsible to vouch for him.

the trial transcripts and applicable law and, within a week's time, had generated a hard-hitting though courteous brief in which I:

1. Explained how the motions were procedurally barred and, thus, merited no further consideration;

2. Meticulously dissected each allegation, demonstrating (often with the judge's own pronouncements) a blatant pattern whereby the defendants had orchestrated a mistrial by overwhelming the court with excessive sidebars and mistrial requests, twisting the *anticipated* meaning of *incomplete* questions and raising objections sometimes days after the alleged infraction had taken place; and

3. Reminded the court of no less than 11 demonstrable violations on the defendants' part.

I knew from the attorney-fee skirmish in Texas that the only way to get an evenhanded result in such a scenario is to argue from a position of objectivity and strength – keep the judge's focus on the facts at hand by avoiding emotional appeals and token self-recrimination. Besides, my strongest procedural argument was that the court had already denied these defendants' oral motions for sanctions, presented on the very day she had declared the mistrial.

Despite the fact that all the factual and legal stars had aligned in their favor, the lead trial attorneys blinked and hired a local ringer. He proceeded to gut our brief and adopt the beggarly attitude of a whipped puppy. I won't bore you with the whole sordid pleading,[91]

---

[91] Montana Eighth Judicial District Court, Cascade County, Cause No. ADV-06-1218(B) – *Plaintiff's Combined Response to the Written "Motions for Sanctions" Filed by Defendants* ... – August 6, 2010.

but here is a sampling of the servile references with which he littered our response:

Plaintiff's attorneys take this Court's declaration of a mistrial <u>very seriously</u> and they stand suitably admonished. They assure the Court that their conduct at the retrial will be impeccable. In sum, although Plaintiff's attorneys are not attempting to excuse [their] trial conduct …. Plaintiff's counsel stand suitably admonished …. Plaintiff's counsel reiterate that their conduct will be impeccable in the next trial. In any event, should there be misconduct, the Court is perfectly capable of dealing with it at the time.
Plaintiff apologizes …. Plaintiff offers several brief points which she hopes the Court will accept in a spirit of mitigation.

The court denied the motions because it was already constrained to do so by case law and statute; therefore, this immediate result was never in doubt. But here is the long term damage my obsequious colleague did with his *summa mea culpa* approach:

- The facts demonstrated that our trial attorneys were faultless;

- The facts also showed defendants had asserted their motions with unclean hands;

- The court's previous order denying their oral motions proved she was aware of these facts;

- By making such a show of contrition, my groveling colleague shook the judge's confidence in her previous grasp of those exculpatory facts; therefore,

- As was evident in her order denying the written motions, she had developed a new mistrust of our trial counsel as a direct result of the Montana Ringer's sniveling.

So, while we escaped sanctions, we did so in the most unnecessarily undignified manner imaginable (not unlike the false confessors of Salem, MA in the late 17th century). Thus, if we ever again encounter this judge, she will treat us like the meddlesome cowards the Montana Ringer needlessly painted us to be. This is yet another example of the primary pitfall associated with hiring a local ringer – he will inevitably take a different approach than yours, regardless of whether it is warranted, if for no other reason than to justify his (a) involvement and (b) extortionate fee.

Finally, the ugly stepsister of self-deprecation is self-censorship. Shared by a distressing number of greenhorns and veterans alike is the timorous notion that one should dilute otherwise descriptive metaphors with the blandest boilerplate jargon for fear that the former *might* offend the delicate sensibilities of a judge. Permit me to illustrate.

Most if not all States have enacted what is commonly known as a "saving statute" which, subject to local nuances, permits a plaintiff to refile his case within one year of (a) a voluntary dismissal or (b) a pre-verdict failure otherwise than upon the merits of the case. In another wrongful death case, we invoked such a statute after filing a voluntary dismissal to save our client's claim from certain disaster at the hands of a State court judge whose rulings had become so erratic that, upon reading one of his orders, a trial judge in a neighboring jurisdiction questioned his sanity. When we refiled in federal court, the defendants moved to dismiss, contending that because a trial had already commenced at the time we filed our dismissal, our current action was barred by that State's saving provision. We countered that, because we had filed our dismissal weeks after the judge had declared a mistrial, the previous trial had been rendered a nullity; therefore, no trial had "commenced" pursuant to the statute. The federal court certified the question to the State supreme court. As luck would have it, the impact of a mistrial on the saving statute was an issue novel to that panel.

In their appellate brief, defendants complained that permitting us to proceed with the federal action would open the door for future plaintiffs to file such dismissals in perpetuity by merely procuring mistrials whenever they perceived their trials going badly. This contention ignored, among other things,[92] a clause in the statute known as the Double Dismissal Rule: "a notice of dismissal operates as an adjudication upon the merits of any claim that the plaintiff has once dismissed in any court."[93] In my response brief, I wrote:

> It is critical to note here that, in every case Defendants cite to buttress their "perpetual dismissal" bogeyman, the court is referring to the legal era predating the instatement of the Civil Rules and, thus, prior to Rule 41's double dismissal provision. In every case that addressed Rule 41, the reviewing court categorically upheld a plaintiff's right to file one voluntary, unilateral dismissal without prejudice prior to the commencement of trial.

My use of the word "bogeyman" caused such apoplexy among our local counsel that I feared a predatory wormhole had catapulted me to an antiquated era when wig-topped men were no less prudish than their petticoat-clad, kerchief-veiled wives. They hysterically proposed that I substitute the word "theory." Shall we compare definitions?

Bogeyman: an imaginary evil character used as an empty threat

---

[92] Though immaterial to my point, it is notable that the defendants themselves had (a) engineered the circumstances warranting the mistrial by lying to the trial judge and (b) moved for the mistrial when we exposed that lie.

[93] Ohio Civ. R. 41(A)(1)

Theory: a proposed explanation based on conjecture rather than fact

Now let us turn to usage. When we talk about someone proposing a *theory*, we ascribe to him an air of innocence – the term *theoretician* evokes the image of a bespectacled lab-nerd bouncing nonjudgmental ideas off his colleague in the mutual pursuit of objective truth. And *conjecture* entails the absence of fact. The purveyor of a *bogeyman*, by contrast, seeks to manipulate his audience with willful disregard for known facts. When we focus dispassionately on the words themselves it is quite clear that, in the context of our brief, *bogeyman* most accurately depicted the defendants' argument.

But what of the plaint that "bogeyman" is an incendiary term whose visceral connotation outweighs its illustrative value? Some employ euphemism out of tact, while others resort to it in ignorance. Still others are motivated by faintness of heart. For the past few years, I've seen a spate of briefs in which a lawyer refers to his opponent's argument as *disingenuous*. I once observed to a group of colleagues, "I can call another lawyer *disingenuous* all day long, but there will be hell to pay if I call him a liar." I think it fair to say this group understood that *disingenuous* is a euphemious synonym for *dishonest*. From their muted and sporadic laughter, I could only deduce that they were uncomfortable acknowledging this fact, even in a casual setting. Very distressing, that.

If I ever had a mentor as a lawyer, it was longtime family friend Russell B. Holloway who, when he learned I was going to sit for the LSAT, poured me a cognac and imparted the following advice: "Don't let your fears or perceptions of the judge, the jury, the onlookers or even your mother temper your passion for the task at hand. Argue every case, and write every motion, as though it were your last."

The oath one takes after passing the bar exam neither imbues him with clairvoyance nor obligates him to divine the bugbears and phobias of strangers. So long as your singular focus is on precision, you are not responsible for the myriad ways in which nitwits and posers have misused the language. So remember that we're all adults here (well, at least we're held to that standard ... theoretically). Do not cater to the misperceptions and hang-ups of sanctimonious simpletons and blushing biddies. If your opponent tosses a putrefying opossum into the room, act the adult you are presumed to be and acknowledge to the court exactly how it reeks.

Get Straight to the Point

Though other authors have addressed this issue, it bears repeating. New lawyers are unduly enamored with the stilted and ostentatious phraseology of a bygone era. I myself was not immune to its allure for some years.

> COMES NOW the Appellee and Plaintiff below, Mary Ann Jones, by and through her counsel of record, *Hughie, Dewey and Louis*, and, for her Appellee's Brief to Appellant/Defendant below's Appellant's Brief, would show this Court that said Appellant's Brief should be denied for the following reasons.

Though my fourth grade English teacher would have slapped me silly for writing such a circumlocutory opener, thousands of pleadings are filed every year with just such an introduction. The responsible writer asks, *Is the phrase COMES NOW a magical password without which the court will not consider my brief? Can the court not ascertain who my client is from the case style? Just what is the message I wish to convey?* The result:

> The Court should deny this appeal for the following reasons.

In a similar vein, many writers spend too long setting out their game plan in the Introduction. After reading one whose author spent page upon agonizing page telling the trial court what he was going to prove in the body of his argument, I wanted to call him up and bark, "Stop telling me what you're going to do. Just do it." No doubt the judge had the same reaction.

When I discussed the first edition of this book with my employing attorneys, one of them shared a poignant observation: "In all my years of practice, I've learned that most trial and appellate judges read the first ten pages of a brief, then they skip to the conclusion. So I lead with my strongest argument and follow up with supportive details."

I end this section with a good example of what my colleague is talking about. In a Montana case, the defendants filed a pretrial motion to limit a category of our witnesses. Commonly referred to as "OSI witnesses," these individuals would testify about similar accidents they'd had in the same model vehicle as the one at issue prior to the accident that had injured our client. Such witnesses tend to prove that a manufacturer had notice of the defect for a certain time before the accident in question. In his response brief, our local counsel delivered his knockout punch at the opening bell:

> Defendant's motion is nothing more than an attempt to prevent Ms. Kroft from proving her case. Defendant has cited no authority (because there is none) to support the proposition that a trial court should tie a plaintiff's hands in the presentation of her evidence merely because a multi-national corporation complains about the costs of defending against that evidence.
>
> As the Court is well aware, the proponent of other accident evidence bears the burden to demonstrate substantial similarity (*Krueger v. General Motors Corp.* – 783 P.2d 1340, 1345-6 – Mont. 1989). Furthermore, to establish her punitive claim, Ms. Kroft must present *clear and convincing* evidence of actual fraud or malice (Mont. Code Ann. §27-1-221). It is therefore incumbent upon her to show that Defendant had notice of the defects in the subject vehicle. It is axiomatic that Defendant's decision to ignore 1 prior incident does not carry the same probative weight as its pattern of ignoring 100 prior incidents. Thus, each witness is critical to Ms. Kroft's case.

Conclusion

The difference between the right word and the almost right word is the difference between lightning and a lightning bug.

-Mark Twain

What the *plain language* locksteppers fail to appreciate is that (a) written expression is, by its very nature, more sophisticated than vocal speech (b) the human mind quickly wearies of seeing the same old nouns, verbs and adjectives time and again and (c) communication is an *active* process *at both ends.* This is why the astute writer (a) always keeps a thesaurus and dictionary within arm's reach and (b) periodically doublechecks the meanings of purported synonyms. This is why the devoted writer never stops improving her vocabulary, and it is why no rule of grammar or citation is sacred. It makes no difference whether you're writing for a county judge or a nine-member appellate panel. Forget legal precedent, political influence and the color of your lucky tie. Your mission as an advocate will never be fulfilled unless and until you can tell your client's story with clarity and passion.

Language is undoubtedly the single greatest invention of humankind. Without a system of communication based on commonality of meaning, science and technology would never have advanced beyond the pebble tools used by *Homo habilis* 2.6 million years ago. The genius of Galileo Galilei, Groucho Marx and Albert Einstein would never have been realized. None of the gadgets and conveniences we take for granted would exist. We would, today, be scavenging for food with only caves to protect us from nature's severity, and we would understand each other no better than a ferret understands an essay written by Ludwig Wittgenstein. As writers, it is both our prerogative and our obligation to celebrate and nurture it. Don't cower from its depth and versatility; embrace it by exploring, expanding and experimenting. Let the Trolls bicker and banter in their arcane conclaves. You owe them no allegiance, because you move in an arena that will not tolerate their tripe. So placate your particular Troll until you have your diploma in hand, then discard her like old underclothes and ...

Excel.

Epilogue

Welcome to the Dark Side - Enter
of Your Own Free Will

One absurdity common to licensed professions is the continuing education component. Caveman level economics and human nature render this requisite nothing more than a token measure used by (a) the overseeing body to prop up its illusory importance to society and (b) the licensee to escape the office and/or hobnob/network and/or write an exotic vacation off as a business expense. Two simple facts expose its fallacy:

- To stay competitive, and therefore profitable, the conscientious professional stays abreast of the latest developments in his field as a matter of course – thus, no continuing education presenter will be able to tell him anything he does not already know;

- By contrast, the remiss professional won't pay any attention to that presenter anyway.

Hollower yet is the ethics component of the continuing education sham. As the recidivism rate among the American prison population handily proves, no amount of instruction will reform a rogue or a predator. By the time your average individual matriculates from high school, his moral code has been so indelibly etched into his psyche that it is immune to verbal instruction. Thus, anyone who insists that a few hours of haphazard "do the right thing" sermons a year will rehabilitate a scoundrel is kidding either himself or everyone else.

When I published the first edition of this book, I saw no need to dwell upon the many examples of chicanery I had seen among my colleagues, perhaps because I clung to the hope that they were rare, atypical incidents. But it now appears to me that, like the *plain language* foolishness in academia, negligence and perfidy have become so routine among certain elements of the practicing bar that, unless upstanding lawyers sound the clarion call, casuistry may become endemic to the entire legal profession.

Though I doubt you'll be able to obtain any such credit from your licensing body, let us consider this section the *ethics* component of this publication.

The Atticus Finch Charade

In 1960, Harper Lee released the literary classic *To Kill a Mockingbird.*[94] The book was adapted to film two years later. Gregory Peck's portrayal of Atticus Finch so impressed me at an early age that I'm certain it played a part in my decision to go to law school. Atticus Finch was a commixture of every quality to which a boy might aspire. He did not shrink from a seemingly futile battle. He faced down a mob for the sake of a pariah. He shot the rabid dog. In the courtroom, he was the paradigm of civil dialectics. He did not give in to trickery. He addressed his opponent with respect. Above all, truth was his bellwether.

The reality is, as with all heroes of the page and screen, Atticus Finch never existed. Despite this fact, it appears to me that an alarming number of the trial judges and appellate panels I've thus far encountered suffer the delusion that a law school diploma magically confers upon its licentiate *AtticusFinchdom*.

For example, many trial judges harbor the naïve expectation that opposing counsel, who have bickered and badgered over pretrial motions, will be able to submit an *agreed* order summarizing the court's findings of fact and rulings. In one of our Mexican cases, despite previous experience with corporate defense counsel who had brazenly inserted into proposed orders the categorical opposite of what he had ruled *on the record*, our judge insisted once again on an agreed order. In frustration, my colleague Mark bristled: "What part of *adversarial proceeding* do these judges fail to comprehend?"

---

[94] J.B. Lippincott & Co.

Of course, it is commendable for a judge to prod and cajole litigation opponents in the direction of honor and integrity. I think we can agree that utopian ambitions must never be forsaken. But the system descends into a farce when (a) lawyers brashly defy those ideals and (b) those charged with disciplinary authority over them turn a blind eye. For the law student who intends to become a practicing lawyer, I will now recount two examples of the most insidious manifestation of *AtticusFinchdom* I have thus far witnessed because, as your predecessor, I owe you a preview of the cesspit into which you intend to dive headlong.

The Snake Charmer Who Bamboozled a Trial Judge and Two Appellate Panels with Total Impunity

In the Oklahoma case I mentioned earlier (in which a wheel bearing failure led to a head-on collision killing five), one of our concomitant theories of defect was that the manufacturer had failed to install a fastener called a *cotter pin* on the wheel in question, which contributed to the abnormal wear upon, and ultimate failure of, the bearings. The cotter pin holds the entire front-end assembly together, and it is the last piece a mechanic would insert after installing, replacing or checking wheel bearings. One of the first responders to view the scene on the day of the accident observed that the cotter pin on the wheel in question was missing. Neither he nor any of his fellow officers found it. Over the next 11 months, no less than four engineers with very respectable résumés independently combed the scene with state-of-the-art metal detectors, but they failed to locate the cotter pin and various other related component parts. Two months after the last of these professionals had explored the scene, the manufacturer's employee "found" the elusive parts, including the cotter pin.

In the 14th century C.E., a Franciscan friar named William of Ockham proposed a principle of logic which is commonly known as "Occam's Razor," and it holds: Of two competing theories or explanations, all other things being equal, the simpler one is preferred. Now, which explanation is more rational: (1) that the parts

240

were there the whole time; therefore this employee's search methods were far superior to those used by cutting-edge investigators (or his metal detector was magically more powerful than theirs) or (2) that someone simply scattered the parts there and ground them in with the heel of his boot just days (or hours) prior to that employee's arrival?

Our accident reconstructionist in the case is a retired highway patrolman who has investigated well over 2,500 accidents *since he left public service*, and has helped to solve murder cases by finding evidence as subtle as a single strand of human hair. His deposition testimony is quite illuminating:

> Q. Okay. And I'm just wondering if you have any other opinions, or conclusions, about the subject of preservation of evidence, as it relates to any other issue besides that, in this case, including the location of parts that were found from the subject [SUV]?
>
> A. No. Obviously, I've always felt like the discovery of those parts were unusual, at best, since I'd looked for them, and several other people had looked for them, and then subsequent to our looking for them, and not finding them, they were found in the area.
>
> I have discussed that with them. But as far as having anything to say – you know, it's my opinion that they, you know, planted or seeded that area with parts, I don't know. I don't know that for a fact.
>
> Q. Do you have any evidence that that occurred?
>
> A. No. Other than, as I say, to go out there and, what I felt like, diligently search for the parts, and then have them found in a situation where they were right at the point we were all searching seemed kind of strange.
>
> ***
>
> My suspicion – I'm not sure how suspicion rises to a thought. But my suspicion is that the parts were

241

not there, in the position they were found in, when I examined the scene and searched for them.

***

Q. Now, you indicate that based on your extremely thorough search, you were very surprised that the objects which were the subject of your search could have been found there approximately three months later?

A. Yes.

Q. And you're still surprised?

A. Still surprised.

Two other experts were unable to positively identify any of these "found" parts as belonging to the subject wheel. Though yet another expert seemed reasonably certain that two of the parts were genuine, no expert for any of the parties in the case was able to conclude to any degree of scientific certainty that the cotter pin "found" by the manufacturer's employee came from the subject wheel. Furthermore: (a) the mechanic who had last serviced the SUV testified categorically that he did not touch the subject wheel and (b) there was no indication in the vehicle's service history that anyone had ever serviced that wheel; therefore (c) any cotter pin found at the scene would have to have been the one installed by the manufacturer when the vehicle rolled through the assembly line ("Original Equipment" or "OE"). Yet, according to Donald Masquerena, the manufacturer's litigation expert upon whom the employee initially bestowed the suspicious parts, the cotter pin "found" at the scene was not Original Equipment:

Q. That's what I was going to ask you. The right side cotter pin and the left side cotter pin on this [SUV] ought to be similar or substantially similar to the right and left side cotter pin of at least the [SUVs] made the same model year, is that correct?

A. That is incorrect.

Q.   How is it different if at all from other [SUVs] made in that same plant during that model year?

A.   That cotter pin is not the OE cotter pin that would have been utilized at the assembly plant.

Q.   So you think that's a replacement cotter pin, is that right?

A.   That's correct.

Q.   How did you differentiate that?

A.   The component part that is utilized in the assembly plant – two things: It is of a different size slightly and a different coating, it's a different part.

If the cotter pin did not belong to the subject wheel, just how did it find its way to the scene of the accident, intermingled with other parts of equally questionable provenance? As an employee of the manufacturer, Mr. Masquerena certainly had the means and the opportunity to plant those parts. A paralegal in our law firm had accompanied Mr. Masquerena on his inspection of the subject vehicle just two days before his fellow employee "searched" the accident scene. She testified that Mr. Masquerena painstakingly photographed the vehicle *and its extant component parts. She further testified that Mr. Masquerena assured her that his colleague would find those missing parts.*

Though we presented these facts to the court, no investigation ensued, and defense counsel was permitted to place this apparent evidence tamperer on the stand at trial. Nor did these peculiar circumstances invoke so much as a yawn at any appellate level.

Every Lie We Whitewash Erodes the Truth

The facts of this case are immaterial to our discussion. Suffice it to say that we had in our hands evidence which is more precise than that on which I raked in pretrial settlements hand over fist in my subrogation days of yore. In her summary judgment brief,[95] a defense attorney to whom I will assign the apt agnomen Wayward Associate spun the following fish story:

> Accordingly, the standard under the old rule that "all facts and inferences raised by a motion for summary judgment [must be considered] in the light most favorable to the non-moving party" is no longer applicable in the determination of summary judgment under Oklahoma law. *Bowman v. Presley,* 2009 OK 48, ¶21, 212 P.3d 1212, 1219.

There are two colossal flaws in this assertion. First, as you already know or will soon discover, the standard of review for summary adjudication is that the facts must be viewed in a light most favorable to the nonmovant. This standard has been beyond question for over half a century (*U.S. v. Diebold, Inc.* – 369 U.S. 654, 655 – 1962).[96] Second, the placement of the *Bowman* citation at the end of the statement suggests that the Oklahoma Supreme Court abandoned the standard in 2009. To the contrary, a cursory review of the opinion confirms that it espoused the standard.

I am unaware of a jurisdiction that does not have the equivalent of Oklahoma's Title 12 O.S. §2011, which provides in pertinent part:

> B. REPRESENTATIONS TO COURT. By presenting to the court, whether by signing, filing, submitting, or later advocating, a pleading, written motion, or other paper, an attorney or unrepresented party is certifying that to the best of the person's knowledge,

---

[95] District Court of Ottawa County, Oklahoma, Case No. CJ-2008-588 – *Motion for Summary Judgment of Defendants Nebojsa Tomicic, Nenad Tomicic and Imperial Eagle Express, Inc., and Brief in Support* – May 26, 2010

[96] There is an extremely rare exception in the event there is in evidence a videotape of the incident at issue which unambiguously contradicts the nonmovant's position (*Scott v. Harris* – 550 U.S. 372 – 2007), but it did not apply to our case. Nonetheless, the Wayward Associate tried to pass this anomaly off as a general rule.

information, and belief, formed after an inquiry reasonable under the circumstances:

> 2. The claims, defenses and other legal contentions therein are warranted by existing law or by a nonfrivolous argument for the extension, modification, or reversal of existing law or the establishment of new law ....

Look again at the Wayward Associate's assertion. She did not propose that Oklahoma *should* no longer follow the standard; she averred that the highest tribunal of the State had already defied the United States Supreme Court by dispensing with it. This key distinction separates a weak argument from a barefaced lie.

In our responsive brief, I thoroughly dismantled her assertion by (a) citing recent local and federal law which upheld the standard and (b) demonstrating that *Bowman* and every other case she had cited for support actually held the opposite of what she claimed. In a footnote, I afforded my junior colleague the opportunity to absolve herself:

So cavalierly have Defendants taken liberties with easily found, and far more handily comprehended, law regarding the summary judgment standard that Plaintiff's counsel have wrestled with their custodial obligations under Title 12 O.S. §2011. Given the fact that Defendants have the option to file a reply hereto, we trust they will use that opportunity to make all appropriate amends; hence, we deem it both prudent and professionally courteous to forego the formal procedure outlined in §2011(C)(1)(a) pending that reply.

Rather than seize the benefit of the doubt I had extended (or, at the very least, offer some semblance of a good-faith argument to salvage her premise), the Wayward Associate devoted the bulk of her responsive brief to feigning indignation at me for exposing her fabrication. No less than three times she contended that, in its

245

enactment of a summary judgment statute[97] which was little more than a restatement of a longstanding court rule, the legislature "changed the wording of the statute," despite the facts that (a) she did not bother to comply with my invitation to come forward with the alleged "former" Oklahoma edict it supposedly modified and (b) the legislative history clearly shows that this particular statute was a brand new codification rather than a revision of any previous enactment. As if that weren't enough, she went so far as to insist upon a logical impossibility – *that the newly enacted statute was, at its inception, a rewording of itself.*

At the subsequent hearing which only our local counsel attended, the judge said:

> I'm going to tell both counsel – all counsel at this point in time. I don't know where you all practice. I don't care where you practice. But if you practice in my court and you give me a pleading which accuses the other party of intentionally misleading the Court, or you start calling people names, you're going to be held in contempt by this Court. I don't put up with that type of conduct by professionals, not in my courtroom and not in anything that people are writing for me to read.

Regrettably, we got no opportunity to take the judge up on his challenge because, in the next breath, he granted summary judgment (which no judge could do unless he were viewing the evidence in a light *least* favorable to the nonmovant), thereby dismissing our lawsuit and leaving us no case in which to pursue sanctions.

I'm sure there are lawyers out there who will disagree with my assessment of the Wayward Associate's assertion. For their consideration, I offer a few authoritative sources. *Dictionary.com* defines "lie" as follows:

---

[97] Title 12 O.S. §2056

Noun

1. A false statement made with deliberate intent to deceive; an intentional untruth; a falsehood.
2. Something intended or serving to convey a false impression; imposture.
3. An inaccurate or false statement.

Verb (used without object)

5. To speak falsely or utter untruth knowingly, as with intent to deceive.
6. To express what is false; convey a false impression.

My 6th Edition of *Black's Law Dictionary* (West Pub. Co. 1990) describes it thus:

A falsehood uttered for the purpose of deception; an intentional statement of an untruth designed to mislead another; anything which misleads or deceives; it means an untruth deliberately told; the uttering or acting of that which is false for the purpose of deceiving; intentional misstatement.

Finally, Oklahoma's Rules of Professional Conduct, Rule 3.3(a)(1) admonishes:

A lawyer shall not knowingly make a false statement of fact or law to a tribunal or fail to correct a false statement of material fact or law previously made to the tribunal by the lawyer.

Though the appellate courts confirmed that the *light most favorable to the nonmovant* standard remains undisturbed in Oklahoma, they completely ignored the Wayward Associate's dissemblance – as did the Bar Association, which prompted a non-lawyer friend of mine to query: "It makes one wonder whom she's sleeping with." By no means do I wish to impugn the sexual virtues of a colleague or any member of a regulatory body. My sole motive in recounting the comment is to illustrate a vexatious reality. So consumed has our legal system become with details of ever diminishing size that the unscrupulous among us who have a particular gift for splitting hairs are able to mask the most cardinal offenses by dissecting them into such minute fragments that they are no longer recognizable. Thus, the venerable art of dialectics too often degenerates into a perfidious burlesque. By sad contrast, it is typically those of us who have not been jaded by this disintegration – non-lawyers – who retain the capability of seeing the waddling, quacking, feathered creature for the duck that it is.

I single out the Wayward Associate because her misrepresentation illustrates the degree of depravity to which members of the bar can fall. Though the line between zealous advocacy and outright dishonesty is sometimes barely perceptible, anyone you ask will agree that it should nevertheless remain inviolate. I have watched colleagues try to redefine it, tiptoe around it and sneak beneath it. Still, I have taken comfort in the fact that they had both the decency and the dignity to never openly defy it. Not only did the Wayward Associate bulldoze that boundary; she did so with that particular strain of arrogance which bespeaks a fundamental contempt for truth and integrity.

In correspondence regarding the matter, the Wayward Associate offered the exculpatory suggestion that her brief may have been "inartfully drafted." Is it plausible for a relatively inexperienced attorney to be so eager to impress her employers that she might accidentally portray an aspiration as fact and misplace a citation? Is it equally conceivable that, once called out for those mistakes, an associate such as she would feel irresistible pressure from managing attorneys to defend an untenable position rather than simply correct the errors? Perhaps, but motives are immaterial – at the end of the day, a lie is a lie, and the liar brands himself indelibly.

In other words, just who is kidding whom?

As a practical matter, the Wayward Associate's lie had no material effect upon the judge, for his principal concern was trying to cajole the appellate courts into taking up an ancillary issue of first impression. Short of that, he was so opposed to letting our case anywhere near a jury that he could not have cared less that the reasons he gave for granting summary judgment were facially inconsistent with logic, law and evidence. But the fact that the Wayward Associate uttered the lie with impunity in this case will only embolden others in her position to repeat it.[98] And, like rumors and urban legends, the true peril of untruth lies in its repetition:

"A lie told often enough becomes truth."
                    - Vladimir Lenin

"If you tell a lie big enough and keep repeating it, people will eventually come to believe it."
                    - Nazi Propaganda Minister
                    Joseph Goebbels

Summation

Suffer no illusions. The legal system is no more perfect than the mortals who administer it. A reflection of the human condition, it is often a moiling sea of bias, prejudice, deception, backbiting and skullduggery from which appellate courts seldom offer a safe harbor. This is primarily because appellate judges by no means hold a corner

---

[98] In fact, the Wayward Associate admitted in writing that this was not the first brief in which she had spouted this hogwash.

on the market of rationality and cogency.[99] As an example, I submit a reviewing court which has a vexing habit of misconstruing its very own rules.

In 2010, we obtained a multimillion verdict, roughly half of which was punitive. The manufacturer promptly appealed. Two years later, after all briefs had been submitted, the highest court of that State dismissed the appeal without prejudice to its reinstatement. Why? Because we had originally sued the dealership in addition to the manufacturer, but at trial we had moved to nonsuit the dealer. Though the trial court had granted the motion from the bench, no written order memorializing this decision had ever made it into the record (2012 Ark. 325):

> Because no order dismissing [Dealership] from this case was entered, there is no final judgment as required by Arkansas Rule of Civil Procedure 54(b).

The parties filed a joint petition for rehearing in which we reminded the court that it had issued an amendment earlier that very year allowing parties to cure a Rule 54(b) "finality deficiency" by abandoning all unresolved claims in their notices of appeal/cross appeal (which we had dutifully done). In adopting this provision, the Court itself had written:

> [I]t wastes parties' and courts' scarce resources to have two appeals in these situations.

How did the ultimate tribunal of Arkansas respond? By affirming its dismissal. Here is its reasoning (Id; emphasis added):

---

[99] By no means do I intend this observation to be a sweeping indictment of all trial and appellate judges. By and large, these individuals are sincere and dedicated, doing the best they can at the mercy of political and temporal constraints. By calling out the rare exceptions, I strive to fulfill my ethical obligation to promote the overall integrity of the commendable though imperfect system I serve.

The Rule concerns abandoning a pending but unresolved **claim**. Similarly, the illustrative cases cited in the Addition to Reporter's Notes concerned pending but unresolved **claims**. The Rule does not, however, allow an appealing party to dismiss a **party** from the action by such a statement in a notice of appeal or notice of cross-appeal.

It is axiomatic that dismissing all of one's claims against Party X operates as a dismissal, *qua party*, of Party X. As if the Court's statement, standing alone, weren't preposterous enough, I asked a local appellate lawyer about it. His response:

> I was in the room when this rule was drafted and when it was adopted. It was specifically for both purposes. The court asked us to draft it for both reasons.

So the parties proceeded to notice and brief the appeal all over again. Five months later, the court handed down yet another dismissal without prejudice so bereft of common sense that one of its own justices wrote a caustic dissent:[100]

2013 Ark. 88

NOTICE: THIS DECISION WILL NOT APPEAR IN THE SOUTHWESTERN REPORTER. SEE REVISED SUPREME COURT RULE 5-2 FOR THE PRECEDENTIAL VALUE OF OPINIONS.

---

[100] In addition to correcting stray punctuation and word form errors in this reproduction, I have omitted irrelative text without indication, consolidated and set off case citations, and deleted those sophomoric parallel citations and signals.

Supreme Court of Arkansas
[Defendant], Appellant

v.

[Plaintiff], Appellee
No. 12–910 | Feb. 28, 2013

Both [parties] filed motions for entry of judgment following the jury's verdict, disagreeing about the exact amount of damages [Defendant] owed. On October 6, 2010, the circuit court entered the following judgment:

> On August 16, 2010 the above entitled cause came on for trial. Twelve persons were duly impaneled as jurors. The case proceeded for trial before said jurors, who were sworn according to law to try the issues joined between the parties. On August 27, 2010, after hearing the testimony and the evidence introduced at trial, the arguments of counsel and the instructions of the Court, the jury returned the following verdicts upon special interrogatories:
>
> *Interrogatory No. 1:* Do you find by a preponderance of the evidence that there was fault on the part of [Defendant] which was a proximate cause of the death of [Decedent]?
>
> A. Yes.
>
> *Interrogatory No. 2:* Do you find by a preponderance of the evidence that there was fault on the part of [Third-Party Defendant] which was a proximate cause of the death of [Decedent]?
>
> A. Yes.

Interrogatory No. 3: Using 100% as representing the entire responsibility for this accident or the extent of the plaintiff's decedent's injuries, apportion the percentage of fault to each person or corporation that you have found to be at fault:

[Defendant] – 50%
[Third-Party Defendant] – 50%
Total 100%

Interrogatory No. 4: State the amount of damages which you find from a preponderance of the evidence were sustained by [Plaintiff], Administratrix of the Estate of [Decedent]:

A. Estate of [Decedent] $383,333.33
    [Plaintiff], Individually $3,918,791.67
    [Son] $100,000.00
    [Relative 1] $100,000.00
    [Relative 2] $100,000.00
    [Relative 3] $50,000.00

Interrogatory No. 5: Do you find by a preponderance of the evidence that [Plaintiff] is entitled to punitive damages[?]

A. Yes.

Interrogatory No. 6: State the amount of punitive damages to which you find [Plaintiff], Administratrix of the Estate of [Decedent] is entitled to by a preponderance of the evidence.

A. $2,500,000.00

Therefore, judgment is awarded to the respective plaintiffs as set out above.

[Defendant] appealed, and this court dismissed the appeal without prejudice for lack of a final order because no written order dismissing [Former Codefendant] had been entered (2012 Ark. 325). The circuit court then entered an order dismissing [Former Codefendant] with prejudice, and this appeal followed.

Even if neither party raises the issue of jurisdiction on appeal, the appellate court is obligated to raise the issue *sua sponte* (*Elis v. Ark. State Highway Comm'n* – 2010 Ark. 196). With exceptions not applicable here, an appeal may be taken only from a final judgment or decree entered by the trial court. [Ark. R. App. P. Civ. 2(a)(1) (2012)] For a judgment to be final and appealable, it must dismiss the parties from the court, discharge them from the action, or conclude their rights to the subject matter in controversy (*Kelly v. Kelly* – 835 S.W.2d 869 – Ark. 1992; *Jackson v. Yowell* – 818 S.W.2d 950 – Ark. 1991). To be final, an order must not only decide the rights of the parties, but also put the court's directive into execution, ending the litigation or a separable part of it (*Kilgore v. Viner* – 736 S.W.2d 1 – Ark. 1987).

In *Thomas v. McElroy* (420 S.W.2d 530 – Ark. 1967), we explained the formal requirements of what constitutes a final judgment. To be final, a judgment for money must state the amount that the defendant is required to pay (Id). In citing Arkansas statutory law, we said that the amount of the judgment must be computed, as near as may be, in dollars and cents, and that the judgment must specify clearly the relief granted or other determination of the action. [Id.; Ark. Code Ann. §16–65–103 (Repl. 2005) (declaring that all judgments or decrees shall be computed, as near as may be, in dollars and cents)] In *Thomas,* we noted that a final judgment or decision is one that finally adjudicates the rights of the parties, and it must be such a final determination as may be enforced by execution or in some other appropriate manner. [*Villines v. Harris* – 208 S.W.3d 763 – Ark. 2005 (holding that, although a previous order set out a formula for calculating damages, the order was not final because it did not establish the amount of damages); *Office of Child Support Enforcement v. Oliver* – 921 S.W.2d 602 – Ark. 1996 (holding that an order was not final where an arrearage in child support was found but the amount of the arrearage was not determined); *Hastings v. Planters & Stockmen Bank* – 757 S.W.2d 546 – Ark. 1989 (holding that an order of summary judgment was not final where the amount owed was not specified in dollars and cents, there were issues that appeared to be outstanding, and the judgment did not dismiss or discharge the appellant)]

Here, the judgment is not final because it does not set forth a specific dollar amount owed by [Defendant]. Instead, the circuit court merely reproduced the jury's answers to the interrogatories and gave no further guidance. Despite the dissent's assertions to the contrary, it is not the form of the circuit court's judgment that concerns this court. Rather, it is the fact that the circuit court has neglected to enter a final judgment amount that is computed, as near as may be, in dollars and cents. It is unclear whether [Defendant] is responsible for half of the compensatory damages listed, half of the punitive damages listed, all of both, or some combination thereof. This problem is further demonstrated by the fact that [Defendant] asks this court on appeal to clarify the judgment so as to ascertain the exact dollar amount owed by [Defendant]. Consequently, without a specific amount, computed as near as may be in dollars and cents, that [Defendant] is ordered to pay, this judgment is not final.

Because we lack a final order, this court has no jurisdiction to hear the appeal. Accordingly, we dismiss without prejudice.

Appeal dismissed without prejudice.

HART, J., dissents.

I am aware that the record in this case is huge. The abstract is 2,208 pages and the addendum, even with the missing items, is 1,201 pages. Even so, this court has previously dismissed this appeal because it found that there was a lack of a final order (2012 Ark. 325), but did not address what they now perceive as an additional problem with the trial court's order. Under this court's rules, the first dismissal was justified, because the final order failed to resolve an outstanding claim against a named party. I cannot likewise approve of today's dismissal.

This case was resolved by a jury verdict. The majority notes that the jury awarded $4,652,125 in compensatory damages and $2,500,000 in punitive damages. The damages were awarded in special interrogatories, which the majority has reproduced in its opinion. In those interrogatories, the jury apportioned the responsibility for the accident at fifty percent to the driver, [Third-Party Defendant], and fifty percent to [Defendant]. Yet, despite the specificity of the award, the majority declares that the judgment is not final because it does not set forth the "specific dollar amount owed by [Defendant]." It is simply not defensible to assert that this judgment is not final because this court does not deign to perform a simple arithmetical operation that is routinely taught in the second grade – division by two.

I am likewise troubled that the majority would fault the trial court because it "merely reproduced the jury's answers to the interrogatories." [Arkansas Rule of Civil Procedure 58 (2012)] specifically authorizes a trial court to "enter its own form of judgment or decree." In this case, the jury was the finder of fact, *not* the trial judge. Except for granting a remittitur or an additur, the trial judge was obligated to accept the jury's verdict.

The majority's decision is not supported by our case law. The cases cited by the majority do not involve jury verdicts. *Thomas v. McElroy* (420 S.W.2d 530) is a chancery case; *Villines v. Harris* (208 S.W.3d 763) is an appeal from county court to circuit court that was dismissed because the county court did not have subject matter jurisdiction; *Office of Child Support Enforcement v. Oliver* (921 S.W.2d 602) is a chancery case; and *Hastings v. Planters & Stockmen Bank* (757 S.W.2d 546) is a summary judgment. Moreover, in *Thomas, Harris,* and *Oliver,* it was apparent from the record that the trial court, sitting as the trier of fact, intended to do additional work on the case. Thus, the majority has not cited a single case where this court has dismissed an appeal because a trial judge has failed to put a jury verdict in a kind of format that this court likes better. Indeed, in *Thomas* this court stated that "strict formality of language used to express the adjudication of the court is not necessary." (420 S.W.2d at 532)

Finally, if it is "unclear" to the majority whether [Defendant] is responsible for half the damages, it must refer only to the black-letter law regarding the construction of judgments. "As a general rule, judgments are to be construed like other written instruments, and the legal effect of a judgment must be declared in light of the literal meaning of the language used." [Am.Jur.2d *Judgments* §74 (2006)] In my view, the judgment is final.

In *Chambers v. Baltimore & Ohio R.R. Co.* (207 U.S. 142, 148 – 1907), the Supreme Court held:

> The right to sue and defend in the courts is the alternative of force. In an organized society it is the right conservative of all other rights, and lies at the foundation of orderly government. It is one of the highest and most essential privileges of citizenship....

While this is a nice, lofty sentiment, it ignores the reality that the very concept of *justice* is a fiction, an arbitrary human construct divined to assuage our fears, a crudely wrought lullaby we intone to divert our minds from the reality that life is fundamentally unfair and there's not one damned thing we can do about it. (If you need concrete proof of this statement, I refer you to the July 5, 2011 acquittal of Casey Anthony.) When I was a young lawyer, just two years out of school, I sat down in the chambers of a small claims judge. He asked me what I wanted. I responded whimsically, "Justice, sir." Without batting an eye, he replied, "No, son, you want fairness. Justice is a fickle friend." This sparked a goodhearted debate pitting Constitutional precepts against personal ambitions, and the salty judge won the argument with the following observation:

"Mark my words, Russell. So long as review at the higher appellate levels continues to be discretionary, justice will remain no less a pipe dream than Marx's opiate of the masses."

Though I could not refute his logic, I refused to accept his deduction for some 17 years. Here's how it happened.

In 2003, a wife and mother of two, though properly belted in the rear seat of an SUV, was ejected and killed when the SUV lost control and rolled several times because of a rear tire failure. In a blatant exercise of reweighing the evidence (and then denying the existence of crucial supportive evidence when it asserted a lack thereof as its reason for reversal), the Fifth District Court of Appeals in Texas vacated our verdict. After a local briefer had exhausted our appellate options in Texas, my employing attorneys asked me to query our national contacts in search of a novel approach that would increase our chances of garnering the attention of the champagne and caviar set who pontificate amidst so much oak and marble. One ally suggested we contact an attorney or two in the High Court's own backyard – that elitist menagerie of legerdemain known as Washington, D.C.

In August of 2012, I contacted a straight talking New Yorker upon whom I will bestow the codename Duke, whose acquaintance I had made (and whom I quickly grew to revere for his uncommon insight into the Big Court) a few years earlier. I asked Duke's opinion on whether there was any merit to the notion that there exists some magical method (or sweetheart law firm) that guarantees a petition will be granted. This savvy counselor, who began his ascent to one of the more prestigious New York firms when I was but one year old, pulled no punches (paraphrasing):

"Name recognition is immaterial. Eloquence is of negligible consequence. I've seen well connected geniuses lose and no-name morons win. The fact is, no one can turn shit into gold. All that matters is whether the Court finds the issue sexy enough to take it up and, even if they do, they will have already decided how they want to rule before the opening brief is even filed."

Toward the end of our conversation, all the evidence at hand prompted me to confess to Duke, "My friend, you have driven the final nail into the coffin of my idealism."

Make no mistake: the best brief does not always carry the day. Allow me to repeat that.

The best brief does not always carry the day. This is why book titles which flaunt some derivation of the word *win* (a) are deceptive and (b) betray their authors as impostors trying to sell you a load of snake oil. As we have seen, reviewing courts do not always favor the most suasive set of facts or the most cogent argument. Because it is administered by fallible human beings with passions and prejudices, "justice" is by no means guaranteed in any juridical system. Thus, one might reasonably say that agenda overshadows truth even in the legal arena.

There are innumerable reasons people decide they want to be lawyers. Whatever is yours, do not suffer the delusion that you will change anyone's mind, or that you will be responsible for currying a landmark decision, at any appellate level. People simply do not possess that great an influence over each other. From the rise of the Nazi party in the 1930s to *Beatlemania* of the 1960s to the 1978 mass suicide in Jonestown, Guyana, the history of human congress proves that people of average intelligence will simply not be led down a path they are not predisposed to take. On the other hand,

259

the fact that the most innovative of arguments will not sway the preconceived opinions of a panel of political appointees (recall my earlier observation about a truckload of money and a trainload of ass) is no excuse to throw up your hands and submit a second-rate brief, because the brief-writer's task is to provide a roadmap for (a) those judges who are already inclined to rule in your client's favor and (b) future litigants.

Human beings come and go, but the written word survives (until the next global catastrophe, anyway). The archival record hungers for honorable and eloquent discourse, and perchance yours will exert sufficient formative influence upon a future generation that sensible reforms will be implemented to stanch the now swelling tide of equivocators and cutthroats. If you recall the quote from President Theodore Roosevelt, the value of the contest inheres not in the outcome but in the struggle itself. Though you may claw your way to the *Holy of Holies* only to be brushed aside, the well written briefs you crafted along the way will stand as your legacy to, not merely legal dissertation, but the time-honored art of dynamic expression. So write for your client, yourself and posterity. After all, everybody dies in the end, and all you will really have in that last nanosecond of consciousness is the satisfaction of, not *pro forma* certificates or store-bought novelties with arbitrary titles etched into their nameplates, but having put forth your finest effort.

Historically speaking, eloquence is its own reward. Just as you have withstood the chatter of the Trolls, the Curmudgeons and the Yapping Chihuahuas, brush off the carping of the liars, the dilettantes and the charlatans, and ...

Be well written.

Printed in the United States
By Bookmasters